WHO'S WHO
OF UNSOLVED
MURDERS

THE
WHO'S WHO
OF UNSOLVED
MURDERS

James Morton

KYLE CATHIE LIMITED

For Dock Bateson
With Love

Picture Acknowledgements

Grateful thanks are made to the following for the use of
their photographs and items from their collections:

Jonathan Goodman: pages 20, 22, 29, 62, 86, 91, 92, 101, 105,
123, 162, 199, 221, 239, 255, 270, 294; Richard
Whittington-Egan: pages 46, 113, 118, 158, 227, 235, 277;
Topham Picture Source: pages 136, 231; London Features
International Ltd: page 150; Express Newspapers: page 119

This edition published in 1995 by
Kyle Cathie Limited
20 Vauxhall Bridge Road
London SW1V 2SA

First published in 1994 by
Kyle Cathie Limited

ISBN 1 85626 203 0

James Morton is hereby identified as the author of this work
in accordance with Section 77 of the Copyright, Designs and
Patents Act 1988.

A Cataloguing in Publication record for this title is available
from the British Library.

Typeset by Books Unlimited (Nottm), Rainworth, NG21 0JE
Printed and bound in Great Britain by Cox & Wyman Ltd,
Reading, Berkshire

INTRODUCTION

The seemingly recent fascination of the public for murder cases – the part-works, the stream of books on famous cases, their reconstruction in loving detail on the television whether in the guise of asking the public to help trace the killer, or of a reconstruction to show how clever the police have been – is not new. Murder has always held an attraction for the public. Crowds would gather at public executions, by no means as turned off at the spectacle as the villain would be. Some, it is true, were there to prevent the surgeons getting their hands on the corpse for experimental and teaching purposes, but the remainder had come for the spectacle and the thrill. The more popular the murderer the more difficulty the hangman had in performing his work. Around the gallows were sold ballads and purported confessions of those to be executed. The more fastidious, such as William Thackeray, railed against the public execution but the fascination remained even after the executions were held behind prison walls. In the 1880s William Marwood, the public hangman, became something of a celebrity and gave lectures which were not always a total success. This was because he chose to air his views on such topics as the Irish problem and the health of the Royal Family instead of giving the public what they wished to hear – an account of his clients and his technique.

Murder trials have always been well attended, with tickets in such great demand at the most popular cases that spectators were only permitted to attend either the morning or afternoon session.

Beginning with Edinburgh detective James McLevy's two-volume recollections in the early 1860s and continuing with almost every well-known detective (and quite a few lesser-known ones), the public has lapped up the memoirs of police officers. Now there is a fashion for the memoirs of the more violent of the country's criminals.

The circulation of the Sunday newspapers thrived on the death-cell confessions of the convicted men and (less frequently) women. Those who defended them became public celebrities in their own right. In 1935 the readers of the *Daily Express* listed Norman Birkett, the year after he had won a spectacular acquittal for Tony Mancini (see The Brighton Trunk Murders), as one of the personalities about whom they most liked reading. Birkett tied for twentieth place with the Aga Khan, and the pathologist, Sir Bernard Spilsbury, was next on the list.

In many ways, however, the most popular category of murder cases has been the unsolved one. Many fancy themselves as a detective – witness the popularity of the game Cluedo – and there is endless entertainment to be had in trying to solve the identity of Jack the Ripper or debating whether William Wallace could have killed his wife and cleaned himself up in the time available. In this book are some two hundred plus cases which for one reason or another have never been satisfactorily determined.

There are three main categories of entries. The first is the genuinely unsolved murder where either no killer has ever been traced or no arrest was made even if the police believed they knew the perpetrator. This category includes such cases as Jack the Ripper. The second is where a man or woman has stood trial and been acquitted. The third category includes the cases where there has been a conviction which has been quashed or which the appellate courts have refused to quash but there is a very real possibility that the wrong people have served sentences. This includes, for example, the famous William Wallace case, where a much more likely candidate on whom the murder can be pinned can actually be named. There are two other categories with fewer entries. The first, such as the Kennedy assassination or, on a less exalted level, the Gold killing, where almost certainly the killer is known but the facts behind the killing and who actually paid for and benefited from it are not. The final category is where deaths have apparently been explained but where there are still genuine doubts about what actually happened. It would be quite wrong, for example, to say categorically that Marilyn Monroe was murdered, but there are enough discrepancies in the facts of the case to raise an argument that it is a possibility. The same applies, on a domestic level, to the sad deaths of the children Susan Blatchford and Gary Hanlon.

The inclusion or exclusion of a case has, I hope, been fairly eclectic rather than eccentric. Most of the cases in the book could probably best be described as domestic rather than political and for that reason I have omitted the so-called terrorist cases of the 1970s when the British police and courts did not display themselves in their best light. This is not that I wish to hide their shortcomings or in any way denigrate the hardships which those wrongly convicted suffered.

I have included many of the famous cases in the western world. An exception is the American South-West in the latter half of the nineteenth century. For example it is impossible even to begin to consider who shot whom over a gambling debt incurred in the St James' Hotel in Cimarron, New Mexico, although there, in most instances, it would probably be fair to lay the crime at the door of the gunfighter Clay Allison. I have, however, included the name of one old friend of the Western fan, that of Belle Starr, if only because one of her lovers went by the engaging name of Blue Duck. Television viewers who watched Larry McMurtry's *Lonesome Dove* will recall he was the villain of the piece. I have included a few of the great gangster killings of the 1920s to 1940s but to include all the unsolved deaths of even the major players (perhaps the police did not try too hard) would swamp this and many another book. I have also included many which, I believe, are more or less unknown.

One splinter case I have not included for two reasons is of interest. The first reason is that the main murder was solved and the second that I could not think where to list it. On 17 June 1974 a severed human leg was washed ashore on Lake Ontario. The post-mortem showed that it had been roughly amputated after death. A local Toronto estate agent then reported his brother, Robert Donnelly, was missing. Robert was a heavy and, like so many, ultimately a losing gambler who had fallen out with other members of a gaming club known as The Circle. Almost certainly he was in debt to a money-lender, Ronald McGuire, and McGuire's sister, Mary Misener. Identification was made on the basis that Robert Donnelly's shoes fit that of the leg. The police were not prepared to move on the basis of such identification and suspicion and Donnelly's brother, Michael, began an investigation of his own. As a result a plot to burn a yacht and kill a lawyer, involving Mary Misener, was uncovered. Ronald Misener then set sail for sunnier climes but Mary Misener was charged with a variety of offences. After a re-trial she was sentenced to six years' imprisonment, five for conspiracy to murder and an additional year for the conspiracy to commit arson. She was then charged with the murder of Robert Donnelly and decided to tell all, blaming her absent brother. As a result of her information the body of Donnelly was dug up from a farm in Lindsay, Ontario. She ran a defence that she knew her brother had killed Donnelly and had buried the body but that she did not know he intended to do so. She admitted driving Donnelly's car to New York JFK airport and leaving it in the parking lot there. She received a further four years for her troubles. Ronald Misener has not been seen since January 1975.

The only complicating matter is that when Donnelly's body was exhumed it was found to have both legs.*

It is curious how unsolved crimes fall into patterns. The celebrated case of Lizzie Borden turned to a great extent on how she could have committed two axe murders in which the flow of blood must have been substantial and not have more than a few spots on her dress. The same applies to William Wallace.

---

* There is a very full account of the case in Derrick Murdoch's *Disappearances*.

In 1993 the Court of Appeal quashed the conviction of the Taylor sisters who had been convicted of the murder of the former lover of the elder of them. Again, very like the Wallace case, the problem was how could they have possibly committed the murder when neither of them had a spot of blood on their clothing which could, in any way, be connected to the victim of a horrendous attack.

Another interesting line of cases is the attack on the courting couple by unknown men. For English readers the classic case is the killing of Michael Gregsten by, the jury found, James Hanratty but there has been a long pedigree including the Texarcana murders and others in America and Canada.

Throughout the book there are references in the American cases to a Grand Jury who returned (or sometimes declined to return) a Bill of Indictment. The Grand Jury, of which there is no longer an English equivalent, sits in private and has the power to question witnesses without a lawyer or the suspect being present and to rule there is a *prima facie* case for a warrant to be issued. In this respect they loosely resemble English magistrates who decide whether there is a case for a defendant to answer before a jury, in which case they commit him to the Crown Court for trial. The American Grand Jury is derived from the English system which was surplanted by the system of the magistracy and which finally fell into disuse in the 1930s. Not all American states use the Grand Jury and some that do also have the equivalent of the English committal proceedings.

A word about the findings a jury may make. Until 1967 in England and Wales a jury of twelve had to return a unanimous verdict. Because of fears, which may have been illusory, that there had been jury nobbling in trials involving major Underworld figures, the requirement for a conviction or an acquittal was reduced to a majority of ten to two. The jury deliberate for a certain length of time, the adequacy of which is at the discretion of the judge, but never less than two hours before a majority decision is allowed. In America the jury must usually return a unanimous verdict but the jury may be composed of a lesser number than twelve. The Scottish system is different again. The jury is one of fifteen members who may return a bare majority verdict. A verdict of 'Not Proven' may also be returned. For the purposes of the accused's record it counts as an acquittal but still remains on court and police files.

At the time of writing, July 1994, I believe that all the cases are extant. It is always possible that one or more will have been solved by the time the book appears in print. A serial killer may always try his luck once too often and a whole chain of killings will be unravelled. This happened in the case of Robert

Black who, on 20 May 1994, was convicted of the murder of Susan Maxwell, who disappeared on 30 July 1982, Caroline Hogg, who disappeared in Edinburgh on 7 July 1983, and Sarah Harper who was abducted on 26 March 1986. He was caught on 14 July 1990 when he attempted to abduct a six-year-old girl on the Scottish Borders and was seen and chased. The girl was found bound and gagged in a sleeping bag in the rear of his car. A month later he received a sentence of life imprisonment and police investigations showed that he was in the area at the time of each of the earlier abductions. At the Newcastle Crown Court on 19 May 1994 he received ten concurrent life sentences with a recommendation that he serve a minimum of thirty-five years. At the time of writing he is appealing against his conviction.

Across the world, on 22 May 1994, a man was charged with the series of so-called Back Packer murders, a previously unsolved series of shootings of young travellers in the countryside near Sydney, New South Wales. If he is acquitted then they too will fall back into the unsolved category.

Sometimes a killer will simply walk into a police station and confess. That is what happened in the case of fifty-seven-year-old Olive Michelle Nixon who was battered to death on 6 November 1947 in a bombed house in the Regent's Park area of London. Her body was discovered by a police officer and for many years he was under suspicion himself. Certainly any thoughts of promotion he had were stifled. Quite by chance he was exonerated when Adam Ogilvie walked into St John's Wood police station in 1956 and confessed to the crime. Found guilty of manslaughter, he was sentenced to ten years' imprisonment.

It is interesting how murder cases are sometimes known by the name of the killer and sometimes by the victim with a preponderance in favour of the former. Given that, in the cases described here, there is no named killer, with one or two minor exceptions all entries are under the name of the victim. Where there has been a named killer, e.g. Hanratty, there is a cross-reference to the victim, Michael Gregsten. Where there has been a series of killings, as in the case of Jack the Ripper, the entry is found under the name of the first victim and, again, there is a cross-reference. Because the stories are inextricable, the death of Violet Kaye appears under Brighton Trunk Murders.

My thanks are due to many people who have mentioned cases to me or helped me research them. First and foremost, I must thank Richard Whittington-Egan for his very considerable help by sharing his encyclopaedic knowledge with me. Jean-Ann Hyslop and Juliet Thomas have also given more help in my research than I could reasonably have asked. In strictly alphabetical order I would also like to thank Julian Broadhead, Jonathan Goodman, Rusty Hoover, the crime reporter of the *Boulder Daily Camera*, Andrew and James Hyslop, Linda Jourgensen, Jennifer Kavanagh, John Kaye, Brian McConnell, Bill Pizzi, John Rigbey, David Sarch, Charlotte Smokler, Edda Tasiemka and the staff at the Law Society and the Public Records Office in Chancery Lane and at Kew. As always this book could not have been completed without the enormous help and effort of Dock Bateson.

Hertfordshire
July 1994

Ahmet Abdullah

A drug dealer and the adopted son of a powerful South-east London family, the Arifs, Ahmet Abdullah, known as Turkish Abbi, had quarrelled with other powerful South-east London interests and was shot in the William Hill betting shop in Bagshot Street, Walworth, on 11 March 1991. He was hit in the back after pleading with his attackers not to kill him. He then tried to use another customer as a shield and managed to escape from the shop before he was shot again. Brothers Tony and Patrick Brindle were charged with Abdullah's murder and stood trial at the Old Bailey in a case where witnesses gave evidence from behind screens and were identified only by number. Tony Brindle said he had not been in the betting shop but had been playing cards and drinking in The Bell public house in East Street, Walworth. Patrick Brindle did not give evidence. After their acquittal on 16 May 1992 Grace Brindle, their mother, told how the boys helped old ladies across the road and how they had wept when their pet budgie had died. The police said the enquiry was closed.

Francis Roy Adkins

O n 28 September 1990, the night of his death, Adkins met two Colombians in the Nightwatch bar of the American Hotel in Amsterdam. He had been the middleman in selling parcels of stolen emeralds in Amsterdam. He had been approached by a Sean O'Neil and several successful runs had been carried out. Then one of the parcels had been stolen from O'Neil and the Colombians wanted their money as a matter of urgency. Adkins persuaded O'Neil to attend a meeting to explain in person what had happened.

According to O'Neil, he had gone to the Nightwatch bar and had seen Adkins with the Colombians. Adkins gestured to O'Neil to continue walking. O'Neil had then heard eight gunshots and had run out of the hotel. He had not known Adkins was dead until he read the papers the next day.*

The death of Adkins is, in a convoluted way, linked to that of the Great Train

---

* The evidence of this was given by a Customs and Excise officer. Earlier in 1991 O'Neil had been acquitted at Isleworth Crown Court of charges relating to £10 million worth of cocaine. Three Colombian co-accused were sentenced to terms of up to eighteen years' imprisonment. Now, although he had previously made a statement, O'Neil could not be found to give evidence in person at Adkins' inquest.

Robber, Charlie Wilson (*qv*), who was shot dead at his home near Marbella. A James Rose had pleaded guilty to drug offences at Chelmsford Crown Court in January 1990, naming Adkins as the leader of the gang. Apparently he had been authorised to say this by Wilson and it was something which, not surprisingly, upset Adkins who had then ordered the execution of Wilson. There was, however, no suggestion that any of Wilson's friends had killed Adkins by way of reprisal. It was an entirely separate matter.

Linda Agostini
(The Pyjama Girl Case)

On 1 September 1934 a girl's body, wearing the top half of the eponymous pyjamas, was found on waste land near Albury, New South Wales, by a farmer bringing a bull back home from market. The body was so disfigured that it appeared at first to have been scalped. In fact, it turned out the girl had been shot and the body set on fire. The first problem was identification. There were difficulties in establishing identity through dental records because a bullet was lodged in her jaw. She was thought to be English and had distinctive ears in that they had no lobes. A Jeanette Rutledge claimed the body as that of her illegitimate daughter, Philomena Morgan, but she had something of a mental history and her claims were not accepted. The body was placed in a formalin tank at Sydney University where, over a period of nearly ten years, desultory identification parades were held.

Meanwhile Mrs Rutledge stepped up her campaign to have the body identified as that of her daughter and a totally eccentric doctor named Palmer-Benbow more or less gave up his practice to try to establish that the body was that of Philomena.

In 1944 a further inquest was arranged and, almost on the eve, Antonio Agostini, a cloakroom attendant in Romano's, a Sydney restaurant, was arrested. He had been interviewed following the disappearance of his wife Linda, a former cinema usherette, some ten years earlier. Then he had been shown photographs and said the body was not that of his wife. Now, he made a confession. The body was taken out of its tank, make-up and a hair-do applied and this time seven people identified it as that of Linda Agostini.

The inquest was devoted to an attack on the identification, with Agostini's

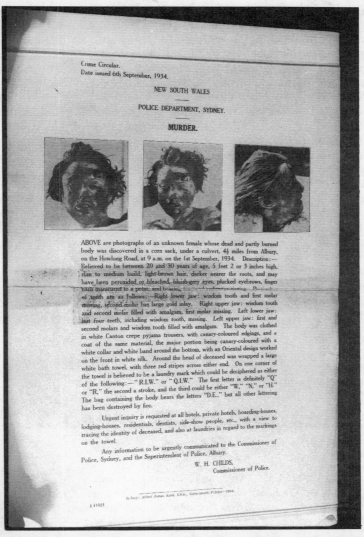

Crime Circular.
Date issued 6th September, 1934.

NEW SOUTH WALES

POLICE DEPARTMENT, SYDNEY.

MURDER.

ABOVE are photographs of an unknown female whose dead and partly burned body was discovered in a corn sack, under a culvert, 4½ miles from Albury, on the Howlong Road, at 9 a.m. on the 1st September, 1934.   Description:— Believed to be between 20 and 30 years of age, 5 feet 2 or 3 inches high, slim to medium build, light-brown hair, darker nearer the roots, and may have been peroxided or bleached, bluish-grey eyes, plucked eyebrows, finger nails manicured to a point, and bearing traces of red enamel staining. Particulars of teeth are as follows:—Right lower jaw: wisdom tooth and first molar missing, second molar has large gold inlay.   Right upper jaw: wisdom tooth and second molar filled with amalgam, first molar missing.   Left lower jaw: last four teeth, including wisdom tooth, missing.   Left upper jaw: first and second molars and wisdom tooth filled with amalgam.   The body was clothed in white Canton crepe pyjama trousers, with canary-coloured edgings, and a coat of the same material, the major portion being canary-coloured with a white collar and white band around the bottom, with an Oriental design worked on the front in white silk.   Around the head of deceased was wrapped a large white bath towel, with three red stripes across either end.   On one corner of the towel is believed to be a laundry mark which could be deciphered as either of the following:—" R.I.W." or " Q.I.W."   The first letter is definitely "Q" or "R," the second a stroke, and the third could be either "W," "N," or "H."   The bag containing the body bears the letters "D.E.," but all other lettering has been destroyed by fire.

Urgent inquiry is requested at all hotels, private hotels, boarding-houses, lodging-houses, residentials, dentists, side-show people, etc., with a view to tracing the identity of deceased, and also at laundries in regard to the markings on the towel.

Any information to be urgently communicated to the Commissioner of Police, Sydney, and the Superintendent of Police, Albury.

W. H. CHILDS,
Commissioner of Police.

An early attempt by the police to identify the Pyjama Girl Case victim, later believed to be Linda Agostini, who is pictured on the jacket of this book.

representatives trying to prove the body to be that of Philomena Morgan. The eyes of the body, which might have helped in the identification, had been removed and suddenly disappeared during the hearing. Agostini's confession really did not stand up. Why had he driven so far to dispose of the body when, many miles nearer, there was a lake said to be bottomless? There were suggestions that he was in trouble with the Camorra, an Australian branch of the Mafia, and was not displeased to be in custody and so out of the way.* The inquest jury found that the body was that of Linda Agostini and her husband was committed for trial.

Now Agostini again changed his tack. Yes, the body was that of his wife. Linda, a constant nag, had been killed by accident in a quarrel after which he panicked. Despite an intervention by Palmer-Benbow who tried to reopen the whole identification question the jury returned what the judge, Mr Justice Lower, described as a merciful verdict of manslaughter. Agostini was given six years and when asked what he wished to have done with the body replied that he did not mind as it was not that of his wife. The body was buried at the State's expense in July 1944 and Agostini was deported to Italy in February 1947 on the completion of his sentence. Throughout his imprisonment he had persistently refused to accept the body was that of his wife. There are good grounds for thinking the body was that of Philomena Morgan, killed by the son of a Sydney detective, something which would account for the enthusiasm the police had for proving the corpse to be that of Linda Agostini. The other body has never been found.

Vince Kelly, *The Charge is Murder*; Eric Clegg, *Return Your Verdict*

Adnan Abdul Hameed Al Sane

On 17 December 1993 the headless and partially burned body of forty-six-year-old Adnan Abdul Hameed Al Sane was found naked, except for his underpants, in a railway arch near Piccadilly Station, Manchester. His head was found some seventy miles away, six weeks later, by a man walking his dog near

---

* Strictly speaking the Australian Camorra was a branch of a Neapolitan gang of organised criminals.

the M6 motorway at Cannock in Staffordshire. It had been mutilated with blows from a machete and was identified from a rare alloy used in dental bridgework.

He had lived in London since 1986, when he retired from partnership in a bank in Kuwait. He had apparently suffered substantial losses with the collapse in the early 1980s of the Kuwaiti stockmarket. It is thought he was abducted from his flat after dining with a business friend in the Brittania Hotel in Grosvenor Square. Although beheading is a traditional form of Arabic punishment the Kuwaiti community said that it was not a normal method of retribution in their country.

Thomas Anderson *see* **Thomas Wendon Atherston**

Edward Andrassy

On 23 September 1935 two naked mutilated corpses were found on Jackass Hill in Kingsbury Run, a poor suburb of Cleveland, Ohio. In each case their heads and genitals had been cut off. The mutilator had displayed some skill in his work. The second body was identified through fingerprints as Edward Andrassy who had a conviction for carrying an offensive weapon. Over the next two years a total of twelve bodies were found, mostly dismembered. Seven were male and five women. All were found in roughly the same area. Of the men only Andrassy was identified. Two of the women were identified as Florence Polillo and Rose Wallace. All the deaths were attributed to the work of the same killer and there are suggestions that the body count may have been as high as forty. Two detectives, Merylo and Zalewski, were assigned full-time to the case and in the ensuing sweep of the underbelly of Cleveland, whilst a number of arrests were made for burglary, assault and robbery they never closed on the killer. Eventually the partnership was dissolved over a disagreement as to whether a potential suspect should be pulled in for questioning or merely kept under further observation.

A private detective, Pat Lyons, who had interested himself in the case, took matters a stage further. Analysing the evidence and the skill with which the bodies had been dissected he believed that the murders took place in a 'laboratory' in the vicinity of Kingsbury Run. Further investigations showed that the two women who had been identified, Florence Polillo and Rose Wallace, not only patronised the same bar but knew each other well. They also discovered that Andrassy frequented the bar. Then information was received that a local man known as Frank often carried knives and threatened to use them. He was identified as Frank Dolezal who lived in the district on Central Avenue. His rooms were searched and in the bathroom stains of long-dried blood were found. It was then discovered that he and Mrs Polillo had lived together at one time.

Dolezal was arrested on 5 July 1939 and made a confession two days later. In it he admitted he had dissected the body of Florence Polillo. His confused story told of a quarrel in which she had tried to take ten dollars from his pocket. He had hit her and she had fallen, hitting her head on the bath. Dolezal then took a knife and cut off her head and arms. He concluded by saying that he had put parts of the body at the rear of the Hart Manufacturing Company on Twentieth Street and the head, lower legs and left arm into the partly frozen Lake Erie. There was some verification of the story. Because of the freezing conditions there was ice on the edge of Lake Erie and open water beyond. Unfortunately for the validity of the confession, the parts of the body Dolezal said he had thrown in the river were found on Fourteenth Street.

Five days later his lawyer retracted the confession on his behalf saying he had been in a daze when he had made it. There was worse to come. The bloodstains found in his apartment were no such thing. The charge of murder was reduced to one of manslaughter. On 24 August 1939, with some considerable ingenuity, Dolezal hanged himself in his cell.

Whether or not Dolezal was responsible for the death of Florence Polillo, the killings had stopped. In January 1939 a letter was sent to the Chief of Police in Cleveland which indicated that the killer, known in the press as the Head Hunter of Kingsbury Run, had moved his operations to Los Angeles. At least that was the postmark on the envelope. In his letter he said a further head was buried on Century Boulevard but it was never discovered by the police. Los Angeles may not have been the next place of work for the Head Hunter because six more victims were found in Pennsylvania in the years from 1938 to 1942 which eliminated Dolezal as the killer.

The great 'Crimebuster' Elliot Ness, who investigated some of the killings, believed that the killer was a young man from an influential family.

Oliver Weld (ed), *Cleveland Murders*

Emily Armstrong

At 4 p.m. on Thursday 14 April 1949, the sixty-nine-year-old Emily Armstrong was found battered to death in an Eastmans dry-cleaners at 37 St John's Wood High Street, London, where she had been the manageress. She had been attacked in the previous hour. There were at least twenty-two severe lacerating wounds on the head and face, and the left side of her skull was shattered. The weapon was not found but was thought to be something like a claw hammer.

Her handbag containing a weekly season ticket and purse was missing and was never found. A heavily bloodstained handkerchief with a floral pattern and a laundry mark H. 612 was found not far from the scene of the crime but it did not lead to any arrest. During the morning a man had made a bogus enquiry about goods he said he had left at the shop some seven weeks previously. He was described as aged thirty and between 5'5" and 5'6" but he was never traced.

One of the suspects was John Allen, the child murderer and Broadmoor escapee. He was not picked out in an identification parade although he had almost certainly been in St John's Wood that day. It was not thought the killer was from the neighbourhood, and indeed one of the locals, then in Borstal, was given ten days leave of absence to try to assist. Army deserters were rounded up but again with no success.

Mrs Armstrong's killing was also linked to the robbery and murder of Dorothy O'Leary (*qv*) and an attack on a shopkeeper in St Helens on 25 May 1949. It was thought possible that the killer was a vagrant or a man who had fled to Ireland.

Peter Arne

On 1 August 1983 the sixty-two-year-old actor Peter Arne was battered to death in his flat in Hans Crescent, Knightsbridge, London. The police were called when another resident in the block of flats saw a bloodstained piece of wood in the hallway. He had been beaten with a firelog and his neck slashed, producing what the pathologist, Dr Ian West, described as a torrential haemorrhage.

Arne, a former Battle of Britain pilot who had appeared in *The Return of the*

Pink Panther and *Straw Dogs*, was due to start work the following week in one of BBC's *Dr Who* series. The cultured Arne, who collected art deco *objets*, was a regular visitor to the arches at Charing Cross station to pick up young and homeless men.

Two days later the passport of thirty-two-year-old Italian teacher Giuseppe Perusi was found, together with bloodstained clothing, by the Thames from which his naked body was later recovered. He had been living rough in London parks. Perusi taught handicapped children and administered a farmers' co-operative in Verona where he was a Communist councillor. He had been having sexual identity problems and had been given leave of absence to holiday in England. He had been seen the day before in Hans Crescent asking for 'Peter'. A handprint of Perusi was found on the bloodstained wall in Arne's flat. Arne's diary showed an appointment to meet Giuseppe.

The coroner returned a verdict of unlawful killing in respect of Arne and suicide on Perusi. 'Everything points towards Giuseppe Perusi killing Peter Arne. He was a depressed man and he talked of suicide to his family. If he had just performed a brutal murder then his mind would have turned to killing himself.' The police said their file was now closed.

Maxine Arnold

On 22 December 1989 thirty-two-year-old blonde Maxine Arnold and her boyfriend Terry Gooderham were shot dead in their Mercedes car in Lodge Lane, a well-known courting spot near Epping Forest. He was an accountant and stocktaker for pubs and winebars across London. He also had a double, if not treble love life. He spent half the week with Maxine and the remainder (Saturday, Sunday, Monday and Thursday) with another blonde, Carole Wheatley, in Chingford. Probably both women knew of his relationship with the other. A police officer found the car in the early hours of the following morning. The car lights were on and the glass of the front offside window was broken. Both Maxine and Terry were wearing tracksuits.

Shortly before 7 o'clock Maxine had been speaking to a friend on the telephone. She had told her she had to take Terry out and would speak again to her later. Maxine's mother arrived a short time afterwards at the Walthamstow flat and found the lights, including the Christmas tree lights, on and the front door double locked. Maxine's clothes were spread over the bed as if she had been choosing what to wear for the evening. Her handbag was still in the flat as were Gooderham's watch and wallet.

The police believe that they had been set up to meet with a contract killer, or that he came to the flat and then forced them to drive to Epping Forest. A packet of cocaine had been left in the car but this, the police believe, was merely to throw them off the scent.

According to a report in *The Sun* newspaper on 27 December 1990, their friends had held a seance in which both Maxine and Terry spoke saying that he had been involved in some way with the Brinks Mat robbery.*

Various theories have been advanced for Gooderham's death – it is generally accepted that Maxine was simply in the wrong place at the wrong time. As one anonymous friend put it: 'It is nothing to do with his love life or his own business but a lot of money is involved.'

One theory is that he was trying to muscle in on the lucrative Spanish ice-cream market and had so upset some other players that a £50,000 contract had been put out on him; another is that some £150,000 had been re-directed; a third that in his job he had uncovered a major fraud. A final permutation is that Gooderham had yet a third girlfriend who organised the killing. Since his own death the name of James Moody (*qv*) has been mentioned from time to time as the contract killer.

Possibly the killing related to the North London gang war which had been simmering throughout the 1980s. 'Sometimes we take out one of them, and then they take out one of ours. Or the other way around,' said a fringe participant.

James Morton, *Gangland*

A6 murder *see* Michael Gregsten

---

* *The Sun*, 27 December 1990. In the Brinks Mat robbery in 1983 some £26 million of gold bullion was stolen from a warehouse at London airport. Despite a number of convictions little has been recovered.

Thomas Weldon Atherston

On 16 July 1910 forty-seven-year-old Weldon Atherston, a small-time actor whose last but one engagement had been at the Battersea Palace in a melodrama *The Grip of the Law*, was found by his son at the base of an iron staircase in the back of the house where his former mistress, Elizabeth Earl (or Earle), had a flat in 17 Clifton Gardens, Prince of Wales Road, Battersea. He was wearing carpet slippers and had been shot. His son, twenty-one-year-old Thomas Frederick Anderson, had been dining with Miss Earl, a former actress who now taught at the Academy of Dramatic Art which would later become RADA.

About 9.30 p.m. a chauffeur, Edward Noice, was driving in Rosenau Road when he heard two shots. He looked and saw a man climbing through the garden of 19 Clifton Gardens. He then saw him on a wall and, after leaping down onto the pavement, running off towards the Thames. Noice drove to the police station. The investigating officer was a Sergeant Buckley who went to No. 17 where the door was opened to him by Miss Earl. She told him she had heard shots fired and that she had seen a man climb a wall. Thomas Anderson confirmed her story.

On investigation of the property heavy breathing was heard and in the doorway of the downstairs scullery the dying Atherston was discovered. He had been shot on the right-hand side of his face near his mouth. Atherston was carrying a rudimentary form of life-preserver, a piece of insulated electric cable wrapped in paper and covered in wool with a loop to pass over the wrist. The police officer found a calling card in the man's possession and asked Thomas Anderson if he knew anyone by the name of Athertone. He replied he knew someone by the name of Atherston and said that was the name under which his father appeared on the stage. He was taken to the police station and asked if the dead man was his father. He said that he did not think so as his father did not wear a moustache. He was told the man was clean shaven and then began to cry saying, 'I saw my father die.'

The case was something of a *cause célèbre*. For a start what was Thomas Anderson doing dining with his father's mistress while his father was downstairs in the empty ground-floor flat in his carpet slippers with a life preserver in his pocket? Various theories have been advanced including the suggestion that Thomas, together with his younger brother and Miss Earl, conspired to do away with Atherston as he was becoming a financial burden to them. Another is that Atherston was killed by Anderson after he discovered his son and Miss Earl together. A third suggestion postulates the existence of a lover who killed Atherston when surprised by him.

An inquest was held and adjourned on a number of occasions for the police to make further enquiries. What did emerge was that there had been a number of burglaries in the area. The man seen escaping was in his thirties rather than a young man like Thomas or his even younger brother. Atherston had suffered a head injury some two years previously and had become increasingly suspicious of Miss Earl, believing that she had another lover; something of which there was no evidence. So far as dining with Thomas on a Saturday evening, he said she had been like a mother to him and had visited her often. There were no signs of a struggle or blood in her rooms. The police indicated they were satisfied that Miss Earl and the Anderson boys had cooperated fully with them.

The explanation is probably that Atherston had been hiding to see if Miss Earl did have a lover whom he would then attack. Unfortunately whilst he was hiding downstairs he encountered the burglar and was shot by him in the ensuing struggle.

Jonathan Goodman, Acts of Murder; Bernard Taylor and Stephen Knight, *Perfect Murder*

Annie Austin

At about 7.30 a.m. on 26 May 1901 twenty-eight-year-old Annie Austin was heard moaning in a cubicle in a lodging house at 35 Dorset Street, Spitalfields, London. She had been separated from her husband for about ten days. When she was examined by a doctor it was found that she had been stabbed in both the anus and the vagina. When he asked her if she knew who had done it she said it was by the man who had come in with her the previous night but whose name she did not know.

She died in the London Hospital on 30 May. The police had been called but did not arrive in time and instead she had told the doctor her story. She said she had slept with the man and then as he was getting up to leave in the early hours she felt a sharp pain as if a knife had been run inside her. She described him as short with dark hair and moustache and a Jewish appearance.

The hostel was managed by a Henry Moore and his wife. His brother-in-law,

Daniel Sullivan, sometimes acted as his deputy. It was he who took her to hospital. The lodging house rules, observed in their breach, were that only married couples should share a cubicle. The manager said that customers were insulted if they were asked if they were married.

At the inquest the pathologist reported no signs of a struggle and that Austin was healthy but for long-standing syphilis. Moore said that he had allowed the man and woman into the premises and that he had sent for Dr Dale and had called a cab for her. His wife, Maria Moore, said she had been up and about all that night but had heard no screams. One of the unanswered questions was when had the man slipped away or if indeed he was part of the hostel staff. Both Sullivan and Moore came under suspicion because for some reason they gave the wrong cubicle number to the police. At first they said she had been in cubicle forty-four rather than the correct number fifteen. Was the street door unlocked before her screams were heard? If so it would indicate that the man had left. If it was still bolted it would almost certainly be the case that the killer had remained on the premises. Her estranged husband was able to give a cast-iron alibi. There was some suggestion that Daniel Sullivan had been the man with her that night but he gave an alibi that he had shared a bed that night with a man named Timothy Batty at 10 Paternoster Row. The coroner took the view that this was not conclusive but in the absence of any contradictory evidence the jury should give weight to it.

The police, who felt the man was known to the lodging house habituees and was being protected by them, clearly had a hard time as the final report reads:

> From the first to the last we have to deal with a class of witnesses that are as low as they can well possibly be and it is difficult to know when they are speaking the truth. In some instances they lie without any apparent motive.
> Although we never despair I fear that nothing further can be done to elucidate this mystery and the perpetrator of this crime unfortunately goes unpunished as a result of the scandalous conduct of nearly the whole of the witnesses in this case. Thomas Divall. (Inspector).

Apart from anything else they had had to pay out the then not inconsiderable sum of £5 to sober people to round up the witnesses and make them keep their appointments with the police.

Axeman of New Orleans *see* Joseph Maggio

Marie Bailes

On 30 May 1908 the mutilated body of six-year-old Marie Bailes was found in a lavatory at the corner of St George's Road, Islington, London. An attendant opened a brown paper parcel which had, he said, been left by a nervous man. Inside, wrapped in a blanket and covered in sand as if she had been buried, was the child.

She had last been seen leaving the local St John's Roman Catholic School on Friday afternoon with a friend. About twelve houses from her home she had separated from her companion and was never seen alive again.

A man was arrested in Derby and released after a witness failed to identify him, as was an inmate of the Wandsworth workhouse. On 22 June during the re-opened inquest, a man in the public gallery shouted out that there were six distinct clues to show that the crime had been committed by a woman. The police, however, said they were unable to shed any more light on the case and the jury returned a verdict of wilful murder against a person or persons unknown.

Olive Balchin

On 20 October 1946 the forty-year-old Olive Balchin was found battered to death on a bombsite in Manchester. A blood-stained hammer had been left by her body. The evidence against thirty-nine-year-old Walter Rowlands was both forensic and that of identification, including a witness who said he had sold the hammer to him. There were also traces of hair and dust, together with blood on his shoe which came from the same group as that of Olive Balchin. On his arrest in a local hostel he had asked, 'You don't want me for the murder of that woman do you?'

He pleaded not guilty but was convicted and sentenced to death. Whilst awaiting trial a prisoner in Liverpool, David John Ware, confessed to the murder of Olive Balchin and the confession became a principal ground of appeal.

The Court of Appeal, however, was dismissive about the idea of calling Ware to give evidence. 'It is not an unusual thing for all sorts of confessions to be made by people who have nothing to do with a crime,' said the Lord Chief Justice. He also commented that questions would have to be asked about Ware's mental

Walter Rowlands, who was hanged on 27 February 1947 for the murder of Olive Balchin.

state. If anyone was to re-examine the case then it was for the Home Secretary who had infinitely more resources. As he was taken down Rowlands shouted, 'I am an innocent man. This is the grossest injustice which has ever occurred in an English court. Why did you not have in court the man who confessed to the crime? I am not having justice because of my past. I am innocent before God.' J. C. Jolly KC was appointed to head an enquiry which acted fast. He interviewed both Ware and Edward Macdonald, from whom Rowlands was said to have bought the hammer used to kill Balchin. Ware retracted his confession beginning, 'I wish to say that the statements I have given confessing to a murder are absolutely untrue. I have never seen the woman Balchin, who was murdered, in my life. I did not murder her and had nothing to do whatsoever with the murder. I made these statements out of swank more than anything.'

He was put on an identification parade in the prison at which Macdonald and the other witnesses were adamant he was not the man they had seen.

Rowlands' appeal was dismissed on 10 February 1947. On the 25th Jolly filed his report and the Home Secretary announced there were no grounds for interfering with the verdict. Rowlands was hanged on 27 February. He had occupied the same cell in 1934 after his conviction for the murder of his daughter. He had been reprieved and released from that sentence in 1940. It was to this he referred when he mentioned his past.

In November 1951 Ware appeared at Bristol Assizes charged with attempted murder. He told the police, 'I have killed a woman. I keep having an urge to hit women on the head'. He was found guilty and sent to a mental hospital.

Leslie Hale, *Hanged in Error*

Harry Barham

At 6.30 p.m. on 14 February 1972, fifty-two-year-old bookmaker Harry Barham was shot dead in his car in Windmill Lane, Stratford, East London. For some years he had held the majority interest in bookmaking businesses in Islington and Holborn. In recent months he had lost and paid £50,000 in personal bets and now he was awaiting trial at the Old Bailey on a charge of evading £160,000 betting duty. He had been killed with a shot in the back of the head and two in the back at close range from a .45 automatic pistol.

In an effort to raise the money to pay the back duty and a fine, that day he had started to buy jewellery cheaply in Hatton Garden and resell it immediately for a profit. By 4 p.m. he had put together £40,000 and the police believe he was the victim of a set-up. Someone had overheard that he was carrying a substantial amount of money – not easy to keep secret in the gossip alley of Hatton Garden where very substantial sums change hands on street corners – and a middleman was sent to him. The aim was to decoy him and steal his money but one theory is that he recognised his attacker and was shot to silence him. He was known to have had tea at Lesley's, a cafe in Red Lion Street in Holborn, and he was seen at about 5.15 that evening cutting up traffic in Russell Square (not the usual way to the East End from Hatton Garden). A witness had taken the car number and reported that he had seen three men in the vehicle.

Another theory on offer was that he had stumbled across a gang planning a major crime and that his death served two purposes. It was said in the underworld that one of his killers was Teddy Machin,* one time enforcer for Jack Spot and now general handyman around town, but, rather like James Moody, after his death there was a tendency to saddle Machin with the blame for all sorts of problems to which he could not respond.

---

* On 23 May 1973 Edward 'Teddy' Machin was shot dead whilst walking near his home in Forest Gate, London. This was the second attack on him within two years. On the previous occasion he had survived what was said to be an attempted contract killing with a value of £500 being placed on his life. Then he had been shot through a ground-floor window whilst asleep in bed in Windsor Road, Forest Gate. After his death Alan Mackenzie was charged with his murder. The prosecution's case was that Machin had been having an affair with Mackenzie's aunt and had been treating her badly, taking money from her and refusing to let her go out without him. The defence was that the gun was Machin's and it had gone off accidentally when Mackenzie tried to take it away from him. After a retirement of five and a half hours the first jury could not agree and, on 6 December 1973, Mackenzie pleaded guilty to manslaughter. He was sentenced to three years' imprisonment.

Edwin Bartlett

On 1 January 1885 forty-one-year-old Edwin Bartlett, a grocer in Pimlico, London, died after eating a large New Year's Eve dinner. He had been unwell for some weeks previously and had been diagnosed as suffering from mercury poisoning. At the time mercury was used as a treatment for venereal disease. Bartlett was also dosing his St Bernard dogs with it. Another of his troubles was bad teeth. An incompetent dentist had sawn them off at the gum line and Edwin had received hypnosis from Leach, the family doctor, to help with the pain.

At the time he was married to Adelaide Blanche, born in Orléans in 1856 and, in theory, the daughter of Adolphe Collet de la Tremouille, Comte de Thouars d'Escury, but it has been suggested that she was really the illegitimate daughter of Lord Alfred Paget. Bartlett had met her when she came to England with her guardian and rented rooms from his family. Theirs was almost certainly a marriage arranged by her guardian. Bartlett would receive a substantial dowry and Adelaide would be kept in modest circumstances well out of the reaches of Society where she might cause a scandal. She would later say that she had only

A drawing of a scene at the Old Bailey during the trial of Adelaide Bartlett. Edwin Bartlett's father is being cross-examined by Edward Clarke QC.

met Edwin once before her marriage but many of her remarks were self-serving. She was allowed to travel in Europe to complete her education before returning to her husband.

Sex between the couple was at best limited. They had tried to produce a family but the child had been stillborn. One of Adelaide's comments was that there had only been a single sexual act. Instead Adelaide had an affair with her brother-in-law, Frederick, who later emigrated to America.

In 1885 Edwin engaged the Rev. George Dyson as a tutor in Latin, history and geography for Adelaide. She would later claim that Edwin had given her to Dyson. In all events they had a close relationship which Dyson maintained was platonic.

The autopsy showed that Bartlett had died from drinking a large dose of liquid chloroform. Dyson had purchased some for Adelaide who, he said, was using it to ease her husband's pain during his final illness. Adelaide told Dr Leach, however, that she needed the chloroform to ward off the unwelcome attentions of her husband who, she said, had abandoned the platonic marriage.

Quite apart from the sexual side there was motive enough. Fourteen months earlier Bartlett had changed his will so that Adelaide had full control of his property on his demise.

The difficulty the prosecution faced was that liquid chloroform was believed to burn both the mouth and throat on contact. Additionally there is a strong and unpleasant odour. It could not, therefore, be administered secretly. In fact it was later established that this theory was a fallacy. The trial judge offered the solution that Edwin may have taken the chloroform to dull the ache from his jaws.

Amidst cheers from the public gallery both Dyson and Adelaide were acquitted. Afterwards Sir James Paget, a Sergeant-Surgeon to the Queen, suggested that, now she was a free woman, in the interests of science she should tell how she had done it. One of the prevailing suggestions is that it was done by hypnosis. Bartlett was clearly a receptive subject and during the weeks before his death he had complained to Leach that he felt he was under a mesmeric spell cast on him by a friend through his wife. The downside of this theory is that it is not believed that a person could be induced to drink a substance such as chloroform whilst under hypnosis.

After the trial Adelaide Bartlett dropped from sight. It has been suggested that she became a nurse and also that she followed her brother-in-law Frederick to America. She died in Boston in the 1930s. In her letter of thanks to Sir Edward Clarke QC, to whose brilliance she owed her acquittal, she wrote, 'I have not been a good woman and my temptations have been terriable [sic] ones, but though I have not kept my vows as I should have done, you will judge me mercifully.'

Sir John Hall (ed), *Notable British Trials*; Yseult Bridges, *Poison and Adelaide Bartlett*; Kate Clarke, *The Pimlico Murder*

Susan Becker

On 1 July 1982 the fully clothed but substantially decomposed body of twenty-year-old Susan Becker was found in a gully about a mile above Boulder Falls, Colorado. It appears she had been dead some ten or eleven days before the body was found. Becker was last seen alive on the morning of 20 June, the day after she attended a friend's wedding. Because of the decomposition of the body it was impossible to say whether a sexual attack had taken place. There had also been severe storms at the time and a combination of hail and rain undoubtedly washed away potential clues. What was apparent was that she had been stabbed thirteen times. Her body and head were wrapped in a lime-green bath towel and her shoulder pack was pushed up around her neck. It would seem she had slid down a very steep hill.

Suspicion fell on a Longmont man then on parole for the killing in 1966 of his fourteen-year-old sister-in-law in Illinois. He was arrested for threatening a woman with a knife and trying to get into her car on the campus of the University of Colorado. He also lived next door to a ninety-four-year-old woman, Orma Smith, whose stabbed body was found eight days after the discovery of Susan Becker, on a campsite in Larimer County. He was never arrested for either of the deaths and was eventually ruled out as a suspect. He was sentenced to one year for menacing the woman on the campus and returned to prison in Illinois.

The police also investigated the possibility that Susan had been the victim of a cult murder. She had died about the time of the summer solstice, there were thirteen stab wounds and they were in a pattern. She was known to have been toying with Rastafarian and Native American beliefs, something which contrasted with her Catholic upbringing.

However, by no means all the detectives who worked on the case were convinced she was murdered. Some favoured suicide, the police theory being that she could have first stabbed herself in the chest and then wedged the knife into some rocks and lunged against it backwards, causing three further wounds. She could then have pulled the knife out of the rock or, if the knife had become lodged in her back, have reached behind her and withdrawn it.

Apart from the physical difficulty in performing this act there were no rocks near where her body was found, but there were rocks further up the mountain and it was thought she might have slid down from that area.

The suicide theory was firmly rejected by her parents who asked, 'How many times can you stab yourself in the back?' They believe she was murdered. She had been associating with a man who had a lodge near where she was found and she often hitch-hiked there. She also liked to sunbathe on the ridge. 'She trusted people too much. She liked people and couldn't believe there were some pretty rotten people around here,' said her mother Ruphene to *Boulder Daily Camera* journalist, Rusty Hoover.

Penny Bell

On 6 June 1991 forty-three-year-old company director and mother-of-two, Penny Bell, was stabbed to death in a car park at the sports centre in Greenford, Middlesex. A sheet of wallpaper and a sample woodblock were found near her body and one theory is that she had been discussing home decorations with her killer. She had drawn out £8,500 in £50 notes from her bank shortly before her death. Other theories ranged from a robbery which went wrong to blackmail. She may have been followed from her home in Denham when she left that morning in her Jaguar XJS. Over 2,000 people were interviewed but no charges were made.

At 9.40 a.m. on the day of her death Penny, who earned £85,000 a year as a director of an employment agency, left her home at Bakers Wood, Denham. She told one workman she had an appointment ten minutes later. An hour later she was found hacked to death in her car left at the Greenford Sports Centre. She had been stabbed some fifty times. The hazard lights on her car were flashing and the windscreen wipers working.

She had been previously married and before and during the present marriage had had a number of lovers some of whom were bi-sexual. Some years before he met his wife Alistair Bell had had a homosexual relationship with a man who had remained a friend of the family. As time went by and no arrests were made

Bell said, 'I realise I am still a suspect. It is very difficult to live with. But it will be that way until there is a trial and the guilty party is put away.'

In the summer of 1992 a former neighbour was arrested and released on police bail to return for further questioning in July. The night before he was due to return to the police station his bail was cancelled and he was eliminated from the enquiries. It is thought that his fingerprint had been found in Mrs Bell's car. The next month the investigation was wound down. Despite an offer of £20,000 reward put up by Mrs Bell's co-director, the police believed that up to thirty potential witnesses had failed to come forward. In December of that year Alistair Bell was given an apology and awarded substantial agreed damages over a story in the *Financial Advertiser* which had linked him to his wife's death.

Kate Bender

This twenty- to twenty-four-year-old, comely or coarse (accounts vary), self-styled healer disappeared, together with her father, William John, her mother and her brother John, from her home fourteen miles east of Independence near Cherryvale, Kansas, in the spring of 1873. In March of that year a Dr William York had asked in the town where he could find something to eat and was directed to the Benders' farm. He was never seen alive again. Versions of the story vary but it seems that York's lawyer brother made enquiries and visited the Benders. They told him William York had never arrived at their farm. The second York declined any food saying he wanted to continue the trail of his brother but that if he failed he would return. Other versions attribute the enquiries to private investigators hired by the lawyer.

The next day the Bender home was deserted and when York returned a full investigation was begun. There were rotting carcasses of calves and pigs in the yard. In the orchard was discovered the body of Dr York together with seven other bodies. As the digging continued more bodies were found. Most had had their throats cut and heads smashed. The *modus operandi* had apparently been that, with the daughter Kate being used as a decoy, whilst the guest was eating the father or brother would creep up behind and attack the traveller.

As for the Benders, their wagon was tracked and found riddled with bullet holes. Of the family there was no trace. According to one version a German who knew the Benders (who were also of German extraction) was hanged and revived three times by a mob trying to make him reveal their whereabouts. Over the years there were a number of 'sightings'. In 1889 a Mrs Almira Griffith and her daughter, a Mrs Sarah Davis, were identified by seven people as being Mrs and Kate Bender. They were brought back to Kansas for trial but released when a marriage certificate for 1872 in Michigan was produced.

Various confessions were made over the years by men who admitted they had been in the attack on the Bender family. One, in 1910, claimed that the bodies had been buried in a twenty-foot well and at the same time the posse which had set out after them had taken several thousand dollars, stolen over the years by the family from their victims. No well was ever found but this may be because the area had been ploughed and sown.

Another version of the story has it that William Bender escaped but was caught for the murder of a man near Salmon, Idaho, in 1884. He was kept in jail overnight but found to have bled to death the next morning. As with an animal caught in a trap he had tried to cut off his foot to free himself. According to journalist William Bolitho a letter was written by the Cherryvale Chief of Police to a firm of San Francisco investigators in 1910.

> Dear Sir, – Yours received. It so happened that my father-in-law's farm joins that of the benders and he helped to locate the bodies of the benders. I often tried to find out from him what became of the benders, but he only gave me a knowing look and said he guessed they would not bother anyone else. There was a vigilance committee organised to locate the benders, and shortly after Old man bender's waggon was found by the roadside riddled with bullets. You will have to guess the rest. – I am, respectfully yours, J. Kramer.

William Bolitho, *Leviathan*; Carl Sifakis, *The Encyclopaedia of American Crime*

Olive May Bennett

The body of forty-five-year-old nurse Olive Bennett was found in the River Avon at Stratford, England, on 24 April 1954. She had been strangled with a long woollen scarf and the body then weighted with a fifty-six-pound tombstone. Until middle age she had led something of a sheltered life but then she took an appointment at the Monroe Devis Maternity Home at Tiddington in Warwickshire. She started smoking and drinking and drew large sums from her Post Office account. Before going off duty she would take endless trouble with her make-up. On the night of her death she was seen drinking in the Red Horse Hotel in Bridge Street and then shortly before midnight standing outside the hotel. Her diary contained the names of a considerable number of men but they were eliminated from the police enquiries. In 1962 two women went to the police to say that on the night of the murder they had been in the churchyard with two men, one of whom had said he would push her in the river and weigh her down with a tombstone. Enquiries were re-commenced and soldiers who had been at the nearby Long Marston Army camp were re-questioned but to no effect.

Leon Beron

December 1910 did not end well for Leon Beron. He was killed on New Year's Eve on Clapham Common in South London. Nor did 1911 begin too well for Alexander Petropavloff, who had at least three aliases, the best known of which was Steinie Morrison. On 10 January he was arrested for Beron's murder. There is little doubt that the 6′3″, handsome, well-built and well-dressed Steinie was a receiver and a housebreaker but did he really lure his acquaintance across London to kill him for a watch and chain? Or was there something much deeper and more sinister in the case, ignored by the Crown, which linked Beron and Morrison to the Houndsditch Murders a few weeks earlier and the Siege of Sidney Street?

Beron's body was found in some bushes on Clapham Common on 1 January 1911. He received a few shillings a week rent from properties he owned but he didn't spend much of it, living as he did in a lodging house for sevenpence a night. Beron did, however, carry on him both jewellery and fairly large sums of money – up to £70, which could then buy a house. His skull had been fractured and he had been stabbed. His money, watch chain, and a £5 gold piece he carried were gone and his forehead was incised with several cuts that looked like the letter 'S'. This, said many a commentator, was the initial letter of the Russian word for *spic* or double agent. A reward of £500 was offered for information leading to the conviction of his killer.

His death came only a fortnight after the Houndsditch murders by Russian anarchists who, whilst carrying out a burglary, were surprised by unarmed police and had shot them dead. Three days into the New Year there had been the famous Siege of Sidney Street in which the murderers had died in a blazing house after a long gun battle with the Scots Guards. Was there any evidence that Beron knew the Houndsditch murderers? No, said Inspector Frederick

Leon Beron's body, as found on Clapham Common.

Wensley, in charge of the investigation. It was, he believed, purely a matter of robbery.

Morrison was on parole for burglary when he was arrested on 8 January in a Jewish restaurant in Fieldgate Street, Aldgate. At the trial there was considerable time spent in argument over whether Morrison had said words to the effect that he was being arrested for the murder. The implication of this was that he had a bad conscience. For his part he said he was told the reason for his arrest by Wensley, who had arrived with four other officers. Wensley said he did not and the arrest was purely for failing to notify a change of address. In this he was later contradicted by junior officers, one of whom felt so bad about things that he made a statement before one of the Police Commissioners. The junior officer, promised immunity, was promptly transferred to Ruislip and resigned from the force within a year.

At its highest what was the evidence against Morrison? There is no doubt that he knew Beron. He was seen with him in the East End shortly before midnight on the night of his death. Indeed this was the evidence which started Inspector Frederick Wensley on Morrison's trail. He also knew the area. Just before his

arrest he had signed on at the local police station saying he had obtained work
in a bakery at Lavender Hill, a few minutes from Clapham Common. He had
given a parcel to a waiter in an East End restaurant saying it contained a flute.
When he gave evidence at Morrison's trial the waiter said it was far too heavy
to be a flute and seemed more like an iron bar. There again, there was evidence
Morrison had been thoroughly unpleasant to him and the man had every reason to hold a grudge against the bully. There were spots of blood on Morrison's
collar when he was arrested. He seemed to have come into money just after
Beron's death. In those days identification evidence was accepted quite readily,
and he was recognised by two cab drivers who firmly put him on Clapham
Common at the time of the murder.

The trial started at the Old Bailey on 6 March before Mr Justice Darling, a
talkative and witty judge. Morrison cannot have helped himself with his arrogant attitude. He declined the recently introduced privilege for an accused to
sit down in the dock and stood throughout the proceedings.

So what was Morrison's defence and where did it go wrong? Almost certainly
he was a difficult man to defend. His defence was an alibi. After midnight he
had been in his lodgings. Some of the witnesses who were called against him to
place him with Beron before midnight were prostitutes and the waiter who said
he had been given an iron bar rather than a flute to mind had tried to commit
suicide, then a felony. Morrison's counsel, Edward Abinger, tore into them,
ignoring a warning from the judge that the consequence would be that
Morrison's character would be put in evidence. The identification evidence was
not strong and Abinger called John Greaves, a medallist of the Royal Institute of
British Architects, to deal with the inadequate lighting at the Clapham Cross cab
rank, which threw considerable doubt on the identification. It was shown
Morrison had at least ten collars and that he was a fastidious dresser. Nor was
he a fool. Surely he would not have worn an unwashed collar for a week –
particularly one stained with Beron's blood?

The difficulty came when his alibi, that he had seen two sisters at a Music Hall,
was effectively broken by Sir Richard Muir, leading for the Crown. The girls
were muddled over their evidence. They could not say who had paid for their
tickets and, worse, they couldn't remember who was on the bill. Morrison did not
help himself when he went in the witness box. He could not give any proof that
the upturn in his finances had not come from Beron's pockets. And then Abinger's tactics in cross-examining the prostitutes rebounded against his client.
Morrison's character was put in evidence – prison record, false names and all.

But when it came to it, the good-hearted Darling was not sure of Morrison's guilt and if he did not sum up for an acquittal he certainly did not sum up for a conviction. He told the jury that Morrison had no convictions for violence and, more importantly, that a foreigner on trial for his life might do things an English person would not do. Merely because he had concocted a false alibi did not mean he had committed the crime. Indeed he reminded them of the Scottish Not Proven verdict. It did Morrison no good. Perhaps the air was too full of Houndsditch. The jury took only thirty-five minutes to convict. In those days a prisoner was allowed to speak before sentence and Morrison now told the court that the money he had came from a bank forgery. It was normal for judges to add they agreed with a jury's verdict but instead Darling told Morrison to be advised by his solicitor and learned counsel. When he added the traditional words 'May God have mercy on your soul' Morrison shouted, 'I decline such mercy. I do not believe there is a God in Heaven either.'

Even though they upheld the verdict it is clear the recently formed Court of Appeal did not like the conviction, but under the terms of the Criminal Appeal Act 1906 there was nothing they could do.

> Even if every member of the Court had been of the opinion that he personally would have acquitted the prisoner the Court must yet have upheld the conviction, unless they were of the opinion that the verdict was so perverse that no reasonable jury would have given it.

Nevertheless, the Court of Appeal and Darling's summing up were enough to save Morrison's life. Churchill commuted the death sentence to one of penal servitude. Morrison was reprieved on 12 April 1910.

Morrison could not accept the verdict. Time and again he petitioned the Home Secretary to have his case re-opened. He was surly, uncommunicative, sometimes violent, continually protesting his innocence. Once he held some warders at bay and as a result was flogged. He is also said to have petitioned for the death sentence to be carried out. When he heard that one of the investigating officers in his case had been killed in the First World War he remarked that, despite his previous belief, there was a God.

He died as he had lived, according to his own rules. A kitten, the pet of the prisoners, lived in the Parkhurst prison bakery. Morrison hated the animal and in a temper threw it on the furnace. For that he was given the No 1 punishment of bread and water. Again he thought himself to have been wronged and so he began to starve himself to death, a considerable task for a man of his physique. He was force-fed for three months and then put in a padded cell. He still refused to eat and died on 24 January 1921 at the age of forty-one.

What was the truth behind the Beron killing? Just why would Morrison take

Beron across London simply to rob him? Surely he could have done it far more easily in the alleyways of the East End. If it was a straightforward robbery why was an S marked on Beron's forehead? Was there anything in the story that Beron was a police informer who had betrayed his fellow anarchists? One theory is that Morrison had been recruited by anarchists to set up Beron who had in some way displeased the group. Perhaps it was his job, but no more, to get him to go to Clapham and he did this by first taking him to East End brothels and then telling him of great delights in South-west London.

Eric Linklater, *The Corpse on Clapham Common*; Frederick Porter Wensley, *Detective Days*

Bible John *see* Patricia Docker

Bingham Family Poisonings

In a period of eight months in 1911 three members of the Bingham family died in suspicious circumstances at Lancaster Castle, England. The first to go was William Hodgson Bingham then aged seventy-three and official resident custodian. He had been in good health until he collapsed with vomiting and diarrhoea on Saturday, 22 January 1911. He died the next day. The medical certificate showed the causes as old age, gastric and intestinal catarrh and heart failure. The hereditary office of castle keeper passed to William's son, James Henry, who invited his half-sister Margaret to come and keep house. She lasted until 23 July when, following four days of vomiting, she died. The cause of her death was given as a brain tumour.

The role of housekeeper now passed to James's twenty-nine-year-old sister, Edith, who lived with the family. She was educationally subnormal and nearly illiterate. She was quite unable to cope and in early August James Bingham engaged a Mrs Cox Walker to take over the housekeeping duties. On Saturday 12 August, two days before Mrs Cox Walker was due to arrive, James Bingham collapsed whilst showing a party of visitors around the castle. He died on 15 August but this time the doctor tentatively suggested arsenical poisoning. The autopsy which followed showed a substantial quantity of arsenic. He had eaten a steak bought in the town and cooked by Edith only an hour before he had collapsed. No others in the household had eaten the meat. An exhumation of William and Margaret Bingham also showed substantial quantities of arsenic in the bodies.

Edith Bingham was arraigned at Lancaster Assizes on 27 October before Mr Justice Avory. Although she was charged with the three murders as was the custom the Crown proceeded on the count of the murder of James. The evidence was mainly circumstantial. A charlady who had seen Edith cook the meat said she saw nothing untoward. So far as Margaret's death was concerned, introduced as similar fact evidence to bolster the case, others had eaten the same food and no one else had become ill. There was no evidence she had cooked anything for William before his death. As far as inheritance was concerned she stood to lose by the deaths in the family. Almost certainly she would be turned out of the castle. Mr Justice Avory summed up for an acquittal and, after a twenty-minute absence, the jury agreed with him.

Black Dahlia *see* **Elizabeth Anne Short**

Keith Blakelock

On 6 October 1985, PC Keith Blakelock was hacked to death during a riot on the Broadwater Estate, Tottenham, London. His death arose from an incident the previous day when officers had searched the house, on the estate, of a Mrs Cynthia Jarrett, looking for her son Floyd. She had suffered a heart attack and had died. There had been a series of difficulties between the police and ethnic minority communities both in and out of London in the preceding weeks and at least a demonstration that weekend, if not more serious trouble, was expected.

There was a large police presence in the area and a substantial presence of local youths. Fighting took place between 7.00 p.m. and 10.30 p.m. A number of shots were fired and pavement slabs were torn up and thrown as were petrol bombs. A supermarket was set on fire. One witness estimated that in less than five minutes more than fifty petrol bombs were made on the streets. Forty-seven wrecked cars were later towed away. Two fire officers believed that the fire from the supermarket might spread to nearby flats and tried to get near the building to discover the danger. They were beaten back by a crowd of youths throwing bottles and were later escorted by police officers to the building where they came under a renewed and more violent attack. They then made a run for safety, chased by the youths. During the chase PC Blakelock tripped and one of the fire officers described how the crowd fell upon him.

> I saw things like machetes, carving knives [and] a pole with a blade set at right angles to it. There appeared to be a frenzied attack going on... The people around were striking up and down with their weapons. I saw eight or ten machetes being used or being held in the air. The officer was surrounded very quickly.

Keith Blakelock sustained forty wounds caused by knives or other weapons. His head was nearly severed from his body and there was a knife driven nearly six inches into his neck.

Reports of the fighting were necessarily confused and at one time local councillor, Bernie Grant, even suggested that PC Blakelock's death might have been caused by another police officer.

Over 300 people were arrested in the course of the enquiries and three, Winston Emanuel Silcott, Mark Braithwaite and Engin Raghip, were convicted of murder and riot on 19 March 1987. Primarily, the evidence against them consisted of their confessions which, said the police, had been contemporaneously recorded. In December 1991 Silcott's conviction was quashed when the Court of Appeal heard evidence that the Crown accepted the evidence of expert witnesses who showed his confessions had not been contemporaneously recorded. Raghip and Braithwaite's convictions were also quashed when the court heard that, because of their low intellectual capacities, the lengthy questioning they underwent could have produced unreliable answers.

The police re-opened enquiries into the killing of PC Blakelock but no further charges were ever brought.

Lord Gifford, *The Broadwater Farm Inquiry*

Susan Blatchford

On the afternoon of 31 March 1970 Gary Hanlon, then aged thirteen, and Susan Blatchford, eleven, left their homes in the Ponders End area of Enfield, Middlesex, and were last seen together about 4.30 p.m. When they failed to return home their parents reported their absence to the police.

In an operation led by Chief Superintendent Leonard Read, earlier responsible for the arrest of the Kray Twins, a total of 4,356 houses, sheds, outhouses, cars, boats, lofts, and any other area where a child could have gone by himself or been taken, were searched. The children could be traced by witnesses to Sewardstone Road, leading from Waltham Abbey to Harlow on the other side of which were fairly dense woods. The police used 250 men, twenty-eight dogs, a helicopter and frogmen – there were two sewage farms and two enormous reservoirs in the area. A team of women police was also employed and the police were helped by hundreds of members of the public searching open fields and other areas.

One theory was that the children might have run off with a fairground show which had been in the area or even been abducted by a traveller with them. Read deputed a team to track down every single caravan and sideshow from that fair but the officers came back with no lead at all.

In the first month there were 218 reported sightings of the children. Four clairvoyants, including Gerard Croiset (*Pat McAdam qv*) who had been so uncannily successful in the Boston Strangler case, were sent samples of the children's clothes by their parents and gave four separate explanations for the children's disappearance, but all said they believed they were alive and still in the Enfield area. They all indicated various places where the children might be found and these were followed up but they too came to nothing.

Then, in a rather vain hope that they might have run away, gypsy camps throughout the country were simultaneously searched in a gigantic and complex operation. At this stage the best the police could hope for was that the children had suffered some tragic accident. There were so many natural hazards in the area. Beside the reservoirs and sewage pits there was the River Lea, as well as acres of woodland. It was a forlorn hope, however. Two months later the matter was resolved.

On 17 June a farmer was out shooting. His dog went into the wood just off Sewardstone Road and would not come out. The farmer went in after him and discovered a kind of hide in which were the two bodies. It looked as though it had been made from branches and twigs and the children had crept inside and had died. Susan's arm was around Gary – although younger, the girl was a much bigger and better developed child than the boy – and this led to the belief that they had died of cold. At this point the newspapers headlined their stories as the 'Babes in the Wood' case. In fact, at one stage, after examinations had been made, some of the experts thought there was no possibility of a third-party involvement. Because of the absence of vital organs the pathologist, Professor James Cameron, was unable to give a cause of death and so the mystery remained.

Read did not, and still does not, accept that a third party was not involved. Susan had been wearing jeans. 'First of all a patch had been taken out which the pathologist said was rats or other animals. That may be, but, more importantly to my mind, her jeans had been ripped completely down each side of the seam as though the trousers had been kippered. They had been pulled off as you strip the skin off a fish. It was impossible to ascribe any explanation for this other than that it had been done deliberately by a third party, and I was determined to find out how.'

He obtained a dozen similar pairs of jeans, and had a young officer wear them. Read then tried to tear them in the same fashion as Susan's and found there was only one way. If he was lying down and Read grabbed hold of the waistband and gave a good pull the jeans then split at the seams. Doing that they came away easily. Another factor in Read's mind was that one of Susan's shoes was found outside the wood and certain of her underclothes were missing. To him there was no other possible satisfactory explanation. He was convinced the children had been murdered.

Now the police stripped the Little Wood where the bodies were found and there was a great deal of debris – bras, condoms, knickers. It was clearly a place where courting couples went and therefore a place for the usual Peeping Toms and sexual perverts. Read's theory was that the children had wandered up there to play and a man had inveigled them into the wood and attacked them.

There was one suspect – a man who had just been released from prison and who had a long history of sexual assaults. Read said:

He had been seen on Day One and although he was not entirely ruled out of the enquiry he was able to account for his movements. Then, later, when he was found abroad almost every night I put two officers on his tail. One night they found him in Enfield with a large knife. That was enough. We plundered him. When we searched his bedroom I could not believe it. In wardrobes, in suitcases, underneath his bed, everywhere, were hundreds of bits of gear he had nicked from clotheslines – panties, brassieres, slips and knickers. He stole them from clotheslines and what he did afterwards with them was his business. There was also other property which was identified as coming from a housebreaking in the Enfield area. All the linen was removed and sifted to see if anything could be traced back to Susan, but it could not.

Once he was lodged in the police station I questioned him again about the children for some time but he would not admit anything. We had no witnesses with whom to confront him, so I could not pursue the matter any further. He was, however, charged with seventeen counts of burglary and housebreaking for which he received five years' imprisonment.

Faced with all the evidence, the coroner returned an open verdict. Read's report concluded that the children had been murdered. He hoped to be able to continue with the enquiry but 'I was told in no uncertain terms that it would be a waste of time and manpower and I was obliged to close the case.'

Leonard Read, *Nipper*

Stanley Bogle

On 1 January 1963 the bodies of Stanley Bogle and Margaret Chandler were found by Lane Cove River in Sydney, Australia. Bogle's body was naked but had been covered to look as though he was dressed. The clothing on Margaret Chandler had been bunched up so that her thighs were showing. They had both been to a party on North Shore. Bogle had been alone because his wife was looking after their young child. Mrs Chandler had arrived with her husband who had stayed on at the party.

Neither body showed any marks of violence, nor was there any trace of alcohol in their blood. Various suggestions have been made as to the cause of death, one being that one partner became unconscious whilst having sexual intercourse and asphyxiated the other. This is, however, hardly consistent with the lack of alcohol in the blood.

At the inquest the court was told that every technique known to modern science had failed to show the cause of death. This was recorded as acute circulatory failure of an unknown cause.

Over the years there have been a number of explanations of the deaths, including the killing by an undetectable poison, something not too fanciful following the death of the Bulgarian, Georgi Markov (*qv*), in London in 1978. Other suggestions have been variations on the conspiracy theory. Bogle was a government scientist and one version involves the Australian Security Intelligence. Another is that Bogle was killed to prevent him taking a position in America and Mrs Chandler happened to be in the wrong place at the wrong time.

A further explanation, which has at least some credibility, is that Bogle gave Mrs Chandler LSD and took some himself, to heighten sexual performance and they accidentally overdosed. A former lover of Bogle's, a Margaret Fowler, who had followed them intending to have a row, did the decent thing on finding them dead and covered the bodies to minimise a scandal. She had apparently offered to give evidence at the inquest but the coroner had refused to hear her testimony.

Margaret Chandler's husband, Geoffrey, was a prime suspect and for a time opinion in the city of Sydney was divided between naming him as the killer, the LSD theory and the conspiracy one. Margaret Fowler left Australia immediately after the inquest and died in London in 1977. Geoffrey Chandler wrote a book *So You Think I Did It* propounding the conspiracy theory. The police officer in charge of the case came down on the side of an accidental dose of LSD about which little was known at the time.

Teddy Bolam *see* **John Coward**

Deborah Lynn Bonner

On 12 August 1982 a slaughter-house worker, taking a break, discovered the naked body of twenty-three-year-old Deborah Lynn Bonner in the Green River in King County, Washington State. Bonner, who had been working as a prostitute, may not have been the first victim because a month earlier the body of another prostitute, Wendy Coffield, had been found a half mile away, also in the river. Over the next two years the number of bodies rose to a massive forty-nine. The victims were women, mainly working in what was called the Sea-Tac strip, a road between the Seattle-Tacoma International airport and Pacific Highway South, on which young prostitutes solicited drivers, offering oral sex for thirty dollars. All the victims were strangled. Several had pyramid shaped rocks inserted into their vaginas. The early victims were almost invariably from lower-income homes, had been abused as children, and had themselves been involved in under-age drinking, drug abuse and petty crime.

At first the police were keen to deny a connection between the various murders but eventually the connection became too obvious for this to be continued. In fact it was not until after the killings ceased in 1984 that it was accepted there had been a serial killer operating. Then, the parents of the dead women became incensed that not enough was being done by the Green River Task Force to discover the identity of the killer, who had left no clues. An FBI profile suggested he was in his mid-twenties to early thirties, was an outdoor type who almost certainly felt he had a mission to remove prostitutes from the streets. It was thought that by putting the victims in the river he may have been symbolically baptising them. Over the years there were two principal suspects. The first, a taxi driver who appeared to know too many details of the killings, and the second a law student, William J Stevens II, who was found to have a pile of pornographic materials in his room and who in fact was an escaped convict, were eliminated from the enquiries. Stevens was returned to prison.

As is so often the case the killings abruptly ceased and it is possible the killer moved his site of operations to San Diego where a similar number of attacks were reported shortly afterwards. Another suggestion is that he moved to the Interstate 70 and continued killing prostitutes whom he threw from a truck. This change in *modus operandi* makes the theory seem unlikely. There have also been suggestions that there was more than one killer operating in the area at the time because only the first few women were placed in the river. The rest were found on dumping sites.

Carlton Smith and Tomas Guillen, *The Search for the Green River Killer*

Betty Jo Booker *see* **Richard Griffin**

Abigail and Andrew Borden

On 4 August 1892 Andrew Jackson Borden and his second wife Abigail were killed in their home at 92 Second Street in Fall River, a small mill town in Massachusetts, where they lived with his daughters from a former marriage, Lizzie (32) and Emma (41). He was a wealthy man with banking and property interests. On that day in August the weather was hot and by the time the Bordens ate breakfast, along with visitor John Vinnicum Morse, Andrew Borden's brother-in-law by his first marriage, at around 7 a.m. the temperature was in the eighties. Breakfast was mutton soup followed by more mutton. The reason was frugality. Mrs Borden had cooked a large joint the previous Sunday and it was now mutton every meal. It was not simply food over which a degree of parsimony was exercised. Despite Borden's wealth there was no bathroom in the house. The only lavatory was in the basement; the only running water in a sink off the kitchen. The heat and the old mutton combined to make the maid, Bridget Sullivan, ill. She stopped cleaning the windows and vomited in the garden. Borden left for his office. Lizzie, overweight and unloved by all except possibly her elder sister, Emma, and her father, was menstruating and unhappy. She was doing the ironing. Borden returned at 10.45 to find the front door locked. He was let in by the maid and discovered the patent lock had been released. Lizzie told him her stepmother had gone visiting a sick neighbour. Borden went into the sitting-room, Bridget went upstairs to rest. Shortly after 11 a.m. she heard Lizzie run upstairs calling, 'Come down, quick. Father's dead. Someone came in and killed him.'

Borden was dead on the sofa, a mass of blood. His head had been split with an axe. A doctor and neighbours were called. Borden had, in fact, been repeatedly hit with the weapon. Bridget was told to go upstairs to get a sheet but, as she said she was too frightened to go alone and that there might be a burglar up there, a neighbour went with her. When they came down the neighbour asked what had happened to Mrs Borden. Lizzie's reply was, 'I don't know but she is killed too, for I thought I heard her come in.' She was in the guest room. She also had been hit with an axe.

As might be expected in a small town, rumour ran rife and the first under suspicion (apart from maniacs at large) was the uncle, John Morse. However he had left after breakfast to ride to a farm some miles away and was able to establish a cast-iron alibi. Next down, so to speak, was Lizzie herself. Apparently a woman 'answering her description' had tried unsuccessfully to buy poison the previous day in two or three pharmacies in the town.

There had been considerable dissent in the family over money. The girls had not been on the closest of terms with their stepmother for some time and Andrew Borden was intending to make a gift of the deeds of a house to his second wife's family. In fact it is suggested that the papers were to be signed that morning. A premature death of Mrs Borden would prevent this and ensure the redistribution of the family wealth in a more orderly way. Lizzie was arrested. Her defence was that she had been in the barn when the murders must have been committed.

The overwhelming problem for the prosecution was the absence of blood on her clothing. It was their case that her stepmother had been killed up to an hour before her father. She, Lizzie, had been seen between the two incidents. She must, therefore, have had not one but two very bloodstained dresses. On the other hand the story of the trespassing maniac who waited an hour to kill Borden after he had disposed of the wife was hogwash.

Lizzie Borden stood trial on 5 June 1893. The evidence against her was the attempted purchase of prussic acid, something which was not admitted, and the fact she said Mrs Borden had been sent a note about the sick neighbour. No note was found. As for her alibi? There were no footprints found in the barn. She did not give evidence in her defence saying that she was innocent and 'I leave it to my counsel to speak for me'. Amidst cheering the jury returned a verdict of not guilty after an hour's retirement.

Lizzie stayed on in Fall River moving to a larger house with her sister – they inherited $175,000 each. In 1897 Lizzie was again arrested, following the theft of two large paintings from a local store. The charges were dropped. She became increasingly estranged from her sister and when she died in 1927 she left most of her $265,000 fortune to an animal charity.

What was the truth? Is it really the case that:

> Lizzie Borden took an axe
> Gave her mother 40 whacks
> When she saw what she had done
> Gave her father 41.

The maniac and Uncle John can be ruled out. That leaves Emma, Lizzie and the maid, Bridget, working independently or in some form of combination. Edmund Pearson in *The Trial of Lizzie Borden* came down firmly against Lizzie. He was convinced the murder had been planned two days earlier. But do poison-buyers then turn into axe-murderers overnight? Pearson's view was challenged by Edward Radin who fixed the blame on Bridget. His argument runs that she was ill and, being made to wash windows, her temper and control snapped in the heat. Another view is that there was a conspiracy between Bridget (whom some say returned to Ireland a wealthy woman) and Lizzie. This would certainly help solve the problem of the blood-drenched clothing. Victoria Lincoln, in *A Private Disgrace, Lizzie Borden by Daylight*, offers the suggestion that Lizzie suffered from a psychomotor epilepsy of the brain usually occurring during menstruation. She argues that the clue to the killings was the house transfer. Lizzie tried to buy poison to kill her stepmother and thwart the property deal. When she failed she took an axe and gave her mother seventeen blows. She then realised her father would inevitably know who was the culprit and to spare him the trauma gave him nine. That, however, still does not get over the problem of the two ruined dresses unless, as with the Wallace killer, she committed the murders whilst naked. Given that Bridget was upstairs skiv-vying she would have had time to wash herself down in the scullery.

Edmund Pearson, *The Trial of Lizzie Borden* and *Masterpieces of Murder;* Edward Radin, *Lizzie Borden, the Untold Story;* Victoria Lincoln, *A Private Disgrace*

John Borg *see* **Barbara Gaul**

Jean Bradley

At 7.30 p.m. on 25 March 1993 forty-seven-year-old career woman Jean Bradley was hacked to death as she put a pack of Coke tins in the back of her BMW parked outside her home in Carbery Avenue, Acton, London, where she lived with her school-teacher lover. A thirty-five-year-old Irish carpenter saw the attacker and gave chase on foot, then in a van and on foot again until they reached the South Acton council estate where he lost him. The man, who was white, about six feet in height and wearing a black sou'wester, had turned and said, 'You'll get it next.' By the morning after she died the police had ar-rested a local sex-pest but he was eliminated from their enquiries.

An arrest was, however, made and thirty-eight-year-old Francis Marnell was charged with killing Jean Brady. The prosecution's case was based on identifi-cation. Marnell was said to have had a history of mental illness and when he was arrested he said he denied attacking Miss Brady but accepted that he might have done so and not remembered. The magistrate, Ian Comfort, who sat until 11 p.m., refused to commit Francis Marnell for trial. He had been able to produce an unbreakable alibi. A social worker had been delivering a meal to him at the time of the killing.

Edith May Olive Branson

During the night of 28 April 1929 the forty-four-year-old Olive Branson was shot at her home in Les Baux, Provence. Before the First World War, in which she had served in France, Olive, the cousin of a former High Court judge, had toured in a circus in Ireland and painted scenes of gipsy life. During the war, whilst her unit was being bombarded, she was rescued by a Colonel Wilson whom she married. The marriage was soon annulled and during the 1920s she moved to Les Baux, staying first at the Hotel de Monte Carlo, owned by François Pinet, and then moving into a small house near the hotel where she lived with her four Great Danes, and where she employed Joseph Girard as her handyman and his wife acted as housekeeper. They did not live in. During this time Olive Branson painted successfully, exhibiting both in Paris and at the Royal Academy. She was clearly a lively lady, writing in a letter the Christmas before her death, 'Frenchmen make the best lovers in the world.'

On the morning of 29 April Girard went to Olive Branson's house. The doors were open with the dogs inside but there was no sign of Miss Branson. He looked around and some twenty-five yards away, wearing stockings and a nightdress, was her body upright in a water tank. She had been shot in the head. In the tank was a revolver.

Initially the police, to whom Girard reported the matter, regarded it as a suicide. Olive Branson's family were not satisfied and they would seem to have had some justification for their scepticism. Not too many people walk in their stockings and climb into a water tank to kill themselves. There were rumours that she had refused work to a passing Spaniard and it was thought he might have taken his revenge.

The next step came when, urged on by the family, a second post mortem was undertaken. This showed there was no water in her lungs. She must, therefore, have been killed before she was put in the tank. The police were galvanised into action and detained Joseph Girard as a material witness. A maid in a Marseilles hotel recognised Olive Branson and François Pinet as regular visitors.

Bloodstains were found in all rooms in the house except the kitchen where the linoleum floor had been wiped clean – a bloodstained sponge was found. Now Miss Branson's next door neighbour, Vernon Blake, an English artist and sculptor living in reduced circumstances, came forward to say he had seen a man on a motor-cycle riding without lights at about 9 p.m. on the night of her death. Pinet's room was searched and two wills were found. It now became clear that Olive Branson had purchased the Hotel de Monte Carlo and the first will bequeathed it to Pinet along with the contents. A second will made a month before her death left the hotel and contents to a distant relation of hers.

A traditional method of a criminal investigation in France is to take the suspect to the scene of the crime and to re-enact the death. Pinet was taken to the water tank and questioned for hours, but continually denied his involvement.

On 8 May 1929 he was charged with her murder. The evidence against him could best be described as slender. He had motive over the loss of the hotel in the second will but he had never destroyed it. He remarked, rightly, that as the second will stood 'She was worth more to me alive than dead'. The investigating officer said he doubted that Pinet was strong enough to have carried her body from the house to the tank. There were suggestions that Miss Branson had been involved with the British Secret Service. Amidst much acclaim by the local community Pinet was acquitted.

After the trial was over, a pamphlet was circulated which suggested that Vernon Blake was the murderer. His heirs collected £40 in damages against the journalist who produced it. Clearly, the murderer was someone well known to the household. The four Great Danes never uttered a sound when he arrived that night.

Harry J. Greenwall, *They Were Murdered in France*

Charles Bravo

On 18 April 1876 at his home The Priory, Bedford Hill Road, Balham, Southwest London, thirty-year-old barrister Charles Bravo ate dinner – whiting, roast lamb, and anchovy eggs on toast – with his wealthy wife Florence, and Mrs Jane Cannon Cox, Florence's companion. Charles Bravo had had a 'jolly' luncheon that day and during the fateful evening Florence Bravo and Mrs Cox had put away two bottles of sherry between them. At about 9.45 p.m. Charles Bravo called out to his wife who, following an illness, slept in a separate bedroom, to get him some hot water. A maid heard this and in turn called Mrs Cox who went into Bravo's room. Before Bravo became unconscious he told Mrs Cox he had taken poison and a doctor was called. He suspected poison and questioned Bravo, who had by now recovered consciousness. Bravo said that he might have taken laudanum for his gums. Florence Bravo meanwhile called for Sir William Gull, the celebrated physician, to whom Bravo repeated his story of laudanum. Gull was convinced that Bravo was dying of an irritant poison and he was right. After the barrister's death on 21 April the post-mortem showed that he had taken or received a dose of between twenty and thirty grains of an antimony. Suspicion fell on his wife.

The whole Bravo ménage was a strange one. Florence had had an affair with a good if elderly doctor, James Manby Gully, which she had apparently given up shortly before her second marriage. 'Need I tell you that I have written to the Dr to say I must never see his face again . . .' Meanwhile Mrs Cox had quarrelled with Bravo. Florence Bravo had inherited her wealth from a former Grenadier Guards officer, Captain Alexander Ricardo, who had died of alcoholism leaving her some £40,000. Bravo seems to have been fairly complaisant about his wife's affair if only because, under the law at that time, he took all her property on marriage. Charles himself had kept a mistress in Maidenhead. Mrs Cox had known Charles Bravo's father, a Jamaican, before Charles' marriage. Curiously Gully also was born in Kingston, Jamaica.

At the first inquest which took place at The Priory the jury, sated with refreshments provided by the widow, returned an open verdict which was quashed by the Lord Chief Justice. Amidst growing suspicion and rumour, a second inquest was held, this time at a local hotel. It now amounted to a trial of Mrs Bravo and Mrs Cox and went unresolved. The jury found wilful murder but added a rider that there was insufficient evidence to fix guilt upon any person or persons.

Florence Bravo did not last long after her husband. The bottle of sherry an evening did for her and she died of alcoholism in Southsea on 17 September 1878. The case has produced much speculation. One line of thought is that she had already murdered the good Captain and, now realising that Bravo had his hands on her money, killed him as well. A second is that because of the series of miscarriages she undoubtedly suffered her mind became unhinged. A third theory is that the villainess was the unattractive forty-nine-year-old Mrs Cox. The line of thinking is that she feared Bravo was about to dismiss her and that she was protecting her own interests and those of her three children. Following the second inquest, at which he was obliged to give evidence, Gully was a ruined man.

Mrs Belloc Lowndes, *What Really Happened*; Elizabeth Jenkins, *Dr Gully*; Yseult Bridges, *How Charles Bravo Died*; B. Taylor and K. Clarke, *Murder at the Priory*

Brighton Trunk Murders

On Derby Day, 6 June 1934, the torso of a young woman was found in a trunk at the left luggage office at Brighton railway station, Sussex. The next day legs were found in a suitcase at King's Cross station, London. An examination showed the body to be that of a woman in her early thirties who was between four and five months pregnant. She had been in the habit of having her feet pedicured. Her skin was tanned suggesting that she had spent some time abroad. Her arms and head were never found. The body had been wrapped in a sheet of brown paper on which the word 'ford', seemingly the second half of a place name, was written. There were also two copies of the *Daily Mail* for 31 May and 2 June in an edition which circulated only within fifty miles of London. A porter at Brighton remembered helping a man with the trunk.

The noted pathologist, Sir Bernard Spilsbury, was called in and with his help the police reconstructed the case as best they could. The scenario they devised was that a wealthy man had made the girl pregnant. She had confronted him

Tony Mancini.

and a quarrel had taken place no later than 30 May, the day on which Spilsbury estimated she had been killed. The man then spent several days thinking about how to dispose of the body before deciding to leave the corpse in the trunk. Her identity was never discovered although it was thought she may have been European. It was believed the man in question had travelled from Dartford to Brighton and a girl who had been in a third class compartment with him gave a poor description. The police could not trace the holders of all the cheap day tickets nor even the makers of the trunk and suitcase.

In the course of enquiries into young women who had not been seen for some time a second body was found in a trunk, this time in the basement of 44 Park Crescent in Brighton. It was that of prostitute, Violette Kaye, girlfriend of Tony Mancini, also known as Jack Notyre, café waiter, club doorman and small-time hoodlum, who was charged with her murder. She had head injuries. His defence was that he had returned home and found her battered to death. The reason he gave for leaving her body in a trunk was that he thought that, because of his criminal record, the police would not believe his story. He was acquitted at Lewes Assizes after a stunning defence by Norman Birkett KC. At the end of the trial Mancini could only say, 'Not guilty,

Mr Birkett? Not guilty, Mr Birkett?' He was told by his counsel, 'Now go home and look after your mother. She has stood by you like a brick.' It is unlikely that Mancini heeded the injunction. Many years later he confessed that he had killed Violette Kaye, maintaining that it was accidentally in a quarrel.

H. Montgomery Hyde, *Norman Birkett*; Douglas Browne and Tom Tullett, *Bernard Spilsbury*

David Brindle

On 3 August 1991 Brindle (whose brothers, Patrick and Tony were charged with the murder of Ahmet Abdullah (*qv*)), was shot dead in The Bell public house in East Street, Walworth, London. Shortly before closing time two masked men burst into the crowded pub, screamed, 'This is for Abbi,' and opened fire. Brindle was shot as he tried to scramble over the bar to safety. A bystander, Stanley Silk, was also shot dead. At first it was believed that this was another in the series of gangland killings which were taking place at the time and was indeed a reprisal for the killing of Abdullah. There were also suggestions that the Brindle brothers were closely related to the notorious Frankie Fraser whose sister, Eva, had married James Brindle, one of a noted South-east London family. This was not the case. If the brothers were related it was only as cousins many times removed.

However, with the death of James Moody (*qv*) an alternative and reasonable explanation emerged. Moody, who was working as a barman in a South-east London public house, had been threatened by Brindle after a fight a few weeks earlier in which Moody had used a baseball bat on him. The killing, it was said, was to avoid reprisals by Brindle.

Frank Fraser, *Mad Frank*

Alan Brooks

On 17 July 1991 publican Alan Brooks, married and with an eleven-year-old son, was dragged from his bar at the Clydesdale public house in Loughton, Essex, frog-marched into the car park and hacked to death by a six-man gang armed with machetes. He had only taken over the pub two weeks earlier. His death was said to be over a drug deal and at the hands of a powerful London gang whom many thought, erroneously, to have retired some years earlier. In June 1994 a man was arrested over the killing but was released without charge.

Sir 'Jock' Delves Broughton *see* **Josslyn Victor Hay**

Keith Patrick Brown *see* **Kelley Lyn Watson**

Eddie Browning *see* **Marie Wilks**

Billy Bryan

On 23 August 1993, seventy-one-year-old Billy Bryan and his seventy-four-year-old widowed sister, Annie Castle, were found dead in the flat they shared in Priam House, Bethnal Green, London. They had literally been frightened to death the previous evening. He was lying on the floor with his hands and feet bound; he had been smothered and had had a heart attack. Annie Castle was sitting fully dressed in a chair with a half-eaten sandwich on a plate at her side. She too had suffered a heart attack, probably brought on by watching the assault on her brother. Her rings had been torn from her fingers. She had never taken them off in some fifty years. The flat had been ransacked and Billy Bryan's CD player had been taken. In all, the property stolen totalled only a couple of hundred pounds. There were no signs of forcible entry and it seems that, despite warnings from her family about the danger of so doing, Annie Castle had opened the door to the killers.

John Buggy

On Derby Day, June 1967 two off-duty Sussex policemen fishing off Newhaven, Sussex, found the body of American-born John 'Scotch Jack' Buggy trussed in wire. The police had suspected for the past few weeks that he had been killed. Sid Kiki, a London betting shop proprietor and a regular police informant, had already told Leonard 'Nipper' Read that Buggy had been killed in an illegal gaming club in Mount Street, Mayfair run by Franny Daniels and his nephew Charles 'Waggy' Whitnall.

Buggy had come to England with the American forces and had established himself as a hard-man. In 1961 he had received nine years' imprisonment for shooting a man outside the Pigalle Club. Whilst in prison he had met up with Roy James, a Great Train Robber, whose share of the proceeds had been handed to a minder for safekeeping who had not kept it safe at all. It was believed that Buggy had been making enquiries into the whereabouts of what was left.

The story in the Underworld was that Buggy had been shot in the club and that his body had been wrapped in a carpet before being taken out to sea. When the police went to the Mount Street Bridge Club there was indeed a smell of fresh paint and a new carpet. There was, however, no help from the members, none of whom had heard or seen anything. Whitnall agreed to be seen with his solicitor in Vienna but nothing came of the interview. In 1973, following information from Donald Wardle, an Australian shoplifter who was serving nine years for blackmail and was no doubt trying to ingratiate himself with the authorities, Daniels, then sixty-three, and Abraham Lewis, who had been working in the club, were charged with Buggy's murder. Wardle maintained he had been in the club on the afternoon of Buggy's death when he had heard three shots. Daniels had come out and told him and the other players to go home. Both men were acquitted.

Leonard Read, *Nipper*; James Morton, *Gangland*

Gerald Bull

On 22 March 1990 sixty-two-year-old Gerald Bull, a Canadian scientist who was making guns for Iraq, was shot dead when an assassin put five

7.65mm bullets in his head outside his flat in the Uccle suburb of Brussels, Belgium. He had opened the door to his attacker. The motive was certainly not robbery because the killer left $20,000 cash in Bull's pocket. Bull had had a lifetime obsession with how objects behave in flight and had made weapons for such diverse interests as South Africa, Spain, Yugoslavia, and China. He had a brilliant career as a mathematician, earning a doctorate at the age of twenty-two. In the weeks before his death he had voiced fears of his vulnerability to friends.

He had been working on the supergun for Iraq and had rejected Israeli requests to desist. He had told associates that he believed Iraq planned to murder him when his work was completed. An Israeli Secret Service official was quoted as saying they had assisted in his death.

The theory advanced by William Lowther is that Bull was killed by the Israelis not specifically over the supergun he was making which would fire projectiles into space, but because he was behind with the main project and was appeasing the Iraqis by helping them with their long-range missile programme.

William Lowther, Arms and the Man: Dr Gerald Bull, Iraq and the Supergun

Harvey Burdell

On 31 January 1857 the forty-six-year-old dentist, possibly a bachelor, certainly a rich and deeply unpleasant man who enjoyed making enemies, was found by his office boy at 31 Bond Street, New York, stabbed to death. His only real attachment appears to have been to guinea pigs which he probably used for experimental purposes. He had, at one time, a servant named Biddy who spoke four languages and slept upright on a stool in the kitchen but it cannot have been she who killed Burdell because she died a year before his death. One story of him is that he had, some years earlier, contracted a marriage and then in the church threatened to call off the wedding unless the girl's father paid him $20,000. The man declined the privilege.

Burdell had no less than twenty-seven wounds to the head and his carotid artery had been severed. He had not been killed in the office because there was blood over the stairs and walls. Burdell must have fought long and hard for his life.

What puzzled the police in their investigations was how not a single one of the other ten boarders at 31 Bond Street had heard a sound during the night.

There was, admittedly, a storm outside that night but the boarders were a curious collection. First, there was Mrs Emma Cunningham, in her late thirties, who may have been a widow but probably was not. She had two teenage daughters and two young sons. She was both tenant and boarding-house supervisor. Her relationship with Burdell was strange. He spent a good deal of time accusing her of theft whilst, in turn, she made counter-allegations against him. The theft related principally to a note of hand given by her to Burdell which he said she had stolen back. The police had been called over the incident and with officers present she had declared herself to be 'his wife by every tie that could be'. She then hit him. She had also brought two lawsuits against him, one for breach of promise of marriage and the other for slander. Burdell had been released on bail of $6,000.

Mrs Cunningham had also been annoyed with him on the day of his death, remarking that his hold on life was likely to be a short one. It was not the first time she had uttered threats. When the police had been called in over the theft she had told an Officer Davis that she would 'have his [Burdell's] heart's blood'. Of the other five boarders, one was Daniel Ullman, then recently defeated for the Governorship of New York. He alone of the adults seems to have had no suspicion attached to him. The next was John J. Eckel, another politician, so fond of canaries that he kept seventeen of them. There was also George V. Snodgrass, a young man with a passion for poetry and women's underwear which he wore, and a talent for the banjo which he was playing when the office boy called for help. There were also two maids.

Mrs Cunningham, who had been breakfasting, appears to have been considerably upset and announced that once again she was a widow. This came as a surprise to both police and neighbours. Despite her remarks during the theft incident it had been thought that if Mrs Cunningham had been involved with anyone it had been with Eckel. However, on the night of the murder she had been in her room with her two daughters.

An investigation was carried out into the marriage, said by her to have been performed on 28 October of the previous year, and a certificate was produced, along with evidence from her daughter, Augusta, that she had been a witness. Further enquiries showed that the clergyman, the Rev. Marvine, could only recall marrying a woman to a man who gave his name as Harvey Burdell. He could not identify either but he did recognise Augusta.

It was thought that the blows had been struck by a left-handed person, which Mrs Cunningham was, and she, together with Eckel and Snodgrass, was arrested and taken to the Tombs prison at Central Street, Manhattan, where they were all held pending the thirteen-day inquest.

The inquest was clearly a sparky affair. One of the maids, Mary Donaghue, reluctantly admitted that she had heard Mrs Cunningham say on the day of Burdell's death that it was 'time he was out of the world because he was not fit to live in it'. Next came the interesting news that Burdell had not lived at 31 Bond Street for several months and had been eating at the Metropolitan Hotel nearby.

Evidence which tended to remove motive from Mrs Cunningham was that of another doctor, a colleague of Burdell, who had told him that he and the widow now had an 'eternal peace and amity'. There was support for this because a paper was found which showed that, in consideration of the withdrawal of the law suits, Burdell agreed to be friends with her and her family and 'I agree never to do or act in any manner to the disadvantage of Mrs Emma A. Cunningham'. The withdrawal of the law suits was said to be six days before the alleged marriage. There was contradictory evidence that Burdell had been heard railing against Mrs Cunningham, and on the day of the wedding one witness placed him in Saratoga.

There was some evidence that Mrs Cunningham had purchased a sword-cane, and a possibly independent witness, who had been sitting on the steps of the house repairing a shoelace, said he saw two men, one wearing a shawl, pass into the house. This was followed first by a cry of murder and then Eckel, in his shirt sleeves, opening the door and telling him to go away. Mrs Cunningham, Eckel and Snodgrass were committed for trial. In the meantime she sought letters of administration of Burdell's estate. The minister, the Rev. Marvine, now changed his testimony and said that he did believe he had married her to Burdell. Public opinion began to swing in her favour. Snodgrass, against whom there appears to have been no evidence at all, was released.

Emma Cunningham stood trial accused of Burdell's murder. Eckel was charged as an accessory. There was ample evidence that Burdell quarrelled with all and sundry. This time the daughters gave convincing testimony that they had slept with their mother all night. Mrs Cunningham was now pregnant with, she said, Burdell's child and knitted baby clothes in full view of the jury, which took five minutes to acquit. Unfortunately Mrs Cunningham was not content to leave matters alone, and pressed her claim for letters of administration. Her doctor, however, reported to the authorities that she was not pregnant and had offered him $1,000 to purchase a baby for her.

On 3 August, the day of delivery, the police arrested everyone at the accouchement including the baby. The outcome was reasonably happy for Mrs Cunningham. She was acquitted on a technicality and went to California where she was said to have made a fortune cultivating grapes. The baby was exhibited for some time and profit for the real mother ($25 a week) with P. T. Barnum's menagerie. Eckel was convicted later of an election fraud and was sent to Albany prison where he died.

Opinion is divided whether Mrs Cunningham could have been so foolish as to kill Burdell on the day she threatened him. On the other hand she was certainly less than adroit in her handling of the baby fraud. It does seem just possible that the whole adult household and the two daughters were involved and had been carefully coached in their parts. There was also a story that Burdell had been a gambler and was in debt to 'Honest' John Burke. That man had, however, a cast-iron alibi for the night of Burdell's death. The *Police Gazette* later had a report that a man named Lewis had confessed to the killing which he said he had committed by mistake. His victim was intended to be another Burdell. Lewis was executed for another killing in New Jersey.

Edmund Pearson, *Murder at Smutty Nose*

Marie Burke

On Thursday 25 May 1989 the sixty-three-year-old American widow, who worked as second secretary in the consular section of the American Embassy in London, was stabbed to death at her £300,000 flat in The Quadrangle, Sussex Gardens, Paddington, with a six-inch knife. She had last been seen about 10 p.m. on the evening prior to her death when she had dined with a friend at The Monkey Puzzle, a local restaurant. Her purse had been taken and, although valuable paintings and antiques were left untouched, at first it was thought that she had been killed by a burglar. A small medallion was missing. Later it was suggested it was because she had discovered a visa racket. Yardie criminals were buying visas at $6,000 a time and it was believed she may have confronted an official involved in the scam. It was thought that someone took the money and blamed Marie Burke when a visa was not forthcoming.

Frances Buxton

On 18 January 1920, the body of fifty-three-year-old Frances Buxton, the landlady for the past five years of the Cross Keys public house in Lawrence Street, Chelsea, London, was found under a heap of burning sawdust. She had been killed by blows to the head and an attempt had been made to strangle her. Her face was almost unrecognisable. A broken quart beer bottle was found in a pool of blood eight feet from her body. It was believed that robbery was the motive because, although some diamond brooches and her silver and gold wedding ring were with her body, the remainder of her jewellery had been taken. It was also possible that the killing was a revenge attack. She had had a number of lovers whom she had infected with venereal disease.

A number of men were arrested and questioned over the killing including Charlie Clay, known as Long Charlie, who was briefly detained. Efforts to trace a man known as Glad Eye, who had been watching her obsessively during the previous few weeks, came to nothing. One anonymous letter put the blame on Edward Cooney of New York, and an attempt to hoax the police was made by John Frank Kingsley O'Connor who said a friend of his had met an Englishman in a French prison who had confessed to the murder. The last letter the police received was from Edinburgh containing only an address. It proved worthless and the investigation petered out in June 1921. There was a brief echo when, during the investigation into the death of Gertrude O'Leary (*qv*), the name of a one-time suspect was brought up.

Terivia Mary Cameron

On 8 July 1982 the fifty-nine-year-old partially paralysed retired nurse was pulled from her blazing flat in Addy Close, Upperthorpe, Sheffield. She was known to smoke in bed and at first it was thought that she had accidentally set her bedding alight. The post-mortem showed, however, that she had been strangled. The motive appeared to be robbery and it was believed that the fire had been started deliberately to cover the murder. No one has been charged with the murder.

Joe Carruthers

At 3.30 a.m. on 13 June 1933, forty-six-year-old Inspector Joe Carruthers, the third-ranking officer in the Calgary, Alberta, police force, was shot whilst investigating a complaint of a prowler. The bullet, fired at not less than three and no more than fifteen feet, came from a .32 calibre revolver and passed through his left side some four inches under his armpit. Death was almost instantaneous.

Four officers had gone to answer the call from Mr A. McGregor, a resident at 2211 Sixteen-a street west in the Scarboro area in the south-west of the city. Carruthers had left his revolver in the police car and was unarmed as he followed Detective James McDonald in the search for the burglar.

Within an hour four men were arrested on suspicion of involvement in Carruthers' murder. A line-up was held but no witnesses could make a positive identification and the men were released.

It was suggested, but never substantiated, that the killer may have been another officer with whom Carruthers had a mutual loathing. One question, which was never satisfactorily answered, was how Carruthers could have been shot at such close range without there being a mark on his shirt. When Henry Brace, the Edmonton ballistics expert, testified at the inquest held a week later at Jacques' Funeral Home, he said that though he thought the bullet came from a heavier gun than the .25 weapon James McDonald was carrying he was not, however, prepared to say exactly what calibre gun had fired the bullet. He had four murder cases under examination at the time and had not given much time to examining the bullet in the Carruthers case.

One of the jurymen, Charles Venables, interrupted the proceedings at the end of McDonald's evidence saying, 'There's a lot of rumours going around and I think they should be cleared up.' Chief of Police David Ritchie replied that whilst he appreciated the juryman's intention he did not think any such efforts on behalf of the police were necessary. 'We are not fighting rumours and have nothing to fear in that regard. When the time comes we will be ready to look after ourselves,' he told the court. He confirmed that McDonald had been carrying a .25 gun.

The jury, after an hour's retirement, returned a verdict of death from a bullet of a gun from some person unknown.

Eliza Carter

At 10 a.m. on Saturday, 28 January 1882 twelve-year-old Eliza Carter left her
elder sister's home in West Road, West Ham, East London, to go to her
parents who lived nearby in Church Street. On the way she took some clothes
into a laundry to be put through the mangle. She was not seen after that until
5 p.m. when she stopped one of her school-friends in The Portway, opposite
West Ham Park. She told her friend that she was afraid to go home because 'of
that man'. She was seen at about 11 o'clock that night in the company of an ugly
middle-aged woman dressed in a long ulster and a black frock.

The next day her blue dress, which had had buttons all the way down the
front, was found on the local football field without its buttons. Despite the offer
of rewards Eliza was never seen again. Remains of arrowroot biscuits were
found in the pockets of her dress and the police thought she might have been
enticed into the park with them.* The buttons of her dress, valued at around
sixpence, had been cut off with scissors. It was thought that it was not impossible that her attacker was a woman. She had been looking forward to receiving
a Sunday school prize the next day.

A considerable number of young girls disappeared in the East End in the last
decades of the nineteenth century. On 13 April 1881 Mary Seward, aged fourteen but described as young-looking for her age and a trifle backward, had
disappeared from her home in West Ham ten doors away from Eliza Carter's.
She had been playing at home for most of the afternoon but about 6 p.m. her
mother told her to go and look for her nephew. The boy was found and given
a ticking off but Mary had disappeared. There was a later suggestion she had
been seen with a gypsy at a fairground. The Home Office put up a £25 reward
and this was supplemented with the proceeds of a charity concert. She was
never seen again. There was now disquiet in the neighbourhood that the Home

---

* Curiously in September 1912 another Eliza Carter was murdered in West Ham. She was
found with her throat cut in the arms of her lover, twenty-year-old William Charles Beal,
whose own throat was cut. She had nearly been decapitated. Beal's defence to the charge of
murder was that it was she who had cut both his and her own throats. The medical evidence
was against Beal. The doctor said that it was highly improbable that the three cuts to Eliza
Carter's face were self-inflicted whereas the cut to Beal's throat almost certainly was. His
appeal against his conviction was dismissed on 26 November 1912. The jury had made a
strong recommendation of mercy on the grounds of Beal's youth. It did Beal, who was
described at the time as probably not of very sound mind, no good at all. He was executed at
Chelmsford prison on Tuesday, 10 December 1912.

Office seemed to value the lives of young girls so poorly and questions were asked of the local Member of Parliament to no great effect.*

Another in the series of so-called West Ham Vanishings is said to have occurred the day before, when a sixty-seven-year-old lady disappeared from her home in Keogh Road, West Ham. In the evening she went to purchase some candles and soap. When, the next morning, the milkman and postman received no reply to their knockings the police were called and an entry was made. The soap and candles were in their place, the grandfather clock had been wound up, the washing up had been done and her bed had been made. But she was never seen again.

Then the Vanishings stopped. Or at least, they were suspended for eight years. They broke out again in January 1890 when three young girls disappeared one after another in a short period of time. Only one body was discovered. Fifteen-year-old Millie Jeffs who had worked as a nursemaid since leaving school a year earlier, disappeared one Friday. She lived twelve doors from the Seward home. At 6.30 p.m. she met her father Charles, a railwayman, on his return from work who gave her threepence to go and buy fish at Bowmans in Church Street. She had not returned by 7.30 and the family began to worry. A search lasting until 2 a.m. produced no result. Nor was there any sign of Millie until St Valentine's Day when two detectives searching for stolen lead smashed the window to 126 West Road, known as The Portway, and in a bedroom cupboard found the body of Millie Jeffs. She had been sexually assaulted and strangled and had struggled violently with her attacker. At her burial in East London cemetery a collection raised £250 as a reward for information, but her killer was never found.

Probably in the case of the young girls the answer to their disappearance is that they were kidnapped for the purposes of white slavery and child prostitution. The elderly lady's vanishing can be explained by the onset of amnesia. It

* Another candidate in the list of vanishings is often given as seventeen-year-old Charles Wagner, the son of a West Ham butcher, who went missing on 1 April 1882. The general story is that his body was found at the foot of a cliff in Ramsgate but that there was no clue as to how the boy got there, nor were there any injuries on his body. This is not correct. He had left his father's home with a bag of gold containing £150. His body was found the next day – his head had been beaten with a screwdriver. He was robbed by John Walters who was immediately arrested and charged with murder. Walters had been recognised as a man who had bought the boy a pair of trousers and had paid in gold coin. When told that a body had been found under the cliffs Walters had replied that he hoped it was not that of his friend who had been with him the previous day but who had gone off with a woman. He was acquitted of the murder and immediately re-arrested and convicted of theft.

is also possible that this story, which unlike the others is not well documented in local newspapers, is simply a folk-tale.

John Cartland

During the night of 18-19 March 1973 sixty-year-old former British secret agent John Cartland was attacked and killed as he camped at Pelissanne near Aix-en-Provence, France. He was returning from a caravanning holiday in Spain with his son, Jeremy. Jeremy was found, suffering from stab-wounds, near their burnt-out caravan.

John Cartland, who ran a language school in Brighton, had been axed to death. He had been killed with two blows whilst a third, delivered with the flat of the axe, split his skull. In his will he left everything to his housekeeper, Janet Gibson, but during his lifetime he had made substantial gifts of property to his children.

The French police detained Jeremy Cartland in isolation before releasing him. He then travelled back to France on a number of occasions of his own volition, telling the investigating magistrate he had heard noises outside the caravan which had been parked in a lonely spot. He had gone out to investigate and had been struck on the head. He woke up to find the caravan on fire. In May 1973 a warrant was issued charging Jeremy Cartland with the murder.

The French appear to have had four theories. First, that John Cartland was killed in a drunken row; secondly, a plot under which Jeremy could inherit £60,000; thirdly, a love affair between Jeremy and a woman over which his father had taken umbrage and finally, that the killing took place at the time of the full moon. The theories were roundly attacked by Jeremy Cartland's solicitor, Michael Relton, who commented, 'They are fantastic, almost unbelievable, everything from Moon madness to murder for gain or love.' Other suggestions, which did not involve his son, included the blackmail by Cartland senior of highly placed wartime collaborators, and, rather more down to earth, that the pair were attacked by car thieves. A further theory was advanced by former Judge Gerald Sparrow, who wrote a number of popular true crime books, that Cartland had been killed by members of the Algerian Nationalist Liberation Front. He said that Cartland had shown him some 4,000 words of notes he had written about his involvement in the Algerian war in the 1950s when, as a British agent, he had made an enemy of Ahmed Ben Bella, the FLN leader.

In July 1973 the French Government decided not to seek Jeremy Cartland's extradition and the enquiry was handed over to the Director of Public Prosecutions who, in January 1974, decided there would be no charges against him.

In May 1983 he brought a libel action against the BBC over a programme *Escape*. Mr Justice Bristow asked the jury, 'Did the film put a question mark over Mr Cartland's innocence?' adding that if it did 'it would be difficult to imagine a more serious injury to his reputation or anything better calculated to injure his feelings'. He was awarded £50,000 libel damages against the Corporation who said they fully accepted Mr Cartland's innocence and had based the programme on his book *The Cartland Affair*.

Joseph 'Danny' Casolaro

In August 1991 the body of the forty-four-year-old freelance journalist was found dead in a bathtub in room 517 of the Sheraton motel in Martinsburg, West Virginia. He had multiple slash wounds to both wrists. His family deny that he was suicidal and question why his body was embalmed without permission and why no post-mortem was performed. At the time of his death he was believed to have been about to receive 'explosive' documents dealing with possible American arms trade with Iran, along with evidence of a computer software program used by the US and the Israelis to spy on military resources of other nations using the same program.

He had also said he was close to breaking a mind-boggling conspiracy he referred to as Octopus, which included an alleged plot to delay the freeing of the American hostages in Iran to sabotage Jimmy Carter's re-election possibilities.

Towards the end of his life he was suffering from blinding headaches and also in the first stages of multiple sclerosis. A handwritten note which said, 'I'm sorry, especially to my son,' was in the room. On the other hand, although the cuts were said to be made by a beer bottle and a half empty bottle of wine was found in the room, there were no traces of alcohol in his stomach.

Casselman Floater

This was the name given to the body of a young woman found on 3 May 1975 by a bridge over the Nation River west of Casselman, some thirty-five miles outside Ottawa, Ontario. The wrists had been bound in front with a man's tie which depicted the emblems of three of the Canadian provinces. Two other less garish ties had been used for her ankles. Her head was wrapped with cloths and around her neck was a linen kitchen towel, decorated with a Gaelic drinking toast and knotted to form a ligature. The post-mortem examination showed she was around five feet three inches tall, aged between twenty-six and thirty and had not had a child. She had poor quality partial dentures in both upper and lower jaws.

Blood spots were found on the roadway over the bridge and it was estimated that she had been thrown into the river, alive but probably unconscious, between 5 and 26 April. At first it was thought that the combination of flashy tie, tea-towel and dentures would make an identification relatively easy, and lead to the arrest of her attacker. Unfortunately the tea-towel, of Irish make, was sold in department stores in Montreal and Toronto as well as in Ottawa for under $1.50. The tie was also on general sale.

As for the dentures, apart from suggestions that they had been manufactured by someone trained in the Third World, where qualification standards were not as high as in Canada, that trail petered out. Although photographs were shown in dental journals and at the Ontario Dental Conference in May 1978, no one claimed the handiwork as their own or recognised having treated the woman.

Derrick Murdoch, *Disappearances*

Annie Castle *see* **Billy Bryan**

Azaria Chamberlain

On 17 August 1980 nine-week-old Azaria Chamberlain disappeared near Ayers Rock, the aboriginal sacred territory, in Northern Territory, Australia. Michael and Lindy Chamberlain, together with their three children Aidan,

Reagan and Azaria, were camping in the evening when Pastor Chamberlain's wife noticed a dingo emerging from their tent. It had something in its mouth and at first she believed that it was one of her husband's shoes. To her horror she later realised it was the baby, Azaria.

Some seventeen yards from the tent there was a drag-mark and depressions in the sand. On 22 August Azaria's bloodstained romper suit was found on the other side of the Rock. She was never seen again. The huge initial wave of sympathy turned against the Chamberlains. The police in their home town, Mount Isa, reported that Mrs Chamberlain had seemed not to care for the baby and did not feed it. The Chamberlains were Seventh Day Adventists and their fatalistic view of the incident – that it was part of God's wider plan – did not appeal to red-blooded Australians. There was also some aversion to the news that Michael Chamberlain had let the press have photographs of Azaria. The Chamberlain children were taunted at school by others who said that dingos did not go into their houses.

At the inquest held on 16 December an alternative explanation for Azaria's disappearance was propounded. It was that, far from the abductor being a dingo, it was a human who had taken her out of the tent and later out of her jumpsuit. The coroner, however, returned a verdict that she had 'met her death when attacked by a wild dingo'.

Six months later the police obtained a second opinion from the celebrated London pathologist, Professor James Cameron, heir to the Spilsbury-Camps-Simpson mantle. His conclusion was that the baby's neck had not been slit by a dingo but by a sharp instrument inflicted before the suit was unbuttoned. On 19 September 1981 the police seized over 400 items from the Chamberlains. Their car was flown to Darwin for examination.

The second inquest was held on 14 December and this time the evidence was very different. Bloodstains seeming to come from a severed artery were found under the dashboard and there were others under the seat. It was said the blood could only have come from a child of less than three months. There was blood and hair in the Chamberlains' camera bag and it was suggested the body of Azaria had been put in that. A London odontologist, Bernard Sims, said that the rips in the jumpsuit were not what he would expect from a dingo, and a textile expert said they were cuts rather than tears. Sims also said that because of the limited opening range of the mouth of a dingo (ten centimetres) Azaria's head could not have been clamped in it. The Chamberlains were arrested.

Their trial took place in September 1982 when the forensic evidence was bitterly contested. By now Lindy was heavily pregnant with their new baby, to

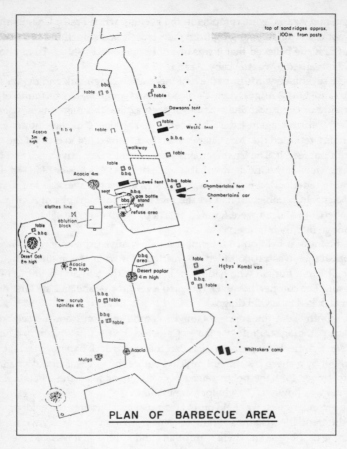

A plan of the scene where baby Azaria died.

be called Khalia. Both the Chamberlains were found guilty. He received an
eighteen-month suspended sentence. She received life imprisonment, but early
in her sentence was released on A$300 bail. On 30 April her appeal was rejected
by a unanimous decision. She was returned to prison. A further appeal to the
High Court was also rejected but, following an enquiry in June 1987, in which
the scientific evidence against her was discredited, Lindy Chamberlain was

pardoned. Her conviction was quashed a year later on 15 September 1988 with Mr Justice Morling saying:

> It follows from what I have written that there are serious doubts and questions as to the Chamberlains' guilt and as to the evidence in the trial leading to their convictions. In my opinion if the evidence given before the Commission had been given at the trial, the trial judge would have been obliged to direct the jury to acquit the Chamberlains on the ground that the evidence could not justify their convictions.

In May 1992 Mrs Chamberlain was awarded A$900,000 compensation. She later wrote a book of her experiences.

John Bryson, *Evil Angels*; Ken Crispin, *The Dingo Baby Case*; Oliver Cyriax, *Crime*; Lindy Chamberlain, *Through My Eyes*

Margaret Chandler *see* Stanley Bogle

Hubert George Chevis

A British Army lieutenant, Chevis died on 2 June 1931 after eating poisoned game. Married with two children he lived in a bungalow at Blackdown Camp, near Aldershot, Hampshire, seemingly without any enemies.

On the weekend before the Aldershot Tattoo, Chevis and his wife had friends in for drinks before dining together. He had ordered a brace of partridge from the local butcher and these were cleaned and hung outside in a ventilated meat safe by the cook, Mrs Yeomans.

Chevis took one mouthful of partridge and exclaimed, 'This is terrible.' His wife tasted one and said, 'It tastes fusty, don't eat any more.' The damage was done. Chevis felt an agonising cramp in his legs, lost all sensation in them and went into violent convulsions. Taken to the Army hospital, he died there at 1 a.m. the following morning. Mrs Chevis, who had merely tasted the bird, was also taken ill but recovered quickly.

The inquest verdict was an open one with the generally held belief that the whole matter was a tragic accident. There things might have rested had not Sir William Chevis, the Lieutenant's father, not received a telegram shortly before his son's funeral. It read, 'Hooray, hooray, hooray!' It was signed J. Hartigan and was posted from the Hibernian Hotel in Dublin. Chevis Senior sent the telegram to the police along with a second missive which read 'It is a mystery they will never solve.' The *Daily Sketch* published a copy of the telegram and in turn J. Hartigan telegraphed them. 'Dear Sir, Why do you publish a picture of the Hooray telegram?'

All the staff and guests at the hotel were interviewed by the Gardai without success. However the post office worker who had received the telegram remembered the man who had sent it and he was linked to the purchase of a quantity of strychnine in Dublin. But there the trail petered out.

At the re-opened inquest Mrs Yeomans gave evidence about cleaning and hanging the birds. Private Nicholas Bulger, Chevis's batman, gave evidence about serving at the dinner table. He had been born in Ireland. He had always been on good terms with Chevis and suggestions that he was an undercover member of the IRA seem ridiculous. Could Chevis have been poisoned by a girl with whom he had an affair and who had been discarded by him? Extremely unlikely. His wife might have had first taste. Could it possibly be that she was the intended target? In his analysis of the case C. J. S. Thompson suggests that the murder was the work of a homicidal maniac who had a fancied grievance against the family. He postulates that, armed with a hypodermic syringe, he had watched the meat safe until an opportunity arose to inject whatever meat was inside. The problem with this theory is that innocent guests could have been the ones to taste the meat.

The most likely explanation is that the birds had fed on berries which had somehow been contaminated. As for the telegrams; they could be nothing more than a cruel and malicious jest. The second inquest jury spent only a further five minutes before returning a second open verdict.

C. J. S. Thompson, *Poison Mysteries Unsolved*; Adrian Vincent, *Killers in Uniform*

Maple Church

The partially clad body of nineteen-year-old Maple Church was found by some children playing in a bombed out house at 225 Hampstead Road, London, on Monday, 12 October 1941. She had been strangled. Her shoes were later found in the basement. Friends had seen her in the company of a soldier and she had said she was engaged. About 10 p.m. the evening before, she had seen a girlfriend onto a train at Charing Cross and it was thought she had been picked up by her killer as she waited for a bus home. Hers was one of a spate of four killings in London that week and in their book Brian Lane and Wilfred Gregg suggest that she may have been an early victim of the sex-killer and soldier Gordon Frederick Cummins, who mutilated and killed at least four women in London in 1942*. Their suggestion is based on the fact that Cummins was billeted about a mile away from where Maple Church's body was found. There does not, however, appear to have been the terrible mutilations practised on the other women.

Robert Jackson, *Coroner*; Brian Lane and Wilfred Gregg, *The Encyclopedia of Serial Killers*

George Clark

On 29 June 1846, PC 313K George Clark disappeared whilst on the night shift at Dagenham, Essex. In 1846 Dagenham was not the urban sprawl of today. It was little more than a village, a number of whose inhabitants smuggled goods from Thames boats over the marshes. The arrival of the police had not been welcomed. Constables had been assaulted and it was believed, both in and out of the force, that a number were quite prepared to turn a blind eye to the locals' efforts to gain more than a marginal living from the scrubby smallholdings. As a result there was a high turnover of men. Those who had been threatened by the locals departed, alongside those who were thought to have been bribed.

Because of the danger, Clark was allowed to carry a cutlass as well as a truncheon. He took over a beat on the edges of the area, replacing PC Abia Butfoy who had been seriously threatened and so transferred. Clark failed to report on the morning of 30 June. His fellow officers said they had not seen him since they had left for their beats at 9 p.m. Sergeant William Parsons reported leaving Clark

---

* Cummins, a leading aircraftsman, was hanged on 25 June 1942 for the murder of a prostitute Evelyn Oatley at her flat in Wardour Street, London W1. He was convicted on fingerprint evidence. A print of his left little finger was found on a tin-opener with which he had mutilated Miss Oatley and which he had left behind in her flat. He was caught when he attempted to strangle another woman in an alleyway in the West End. He was disturbed by a passer-by and fled, leaving behind his gasmask through which he was traced.

at The Four Wants crossroad. He had seen him again at 1 a.m. Clark had failed to meet PC Kempton shortly after that; nor had he kept his next official appointment with Parsons at 3 a.m.

The search for Clark continued throughout the day and recommenced at dawn on the Thursday. PC Kempton told a local farmer, Ralph Page, he thought it was a bit of a waste of time, saying he thought the body was in one of the cornfields and would not be found until harvest time. Three other police in the search said much the same thing to the farmer. On the Friday night, on the way to drag a pond, a damaged police truncheon and then a bloodstained cutlass were found in a hedge near the already decomposing body of Clark. He was on his back, his legs crossed and his right hand clutching a handful of corn. His face was bruised and there was a large cut along the top of his skull. There were cuts to his back and neck. His money, watch and rattle were still in his pockets, which effectively ruled out robbery as a motive.

Various theories for the killing were on offer. The first was that it was a mistaken identity case with the unfortunate Clark being mistaken either for Butfoy or his sergeant, Parsons, both of whom had fallen foul of the Walker brothers, local villains.

At the inquest, to no one's great surprise, the Walker brothers said that they were innocent. More importantly there was evidence from Page's wife, Elizabeth, that after the discovery of Clark's body she had invited three of the officers to supper. It was then that Kempton had said that Parsons had not been on duty for most of the night of Clark's disappearance. He had, apparently, reported sick and Kempton had finished his duty for him. Kempton and another officer, Jonas Stevens, who had fainted at the sight of Clark's body, both denied this. Parsons denied any absence from duty and in this he was backed by the constables under his command.

The coroner wished to know about Clark's box in which he kept his possessions at the police station and why it had been broken open, and whether Clark was disliked by his colleagues. Was he lending them money? Had there been arguments over religion? PC Isaac gave evidence that Clark had broken open his own box but put his disappearance much earlier in the night. Clark had not kept a rendezvous at Miller's Farm at 11 p.m. that night.

Suspicion was now transferred to Parsons. Mrs Page stuck to her story that Kempton had told her Parsons was not on duty. She was contradicted by a witness who in turn was contradicted by a juryman who said that the witness had told him Kempton regularly did Parson's duty. Parsons interrupted to say he believed that he was being set-up as the murderer. He denied he was, saying he could produce a number of witnesses who would deny the statements made by Mrs Page. To further confuse matters, Julia Parsons, the sergeant's sister, told the jury that she had seen Parsons and Clark together about 9 p.m. that evening. Parsons was on a horse with Clark walking beside him. She went on to say he had been home around midnight to write up his report and had left again at 1 a.m., not returning for a further eight hours.

Parsons first produced evidence that he had been served a pint of porter by the landlord at the Cross Keys public house around midnight and then called a carter who had seen him on horseback between three and four in the morning. The coroner said that he accepted Parsons had been on duty all night. The problem was now whether Kempton had said he had taken the sergeant's duty and if so why. The inquest was further adjourned.

On 12 August 1846 Dennis Flinn, John Hennessy and Eileen Rankin were brought before magistrates at Ilford on suspicion of murdering Clark. The evidence depended on a rambling confession by Eileen Rankin to an Irish labourer, Michael Welch, to the effect that Hennessy and Flinn had been involved in a fight with a policeman who was found dead the next morning. The case was remanded a week, during which time it was established both men had a perfectly good alibi.

On 18 August *The Times* reported that several Dagenham policemen had been arrested on a charge of murder. In fact Kempton, Hickton, Farnes, Butfoy and Parsons had merely been suspended. The inquest was re-opened.

Butfoy gave evidence first, admitting he had told lies. He had not seen the sergeant that night. He had not even been on duty. Parsons and he had been to a police court earlier in the day and he, Butfoy, had got so drunk that he was excused duty. He had no explanation for the death of Clark, he told the jury:

> only it looks strange that the sergeant does not account for his time from half past nine o'clock until 11 and that Clark was not seen by a man who was invariably in the habit of seeing him at 11 o'clock at the Four Wants.

Kempton went next, admitting to taking over Parsons' duty at midnight. He had expected to meet Clark but the officer had not appeared. Farnes now retracted his statement that he had seen Parsons previously and that he had changed his story at Kempton's request. Parsons' response was a simple denial. 'They have sworn falsely.' When it was pointed out that they now all contradicted him, he replied, 'I can't help that.'

There was further damaging evidence from Luke White, a labourer, who said he had seen PC Clark on duty at 10. 30 p.m. and who had agreed to wake him up between three and four, a service regularly offered by the police. A porter, Henry Clements, then said that he had seen Parsons in the public bar murmuring, 'Poor fellow, I wish I had not done it now'. Clements had asked, 'Done what?' Parsons did not reply but since then he said that Clements said he had been threatened by Kempton.

But suspicions soon shifted from Parsons. It was discovered that the hymn-singing, tract-bearing Clark had two girlfriends, the second of them a married, though separated woman, Susan Perry. Her husband, James, said to be very jealous, had been seen in a Dagenham public house the night of the murder. An officer was instructed to become friendly with Perry and to try to worm out any confidences from him. He failed to do so.

On the last day of the inquest yet another witness was called. This time a PC George Dunning gave evidence that he had heard Parsons quarrelling with his sister, Julia. Parsons had begun to cry and later had threatened to throw her down the stairs if she did not hold her tongue. Julia Parsons admitted the quarrel but maintained it was to do with family matters.

When it came to it the coroner told the jury that in his opinion both Butfoy and Parsons were lying and the jury must make up their minds whether there was sufficient evidence to bring in a verdict of wilful murder against anyone. The jury returned a verdict of murder by persons unknown.

The charges of perjury against officers Farnes, Butfoy and another named Stevens were dropped. They had not been on oath when first examined. Therefore whilst they may have lied, they could not have committed perjury. They were dismissed from the force and now appeared as the main prosecution witnesses against Parsons, Hickton and Kempton for conspiracy to pervert, and against Kempton and Hickman for perjury.

At their trial, Kempton and Hickton were found guilty and each received a sentence of seven years' transportation. In the end neither served the sentence. Hickton had his commuted and Kempton too was released on a petition by his father. He had, after all, had 'only one report for neglect of duty'. Parsons was acquitted at the Old Bailey in 1848 on the direction of Lord Justice Denman, who ruled that the sergeant had not been conspiring to defeat justice but only to cover up his own dereliction of duty.

In 1858 Mrs Page came forward to tell the story that the murderers were her husband Ralph, conveniently dead, and three other men, one of whom had already hanged himself and another gone to Australia. The third, George Blewett, was acquitted when a grand jury refused to return a true bill of indictment.

One theory was that Clark had been killed because of his refusal to turn a blind eye to smuggling. There was support for this when, later in 1858, the police received a letter from Australia to the effect that Clark had been killed when he came upon some tobacco smugglers. A final version of his death was that he was killed because of the affair with Perry's wife.

Joan Lock, *Dreadful Deeds and Awful Murders*

Jane Maria Clouson

The seventeen-year-old housemaid to the wealthy and snobbish Pook family from Greenwich, South-east London, was killed on the evening of 25 April 1871. Earlier that month she had told Mrs Pook that she had been seduced by twenty-year-old Edmund, the son of the house, and was pregnant. She was dismissed, took rooms nearby and on the advice of friends sought out Edmund. She was later heard to say that Edmund had agreed to stand by her and that she was going to the country for her confinement. She also said she was meeting Edmund on the evening of 25 April.

At about 4.45 a.m. on 26 April she was found in Kidbrooke Lane by a passing police constable. She had been badly beaten with a packing case hammer and died later in hospital. The evidence against Edmund was strong. The girl was indeed found to be pregnant; there were bloodstains on his clothing and some identification. He was vigorously defended by a local solicitor also called Pook although he was no relation. His trial took place at the Old Bailey on 12 July 1871. Evidence was called to show he suffered from nosebleeds; the Pooks denied vehemently that their son would have associated with a 'skivvy' and, with the Lord Chief Justice summing up in his favour, he was acquitted in 20 minutes.

It was not the end of the matter. Newton Crossland, a rich Londoner enraged by what he considered to be a gross miscarriage of justice, published a pamphlet, *The Eltham Tragedy Revisited*, accusing young Pook of the murder. Pook, egged on by his family and namesake who established a fighting fund, sued. This time he was obliged to give evidence – he had not been permitted to do so at the criminal trial – and was savagely cross-examined by Sergeant Parry acting for Crossland.* Nevertheless Pook won the case and £50 damages. He was

---

* A Sergeant was roughly equivalent of Queen's Counsel.

successful in three other similar actions brought against people who were prepared to air their views on the jury's verdict and to pay for the privilege. Despite
this the Pook family was socially ruined and left the locality. A monument was
erected to Jane Maria Clouson which reads, 'She was agreeable in manner,
amiable and affectionate in disposition.'

Maxwell Confait

On 22 April 1972, a fire broke out in a house in Doggett Road, Catford,
South-east London, and in a room on the first floor firemen discovered the
body of Maxwell Confait, a transvestite prostitute. Within days three boys,
Colin Lattimore, Ronnie Leighton and Ahmet Salih, were arrested. All confessed
to the murder of Confait and the subsequent arson. At the time Lattimore was
eighteen but was said to have a mental age of eight. He had been diagnosed as
educationally subnormal and, later, psychiatrists were to say he was highly
suggestible 'so that the slightest indication of the expected answer will produce
it'.

Leighton was fifteen and, although considerably brighter than his friend
Colin, he was described as 'borderline subnormal' and 'really an immature,
inadequate, simple dullard'. Salih was described as reasonably intelligent. He
was just fourteen. The boys were arrested after a policeman had seen two of
them running from a fire which had been started in a shed in a nearby park.

The crucial question for the prosecution was the time Confait died. The doctors at the committal proceedings put the time of death between 6.30 and 10
p.m., basing their conclusions on the onset of *rigor mortis*. Once the case was
committed the boys were obliged to give details of any alibis they had under the
provisions of the Criminal Justice Act 1967. Lattimore, for example, who had
allegedly admitted strangling Confait, had a watertight alibi for the night of his
death. Independent witnesses could trace his movements from 6 p.m. to 11.40
p.m. Another had seen him at home at 11.45 p.m. and his father could place him
in the house at 12.35 a.m. Now the goalposts were shifted and the medical
evidence put the time of death at about 1 a.m. The alibis were useless and the
confessions stood.

The boys were convicted in November 1972 – Lattimore of manslaughter on
the grounds of diminished responsibility; Leighton of murder and Salih of arson. Lattimore was ordered to be detained under the Mental Health Act without

limit of time, Leighton during Her Majesty's pleasure and Salih to four years' detention. Their appeals were dismissed.

Their families did not accept the verdicts and in June 1975 the Confait case was referred by Roy Jenkins, then Home Secretary, back to the Court of Appeal. Over the years this has been something of a graveyard for the hopes of appellants but on this occasion their convictions were quashed. At the appeal in October 1975 it was established by further medical evidence that Confait's death took place 'some appreciable time before midnight'. Lord Justice Scarman said the effect of this fresh medical evidence was:

> to destroy the lynch-pin of the Crown's case and to demonstrate that the version of events contained in the admissions relied upon by the Crown cannot be true.

He accepted that it was still possible that their confessions to the arson at 27 Doggett Road could be correct but added their statements could not be regarded as 'sufficiently reliable evidence standing as they do, alone, to justify the convictions for arson which were based solely upon them'.

Sir Henry Fisher, a former High Court Judge, was appointed to hold an enquiry. It was held in private and in his report his findings went as follows: (a) Lattimore's alibi was genuine and he could have taken no part in the killing, (b) Leighton and Salih could have taken part in the killing and (c) all three could have set light to 27 Doggett Road. He could not accept that the confessions could have been made without at least one of the boys having been involved in the killing and arson. The most likely scenario was, he thought, that Lattimore's confession to his part in the arson was true and that he had been persuaded to confess to the killing by either Leighton or Salih. He thought Leighton and Salih's confessions to the arson were true and that their answers to the killing had been falsified to include Lattimore. They had both been involved in the killing.

Sir Henry had it almost completely wrong. In January 1980 the then Director of Public Prosecutions, Sir Thomas Hetherington, received 'new information' about the case and Sir Michael Havers, the Attorney General, told the House of Commons eight months later that he too was satisfied that Confait had, in fact, died before midnight on 21 April.

> I am also satisfied that if the evidence now available had been before Sir Henry Fisher he would not have come to the conclusion that any of the three young men was responsible for the death of Confait or the arson at 27 Doggett Road. Counsel has advised, and the Director of Public Prosecutions and I agree, that there is insufficient evidence to prosecute any other person.

The new information had come through Inspector Eddie Ellison who had investigated the story of a man who claimed he was being blackmailed for a murder he had committed. He and another man maintained he had seen the other kill Confait but not to have been involved himself. It was not thought there was sufficient evidence to prosecute either of them.*

The Confait case was the start of the road which led to the Police and Criminal Evidence Act 1984 and the Prosecution of Offences Act 1985, the second of which saw the foundation of the Crown Prosecution Service.

James Morton, *Bent Coppers*; Christopher Price and Jonathan Caplan, *The Confait Confessions*

Margaret Cook

On 10 November 1946 Margaret Cook, a thirty-year-old 'exotic dancer' who had served a Borstal sentence, was found shot in an alley outside the Blue Lagoon Club in Carnaby Street, London. The police wished to interview a man between twenty-five and thirty, height between 5'8" and 5'9", clean shaven and wearing a dark pork pie hat and a Burberry style raincoat. It is probable that she was killed after an argument with a boyfriend or client. She had been warned that her new boyfriend carried a revolver but no one knew his name. No one was arrested.

Andre Cools

On 18 July 1991, Cools, a former deputy Prime Minister of Belgium, was shot in Brussels in the throat and left ear as he walked to his car with his mistress, Marie-Helene Joiret, who was shot in the kidney but survived. The gunman was said to be in his thirties, wearing denims and sneakers. Cools' death came a matter of days after he had been given Bank of Credit and Commerce International (BCCI) bank statements and other documents which

---

* The next year the Home Office offered the youths a total of £65,000 in compensation for their wrongful imprisonment.

suggested that civil servants had been 'sweetened' to secure the use of Belgian airforce freighters to ship cargoes of supergun propellant to Iraq. The material was for Project Babylon, the Iraqi guns designed by Gerald Bull (*qv*).

Pamela Coventry

On 19 January 1939 the body of eleven-year-old Pamela Coventry was found in a field near Hornchurch, Essex. She had disappeared the previous day after lunch, walking back to her school in Benhurst Avenue. She had been watched on her way by her step-mother. When Pamela did not return for tea and the step-mother learned that the girl had not been at school during the afternoon she called the police.

Pamela's dress had been tied around her neck but the rest of her clothing was missing. Her legs had been tied with tarred string and black and green insulating wire. She had been raped and strangled and had clearly fought against her attacker. She had a number of bruises and scratches on her face and head and had suffered a nosebleed. A cigarette end was found on her body, under which was a rotting mattress. The pathologist, Sir Bernard Spilsbury, estimated that she had died before 2 p.m. the previous day.

Over the next two weeks some of her clothing was found at Elm Park station where a parcel wrapped in the *News Chronicle* for 11 January was found, tied together by black insulation wire.

On 28 January the police searched a house in nearby Coronation Drive and took away tarred string and insulation wire along with copies of the *News Chronicle* from 4 to 12 January. Only the issue of the 11 January was missing. They also took away a blood-spotted raincoat. On 2 February, Leonard Richard, who lived in the house, was charged with Pamela's murder. The police case was that he smoked the same brand of tobacco and used the same cigarette paper as the butt found on the child's body.

The quality of the evidence was not dissimilar to that in the case of Vera Page (*qv*). The insulating tape and wire were common enough. The blood on the raincoat could not be tied to that of Pamela's. The tobacco was popular as was the *News Chronicle* and there was evidence that some 60,000,000 cigarette papers of the same type were in circulation at any one time. The jury stopped the case, sending a note to the judge to say they had heard sufficient evidence. Richardson was acquitted. There were no further arrests.

D. G. Browne and T. Tullett, *Bernard Spilsbury*

John Coward

Just before 3 a.m. on 29 September 1921 John Coward was found shot to death in a curtained Buick motor car a short distance from the mining town of Carbon, Alberta. He was half lying across the front seat with his left hand still on the steering wheel. The ignition of the car was still on and it was in gear. His watch, $79 in cash and a $400 cheque were still in his possession so, it would appear, robbery could be ruled out as a motive.

Coward had been seen on his journey earlier in the evening after he had left the Gallagher coal mine owned by John Gallagher. Gallagher was negotiating with the Peerless Carbon Coal Company to sell his mine and was now in the habit of passing the day's takings to Coward. According to Gallagher, earlier in the evening before Coward's body was found he had been with him to see another miner, Teddy Bolam, whom he had dismissed some weeks earlier, and had collected $75 from a local Mennonite community. Gallagher said that he had been dropped off by Coward and had walked back into town.

The police enquiries started with Gallagher, who had once been a member of the Royal North West Mounted Police (RNWMP) and a constable with the Alberta provincial police. A womaniser, he had also been instrumental in breaking up embryonic miners' unions and was suspected of being a bootlegger. As for Coward, he had once been manager of the Stirling mine which had gone bust and, so Gallagher said, there was residual resentment over unpaid wages.

When the body was taken for examination a rare .38 flat-nosed bullet which appeared to have been filed down was discovered. There were two other bullet entries and wounds but no more bullets were found. Gallagher was known to have had a similar bullet to the one found – albeit four years earlier. When asked where the .38 revolver was he said at his home. From then on it would appear the police became convinced Gallagher was the killer. He was arrested on the wholly spurious charge of contributing to the delinquency of a minor – the five-year-old daughter of a witness who was backing Gallagher's story of leaving the car – and kept in custody. His contribution to the child's delinquency was that he was living with her mother but not married to her. His property was now searched more thoroughly. Detective Lesley found that the ammunition in Gallagher's belt had been changed. The previous day it had contained a .38 snub-nosed bullet. Now this had been replaced with a more ordinary .32.

On the Saturday Gallagher pleaded guilty to the delinquency charge and was remanded in custody for sentence. On the Sunday morning a snub-nosed .38 slug was found some seven yards from where the rear wheel of Coward's car had halted.

When the inquest began on 6 October Bolam, the miner, gave evidence that Gallagher had been to his shack on the night of the killing but after he left Bolam had been watching the path down which Gallagher had said he had gone but had not seen him. If Gallagher had given details of the route correctly he should have been visible from Bolam's shack. There was also evidence from Carl Hedberg, who might himself have been a bootlegger, who said he had seen Coward's car pulled to the side of the road with its headlights on. He also gave evidence that he had known Gallagher during the latter's time in the Alberta provincial police force and that he had a .38 gun. Mrs Dorothy Bruce, with whom Gallagher had been living, provided an alibi for him saying he had returned from the Mennonites at about 7 p.m., they had had supper after which he had gone to check the horses and they had then gone to bed. The first she had heard of the murder was when the police came the next day. Reluctantly she admitted to Chief Inspector Nicholson, who conducted the police case, that it was possible Gallagher had become mentally unbalanced.

Gallagher's evidence was simple.

> I left Bolam's shack at about 7.10 and walked a few paces to where Mr Coward was waiting in the car. I jumped on the running board and with Mr Coward driving at a slow pace I told him that I had joshed Bolam about having to get off company property. I was just a short distance from my shack at this time, so I bade Mr Coward good night and jumped off the footboard and went home by way of the railway track.

Gallagher denied he had a gun, saying that he collected military paraphernalia and had many swords, badges and shells. What about a motive? There was some suggestion that Gallagher was about to lose his mine, rather than sell it, to the Peerless Carbon Coal Company and that Coward had been appointed manager over Gallagher.

The jury returned a verdict of death by 'bullets fired from a revolver in the hands of a person or persons unknown'. Nicholson was not satisfied. He arrested Gallagher and charged him with murder. What was the sum of the police evidence against Gallagher? It appears that he had refused to help move Coward's body and this was deemed to be a suspicious circumstance. There was the finding of the .38 bullet and the subsequent switch of bullets. Mrs Bruce, now assured her daughter would not be taken from her, gave evidence that Gallagher had indeed had a gun. She also gave evidence that changed the time of return from Bolam's shack to half an hour later. She also said she had given him a gun some years previously, had taken it back and put it in a drawer from where it had disappeared. There was now more evidence on the negotiations for the take-over of Gallagher's mine. He had been replaced by Coward as manager, said one officer, even though the take-over was not complete. Gallagher had not been invited to meetings but on the afternoon of Coward's death had learned that he was no longer in charge of what had been his mine. The alternative version for Coward's death and one which the police were not inclined to pursue was that miners from the Drumheller Valley, whose strike Coward had broken some years earlier, had sworn vengeance on him.

Gallagher's trial before a judge and jury of six began on 18 January 1922. Now he was represented by Alexander Sinclair, a forceful Calgary lawyer, and the prosecution's case took its final shape. Gallagher was indeed being replaced as manager of the mine but, according to a witness, he did not know of his sacking at the time of Coward's death. Witnesses were called to say that Gallagher had shot at them in the past, thus negating his story that he had no revolver. It was accepted that blood would be expected to be found on the clothing of the murderer but although Gallagher's clothing had been sent for examination no bloodstains were found. Mrs Bruce was now convinced Gallagher had arrived home at 7.30 p.m. and had gone to see to the horses half an hour later. A witness was produced who said he had heard shots at 7.15 p.m. This would fit neatly the timings required by the police. Gallagher was out of his ground. If he and Coward had left Bolam at ten past seven it would have taken five minutes to drive to where Coward was shot and Gallagher could then have walked the distance home in eleven minutes getting him back at 7.30, as Mrs Bruce now said. Bolam now strengthened his evidence saying he had kept watch from both windows and had not seen Gallagher. Gallagher did not give evidence. The jury retired for five hours and returned a verdict of guilty with no recommendation for mercy. He was sentenced to be hanged in Calgary on 15 April 1922.

Sinclair began to prepare the appeal and was greatly helped when it was discovered that Teddy Bolam had received a large sum of money after the case. He then left for a trip to Mexico but only reached Calgary where he and his money were separated by the attentions of a prostitute. On 28 February 1922 he was killed in the Fuller mine at Carbon. It seems he had been working alone when the ceiling, carelessly shored, had collapsed on him. He was known as a careless workman and it might be that the accident was simply that. There was, however, a body of opinion that said someone had crossed from the Shannon mine into the Fuller workings and hit Bolam on the head before pulling down the timbering.

Gallagher's appeal was allowed on the grounds that the judge had inadvertently referred to the defendant's failure to give evidence. A new trial was ordered. Public sympathy had always been with Gallagher and it now swelled as the man's war record was disclosed. Before that he had suffered spinal injuries when he had been thrown from his horse whilst in the RNWMP. Now, it was learned, at the second battle of Ypres in April 1915 he had suffered ear damage when a cannon had fired prematurely. Later at Ploegsteert he had been buried by a German shell. He was now completely deaf and could only lip-read, something he did with such skill that only his close friends knew of his disabilities.

Better still from the defence point of view, three of the rare flat-nosed .38 bullets were sent to a Calgary detective agency with an anonymous note warning people to keep out of Carbon.

The retrial began on 22 May 1922. Bolam was gone and so was Daniel Sherry who had 'found' the second .38 bullet. He had left the area. With the prosecution evidence substantially weakened and after he had given evidence, Gallagher was acquitted, following a four-hour retirement by the jury. It was a decision which was greeted with acclaim in which, curiously, police officers joined.

It was not the end of the matter. Rival theories flourished. The first was that Gallagher had indeed killed Coward but that he had been helped to flee the scene. The second was that Coward had accidentally stumbled over some illicit activity and had been killed to keep him quiet. There had, after all, been considerable bootlegging activity in the region.

On Sunday, 8 December 1923 the body of the mine operator, Jesse Fuller, was found on Shannon mine land. His throat had been cut and the autopsy showed that he had been struck with a piece of wood on the side of the head with such forced that his right ear had been nearly torn off. He had operated the mine on his own and had then sold out to the Carbon Coal Company. He had, it seems, borrowed money from Gallagher who had been to see him earlier in the week, when he asked his daughter, Stella, to sign a promissory note for $300 which, he said, Fuller had borrowed previously. Medical evidence established that

Fuller had been killed between Thursday and Friday night. He had been killed elsewhere and the body placed on Shannon land. Gallagher hired Sinclair to represent him at the inquest. Fuller's daughter gave evidence that her father had left her two notes which she had burned. In one of them he had told her to get in touch with Gallagher who 'will do everything for you'. Gallagher told the coroner's jury that he assumed it had to do with Fuller's financial mess. The verdict was death by a person or persons unknown.

It is difficult to see why Gallagher should have killed Fuller. Just what had he to gain? But then why was the man regarded as a quiet, inoffensive and broke miner killed at all and with such ferocity?

If, as it appears, he did not know he was being replaced as mine manager by Coward why should Gallagher kill him either unless, as Mrs Bruce hinted, he was becoming unbalanced. Was Bolam's death an accident? Probably not when allied to the change in his evidence, the money he suddenly received and lost just as quickly. But on whose behalf was he killed?

In extreme financial difficulties over the payment of his legal costs Gallagher was convicted on 10 June 1924 of setting fire to buildings on his property. He was given a sentence of life imprisonment, reduced on appeal to one of ten years. After the completion of his sentence he went to England.

Frank Anderson, *The Carbon Murders Mystery*

Harvey and Jeanette Crewe

The New Zealand police never really came anywhere near establishing who looked after Rochelle, the baby daughter of Harvey and Jeanette Crewe, for five days after her parents had been killed in their farmhouse in Bitter Hill, twenty-five miles south of Auckland.

The Crewes, whose absence was discovered on 22 June 1970, lived and worked a 365-acre farm not far from a larger spread owned by Jeanette's father, Len Demler. Whilst, in general, the Crewes were neither popular nor unpopular in the community – Harvey Crewe was said to have a violent temper – there had been a series of unfortunate incidents following their marriage. In 1967 their home was burgled but only Jeanette's valuables had been taken. The next year Harvey Crewe returned home to find the spare bedroom ablaze. In 1969 a hay-barn was set alight.

Initially, when there was no word from them for five days in June 1970 no one worried too much but, when there was no reply to his telephone calls, eventually Demler rode over and found Rochelle in her cot, soiled and hungry but by no means starving, nor suffering from hypothermia. There were bloodstains on the carpet and a laid-out meal on the table. Of the Crewes there was no sign.

Demler, who was later roundly criticised for his behaviour, left the child in her cot and drove home to telephone his stock agent before calling for assistance. He was later to attract further comment because, instead of searching for the bodies, he went to a party. Jeanette's blood was found in his car but it was later established she had driven in it earlier.

The movements of the Crewes over the previous days were traced. On the morning of 17 June Harvey Crewe had discussed the purchase of a bull with a stock agent. In the afternoon the Crewes went to a local stock-clearing sale and were seen leaving in their green Hillman car at about 4 p.m. The car was seen at the south end of the farm an hour or so later. The Crewes were never seen alive again.

The police investigation showed that there were bloodstains and brain tissue on Harvey Crewe's armchair, leading them to believe the couple had been killed in their home. At first the police focused on Len Demler as the principal suspect. There had been ill-feeling in the family over the will of his wife, Maisie. She had cut her daughter Heather from her will because of what she saw as an unsuitable marriage. In turn Demler had cut Jeanette from his will. At the time of his death Harvey Crewe was negotiating to buy Demler's half share in his farm. It would seem that Demler would then be evicted from his own farm. This, coupled with the fact that Jeanette's blood was found in Demler's car, was sufficient for the police to regard him as a prime suspect.

The Crewes were found two and three months later respectively. On 16 August Jeanette's body was fished out of the flooded Waikato river. She had been shot through the head with a .22 bullet. She had also been beaten but there was no evidence of a sexual attack. The body, clothed, had been wrapped in bedclothes and bound up in farm wire. A month later Harvey's body, again with a bullet in the head, was fished from the same river. His body had been weighted with an axle.

Suspicion shifted from Demler and now the best, if not very likely, suspect was Arthur Allen Thomas, a thirty-two-year-old farmer who had certainly been fond of Jeanette both at school and before her marriage. There was, however, really no evidence against him. The axle with which Crewe's body had been weighted was traced to a 1929 Nash motor car in 1958 and then to a trailer owned by Thomas's father. In 1965 the trailer was taken to have its axle assembly removed and when it was collected it may or may not have still had the axle. Stub axles which matched the one used as a weight were also found on a tip on Thomas's farm. Certainly there were no fingerprints matching his at the Crewes' home but a matching cartridge case from his rifle was found in the Crewes' garden. The theory was that this had been dropped when he fired the first shot or reloaded.

An 'unspeakable outrage' was how the Royal Commission described this piece of evidence after Thomas, convicted in 1970 following a re-trial, had served nine years of his life sentence. Throughout his defence he had alleged the cartridge had been planted and he was assisted when a friend of the Crewes, who had initially helped the police search the property, said that the area where the cartridge had been found had been thoroughly sieve-searched. In 1978 the author David Yallop published *Beyond Reasonable Doubt?* and also claimed he knew who had fed Rochelle. Thomas's case was taken up by Pat Booth of *The Auckland Star*. In turn this led to a Royal Commission appointed by the Prime Minister, Robert Muldoon.

The Commission found that two detectives from the police had planted the cartridge and that it would be unsafe to make any assumption of Thomas's guilt from the axle. He was awarded £400,000 in compensation and bought a dairy farm with the money. The detectives who planted the evidence were not prosecuted and indeed the police have never accepted the Royal Commission's findings. It is thought Rochelle Crewe grew up in America before returning to New Zealand under another name.

The theories for the murder range from a suicide-murder by the Crewes, which means someone must have cleaned up after them and disposed of the bodies, to murder by a stranger. Even in this decade there is a reluctance in Auckland to discuss the case in detail, with hints that it had been a contract killing. But who fed the child and, for that matter, the Crewes' kennelled hunting dogs during the five days?

David Yallop, *Beyond Reasonable Doubt;* Richard and Molly Whittington-Egan, *The Bedside Book of Murder*

The Reverend Hubert Dahme

On 4 February 1924 the vicar at St Joseph's Church was shot dead on the main street of Bridgeport, Connecticut, in front of a large crowd. There appears to have been no motive for the killing. Two weeks later a twenty-eight-year-old alcoholic, Harold Israel, confessed after extensive police questioning. He had, he said, been starving and was filled with an uncontrollable rage. The only good supporting evidence was from a waitress in a nearby cafe who said she could identify Israel. He was defended by Homer Cummings who could not understand why Israel should be starving when he could have pawned the gun for at least five dollars. Israel now told Cummings he had confessed merely to be left alone by the police and that he had been in a cinema when the shooting had taken place. Cummings made enquiries and discovered that the waitress could not have made any proper identification through the steamed-up windows of the cafe. She confessed she had made the identification for the reward money. Israel was acquitted and, according to folk history, gave up alcohol and became a wealthy timber merchant. Cummings became Attorney General under the Roosevelt administration. No one else was arrested for the killing of the priest.

Colin Wilson, *The Mammoth Book of True Crime*

May Daniels

On 6 October 1926 May Daniels, a probationer nurse at the Chiswick and Ealing Isolation Hospital, West London, disappeared during a trip to Boulogne with a colleague, Nurse Marcella McCarthy. The previous day they had gone to Brighton for the afternoon, had lunch in the famous or infamous Sherry's and walked to the Palace Pier where they noticed a day trip to Boulogne. According to Nurse McCarthy, Daniels said she would like to go and that they could apologise to the hospital matron the next day. They left on the 9.40 excursion boat. Miss Daniels took with her curling tongs and a hairbrush, a hypodermic syringe and some morphia tablets. The return halves of the 12/6d tickets were never found. The boat did not arrive until about 2.45 p.m. It was due to return at 5.10 p.m. Neither of the girls caught it.

When later Nurse McCarthy made a sworn statement for the benefit of the French authorities she said that just before they returned to the boat Daniels went to the lavatory opposite the Post Office. McCarthy waited for her, searched and could not find her, and then made enquiries but, as she could not speak French, she was ignored. She went back to the boat but arrived only in time to see it go. She returned to the station to look once more for her friend. By now it was getting dark and so, as a Roman Catholic, she looked for a convent for help. She could not find one and spent the night on a bench in the waiting-room at the railway station. The next morning she found someone to take her to the convent. There she was fed and given the address of the British consulate. Poor Nurse McCarthy was not good at directions and ended up back at the convent where she spent another night. She was then taken to the consul the next morning who gave her a temporary passport. She returned to the convent where she stayed until she caught the boat on Saturday 9 October. She went at once to the hospital with her sorry tale. She was sure that whilst Daniels was with her she had spoken to no men.

May Daniels' body was found six months later in a field in Wimille, about two miles from Boulogne. Around the body were the syringe, curling tongs, morphia tablets, a bracelet, handbag and hairbrush. The body had been subject to the ravages of a winter in the French countryside and the doctor who first examined her thought she had been strangled. The next month his opinion was confirmed by Dr Charles Paul, a noted Parisian pathologist. He supported the local doctor's finding that it appeared that she had been held down by a man kneeling on her.

Before May Daniels' body had been found, Nurse McCarthy told of how a middle-aged man had eyed them in Boulogne and then followed them. Could this man have persuaded May Daniels to go off with him? Rumour now abounded about both girls and Nurse McCarthy, who must have had good connections and no little money behind her, took the advice of the well-known firm of Lewis and Lewis and had herself examined by a doctor. She was *intacta*. On the advice of leading counsel, Roland Oliver KC, and Sir Travers (later Mr Justice) Humphreys, she made her sworn statement but declined to return to France for an oral examination. Libel proceedings were threatened against anyone who spoke ill of Marcella McCarthy.

The matter was complicated when the British consul decided that Nurse McCarthy had been to see him on the 7th and not the 8th of October and worse followed when an Egyptian, Suliman, said that the manager of the British YMCA in Boulogne had offered him £50 to perform an abortion on Nurse Daniels. He had been told that if he declined a woman, whose name he gave, who was with Miss Daniels, would have to do it. The manager firmly denied the allegation, saying that the only time he had met Suliman was when the man had tried to borrow money from him. Later a letter was sent to the French police by a man who said he had seen two women in Brighton, in the company of men who looked like Egyptians, on the day before the trip to Boulogne. He seems never to have been called to France to give evidence.

In September 1930 a criminal, Charles Gras, made a statement that he had killed both Nurse Daniels and Florence Wilson (*qv*) but he was not believed. Later a man arrested on a charge of theft in Boulogne was denounced by his wife who said he had confessed to her. A gold watch was found in his home but the Daniels family said they did not believe she had a watch of any kind at the time of her death.

The possibilities seem to be that she committed suicide, something that her family would not believe, that she died as a result of an abortion or that she was indeed strangled.

Harry J. Greenwall, *They Were Murdered in France*

Paul and Wayne Darvell *see* **Sandra Phillips**

Helen Davidson

On 9 November 1966 Helen Davidson, a fifty-four-year-old doctor who had practised in Amersham, Buckinghamshire, for some years, disappeared from her home in North Road. She was married to a retired bank worker, Herbert Baker, who had a part-time job in the locality. In the morning they worked in the garden and then, shortly after 1.30 p.m., he went to his job. When he returned he found she was out in her Hillman car along with her wire-terrier dog, Fancy. When she did not return he contacted friends and finally the police. In the early hours of the next morning her Hillman was found in a lay-by on the Amersham-Beaconsfield Road. The doors were locked with her handbag and binoculars' case still inside. At 2.15 p.m. her body was found in a clearing at

Highfield Grove, part of Hodgemoor Wood, some eleven hundred yards from her car. Her head had been battered beyond recognition. Her coat was still buttoned and the binocular strap still around her neck. The glasses themselves were nearby. Fancy was cuddled against the body.

Forensic evidence showed that she had died immediately from a single blow across her forehead. Her killer had then continued to batter her. The murder weapon, a branch of a poplar tree, was found nearby.

A number of suggestions for the reason for the killing were advanced and mostly dismissed. There had been no sexual attack and the motive was clearly not robbery. It was suggested the attacker might be a vengeful patient or that she had surprised a courting couple or indecent exposer who, recognising the doctor, killed her to prevent his own identification. The attack was almost certainly unpremeditated because of the weapon used.

Investigation was made of a particular man who left the area and went to Australia where his behaviour was peculiar – he advertised for the purchase of a Flying Saucer. Later he returned to England where he was convicted of an assault on an elderly man. In an interview with Anne Edwards in the *Bucks Free Press* in February 1986 he said, 'I have not pleaded innocent yet. I have not pleaded guilty yet. Time will tell. Destiny will tell. I have said to the coppers that I could have had a bloody blackout and I could have done it.'

Bernard Taylor and Stephen Knight, *Perfect Murder*

Fabian Del Rosario

The twenty-year-old college student was last seen on Friday 28 August 1987 in Boulder, Colorado. At 6.15 p.m. he telephoned his girlfriend, Elizabeth Bader, who worked for Aspen Eyewear, to make arrangements to collect her for a dinner date between 7.30 and 8 p.m. He told her he had to telephone and meet another person before he collected her. He never showed up at her apartment and she reported him missing the next morning. His bloodspattered sports car was found on 31 August in the Crossroads mall parking lot. There were a substantial number of '0' type bloodstains, the same as Del Rosario's group. The police thought that he had been killed elsewhere and the car and body then dumped.

Over the weeks it transpired that Del Rosario was a small-time cocaine dealer and one theory was that in trying to extend his empire he may have trodden on more important toes than was wise. Although he was on a full grant at the University and therefore deemed to be in need of financial help, he was able to take trips to Hawaii and Las Vegas and made several visits to Miami where his Argentinian family owned an aquarium business. He had spent most of the summer with his girlfriend touring Europe.

This was another of the numerous cases in which psychics offered their assistance, one saying that the body was located in a mine-shaft. As police Lieutenant Jerry Hoover pointed out, 'It's a distinct possibility given the number of mine shafts in Colorado and it's the first thing that seems to come to people's minds.'

A private investigator was instructed by the family but no substantial leads were ever traced. Elizabeth Bader left her job shortly after Del Rosario's disappearance and moved from the area.

Jack 'Legs' Diamond

The legendary gangster was shot dead in his room in Albany, New York, on 18 December 1931 in what was a typical gangland execution. Born in 1896 Diamond had begun his career as a sneak thief in New York, working his way up to become an enforcer and bodyguard to Jacob 'Little Augie' Orgen, then a leading racketeer. Diamond, who was given his nickname either because of his prowess on the dance floor or because of an ability to outrun pursuing police officers, was shot in the arm and leg when Orgen was killed on Norfolk Street in the Lower East Side in 1927. Once out of hospital Diamond divided Orgen's businesses with the killers, Louis Lepke and Gurrah Shapiro, retaining the bootleg liquor and drugs trade for himself. He opened a club, the Hotsy Totsy, on Broadway between 54th and 55th and it was from there a number of gangland killings were carried out. Diamond was eventually obliged to absent himself from the scene for a time when, in 1929, he and his right hand man, Charles Entratta, killed a rival, Red Cassidy, in full view of both employees and customers. Both men fled and then organised a series of contracts to eliminate the witnesses and so undermine the police case against them. They duly surrendered and were charged but released because of a lack of evidence. In his absence Diamond's business was taken over in a large part by Dutch Schultz.

Over the years, because of his ability to survive assassination attempts (1924,

1927, 1930, 1931) he traded on the reputation of being a man who could not be killed. He could, however, be convicted. In August 1931 he was convicted of operating an illegal still. He was fined $10,000 and given a four-year jail sentence. He was released on bail pending an appeal. By this time he had fallen out with most of the other leading Underworld figures, first because he could not be trusted and secondly because he wanted a larger share of Joey Fay's nightclub rackets and the bootlegging from Waxey Gordon. It was never known which, if either, of these operators organised the contract on Diamond. He was asleep when three men entered his hotel room. One held him by the ears and the others shot him in the head.

Phyllis Dimmock

On 12 September 1907 Phyllis Dimmock, a prostitute, was found murdered at her two room lodgings in Camden Town, North London, by her common-law husband, Bert Shaw, on his return from night shift as a railway dining-car attendant. She had had her throat cut. Although it seems barely credible, apparently Shaw – who had the cast-iron alibi that he was on the London to

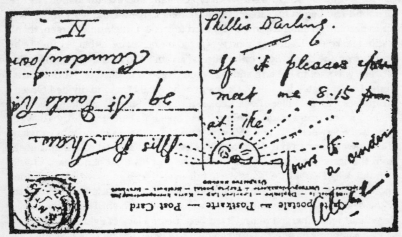

Robert Wood's postcard to Phyllis Dimmock, illustrated with a cartoon of a rising sun.

Sheffield train – had not known that she was carrying on her trade whilst he was away working. In the flat was a letter inviting her to meet a man 'Bert' on 11 September and another with a picture of a Rising Sun to suggest a rendezvous at that public house. Scotland Yard publicised the drawing and Robert Wood, a young artist, came forward to identify it as his work. He had, he said, met Phyllis Dimmock in a public house and she had asked him to draw something nice on a postcard.

He was arrested when a prostitute and former girlfriend, Ruby Young, was asked by him to provide an alibi. Instead she went to a journalist friend and the police were informed. The evidence against Wood was strong. He had a distinctive walk – his shoulder twitched – and there were several identifying witnesses. He was fortunate to be defended by Edward Marshall Hall KC who persuaded the jury that, because of poor street lighting, the identifying witnesses were mistaken. Hall was also able to cast doubt on the authenticity of the letter which another client and suspect, Robert Roberts, said had arrived at the flat whilst he was there. There was some resentment that Ruby Young had betrayed Wood. He made a good impression in the witness box and, with a favourable summing-up, was acquitted, to the delight of the public gallery. It was the first time a defendant had given evidence in a murder case and been acquitted following the section of Criminal Evidence Act 1898 which permitted an accused to give evidence on his or her behalf. The body of opinion is that Wood, who later emigrated to Australia, was fortunate in his defending advocate. Wood's champions suggest that Shaw, despite his seemingly impregnable alibi, could have caught an earlier train and jumped off whilst it was outside St Pancras Station. Yet another suggestion is that the murderer was another lodger in the house.

Sir John Hall (ed), *Notable British Trials;* L. Gribble, *They Got Away With Murder;* N. Warner Hooke and G. Thomas, *Marshall Hall*

Gwenda and Peter Dixon

Two experienced walkers in their early fifties, Mr and Mrs Dixon disappeared whilst on a tour of Pembrokeshire, England, in June 1989. They left their home in Oxfordshire on 19 June to camp at Howelston Farm Camp Site at Little Haven which they used as a base. On Sunday 25 June their son, Timothy

Edward, joined them for a meal in a local hotel and the next day all three walked
the coastal path from Portglais to St Justinians. They also spent next day together when they went to St David's Cathedral and on a 1000 island cruise
around Ramsey Island. Their son returned home and on Thursday 29 June the
Dixons left the farm to walk the coastal path towards Dale. They were never
seen again. When they had not returned home on 3 July they were reported
missing by their son. Their bodies were found on the coastal path. They had
been shot. Witnesses said that they had heard gunshots at about 11 a.m. on 29
June.

It was thought that robbery was the motive. Peter Dixon's National Westmin-
ster card was used on June 29 at 1.36 p.m. when £10 was withdrawn. It was used
again at 4.09 on the same day in the same bank when £100 was withdrawn. The
exercise was repeated at Carmarthen on 30 June at 2. 59 p.m. and at 7.14 a.m. in
Haverfordwest on Saturday 1 July. A scruffy looking motorcyclist was seen at
the relevant times and he must have obtained the PIN number from Dixon. A
second man, thought to be German, was seen in the company of the motorcyclist but it was never established whether they were travelling companions.

Another theory is that the Dixons were killed because they stumbled accidentally on an IRA cache and a third is that they were killed by James Moody (*qv*)
who was believed to be undertaking occasional work for that organisation.
There has been no hard evidence to establish either theory.

Patricia Docker

On the night of 22 February 1968 Patricia Docker was found naked in the
door recess of a lock-up garage. She was the first of the victims of a short-
term Scots serial killer known as Bible John who murdered at least three women
between February 1968 and October 1969. Each of the women, Patricia Docker
(25), Jemima 'Mima' McDonald (32) and Helen Puttock (29), had been picked up
by Bible John at the Barrowland Ballroom in a poor quarter of Glasgow.
McDonald was found partly clothed in a derelict tenement and Puttock fully
clothed lying against a wall. There was no evidence of sexual assault but the
women, who were all strangled with a belt or tights, were all menstruating at
the time of death. Helen Puttock's sister, Jeannie, had at one time spoken to
Bible John and recalled him as a six-foot man between twenty-five and thirty

with beautifully barbered red hair. He smoked and quoted sexual and other passages from the Bible, hence his soubriquet. He said he was a teetotaller.

The killing of Puttock, found with a sanitary towel in her armpit, was the last in the series. In 1983 a man who had been in Australia recognised an artist's impression of Bible John, circulated by the Crown Office, as a friend with whom he used to visit Barrowland. The friend was traced to Amsterdam but apart from being a lookalike there was nothing to link him with the killings.

Charles N. Stoddart, *Bible John*

Kenneth Stuart Dolden

On Saturday 9 November 1946 twenty-four-year-old Kenneth Dolden, the son of a solicitor and on demobilisation leave from the RAF, was shot in his parked car in Epping Forest, Essex. He was with his fiancée schoolteacher, Jacynth Bland, and they had been to a dance at a technical college in Walthamstow. They had then parked in a glade at Fairmead Bottom between Woodford and Loughton and moved into the back seat.

They had been there for about half an hour when a rough looking man, wearing a grey cloth cap pulled down and a muffler over his mouth, ordered Dolden to get out. He was then shot three times, once with the .38 revolver pressed against his body. The attacker then ran off leaving Miss Bland to find help. She ran to another parked car and was driven to a phone box where the driver, who gave his name as Brown, rang the police and then said he was driving back to help Dolden. He was not seen again.

In a dying declaration, Dolden said that he thought the man was after his car but Scotland Yard discounted this. There had been no major crime in the area necessitating a car to be stolen for a getaway and in 1946 the police could not believe that a man would be killed over a car which could only be used for an hour or so. The gun was never found.

At the inquest Mrs Isabella Wilson, who had been in the second parked car, said that she had accepted a lift from a tubby Jewish-looking man with a moustache, height 5'6". He had told her his name was Bill Brown and that he was a motor car salesman from Dalston. She said they had been sitting smoking and that Brown had not left the car from the moment they had parked. Despite appeals the police were never able to trace Brown.

Dolden's background was exemplary and for a time it was thought that a jealous husband had followed his car by mistake. In turn this theory was abandoned. No other cogent suggestion was offered in its place. In 1948 it was thought that the murder had been committed by a man then serving a life sentence for murder. The police interviewed a prisoner at Pentonville but no charges were ever brought.

Philip Yale Drew *see* **Alfred Oliver**

Arthur Duncan

On 2 July 1917 Arthur Duncan became the first Calgary, Alberta, policeman to be killed on duty. He was shot whilst patrolling his beat between 8th Avenue and 8th Street SW. No one was ever arrested for the crime and it is thought that he surprised a burglar. In 1979 an elderly man in British Columbia claimed to know the facts of the killing but nothing new was uncovered and the crime has remained unsolved.

Joseph B. Elwell

The body of cardplayer and womaniser Joseph B. Elwell was found by his housekeeper, Mrs Mary Larsen, at about 8 a.m. on 11 June 1920 at his home on West 70th Street, Manhatten, New York. He had been shot in the head by a .45 revolver. He had died within the previous half hour for he had a letter in his hand which timed the crime to after the morning postal delivery.

Elwell had been a professional bridge player whose books – *Elwell on Bridge* and *Elwell's Advanced Bridge* – ghosted by his more literate former wife Helen Darby, had been a great success. Aged forty-five at the time of his death, he gave the impression of a handsome youthful man. In fact his wavy hair was from one of his collection of forty wigs and he also wore false teeth. However, he was still attractive to women and had a 'love index' comprising the names of over fifty wealthy women with whom he had been, or was currently, involved.

Quantities of women's clothing were found in his home including a pink kimono, the owner of which was able to provide an alibi.

The police, however, discounted the theory of a female murderer. First, the argument went, a .45 revolver is not a woman's gun. Secondly, Elwell had been found without his teeth and wig and it was thought he was too vain to open the door to a woman when not properly dressed. Suggestions as to his killer included one from the pool of jealous husbands or someone connected with his

Joseph B. Elwell.

gambling. An even more fanciful suggestion was that it related back to World War I, in which Elwell had supposedly been a spy for the American government. No one was ever tried for the murder. Those who favour the killing-by-a-woman theory suggested that there might be an element of double bluff in the murder. The use of the .45 and the subsequent removal of the wig and teeth might have been simply to deflect suspicion from a female killer.

22nd Earl of Erroll *see* Josslyn Victor Hay

Starr Faithfull

At about 6.30 a.m. on Monday, 8 June 1931 the body of a young woman was discovered on Long Beach, New York. She was wearing a silk dress with a belt and sheer and undamaged silk stockings. Apart from that the body of twenty-five-year-old Starr Faithfull was naked. An initial autopsy showed that she had drowned in deep water. Twelve hours after the body was discovered her stepfather, Stanley Faithfull, appeared at Nassau County police station to enquire whether the body was that of his daughter. He identified it and then said he believed she had been murdered. He had reported her missing the previous Friday when, he said, she had stepped out to have her hair done. A second autopsy showed that Starr had suffered a bad beating and there was sand in her lungs, which would negate the deep water theory. On his way home Faithfull was trapped by reporters for a statement. He described 'his daughter' as a 'light-hearted, happy, tranquil-minded girl'. No, she had no interest in men and no reason to be in the Long Beach area since the family lived in Greenwich Village. She had been perfectly happy the night before she left home.

It was almost a question of 'watch my lips and count my lies'. First, Stanley was only Starr Faithfull's stepfather. She had been born on 27 January 1906 and her parents were Frank Wyman II and Helen MacGregor Pierce. They had a second daughter, Tucker, but then the relationship deteriorated and they separated in 1918. He went to Paris and was divorced six years later. Helen, meanwhile, came under the influence of her second cousin, Martha, who was married to Andrew Peters, the Mayor of Boston. Secondly, Starr was certainly not a 'light-hearted, happy, tranquil-minded girl'. She was fixated with drink, drugs and men.

By 1918 Starr had been exhibiting displays of moodiness and secrecy which some would say are the classic signs of child abuse. In her case they would be

Starr Faithfull.

right. Peters probably had some sort of relationship with her from the time she was eleven. Mrs Wyman married Stanley Faithfull, a none too successful businessman, on 7 February 1925. If the Starr Faithfull version is correct, her union with Peters was finally consummated on 26 June 1926 in the Astor Hotel on Times Square after he had taken her to a Broadway show. Now she told her mother the whole story of chloroform and sex books, petting and perverted sexual acts.

The upshot was that Starr needed rehabilitation and the next year the Faithfulls, with the help of their lawyers, extracted $25,000 from Peters. They kept four-fifths. Starr had had to give evidence to Peters' lawyers and had not enjoyed the experience. The rehabilitation consisted of time

with a psychiatrist and trips on liners, the latter of which certainly pleased Starr. The psychiatrist recommended that another part of the rehabilitation consist of a normal affair and the Faithfulls selected an old friend, Edwin Megaree. In addition to her relationship with Megaree, Starr was behaving in an increasingly uncontrolled and uncontrollable fashion. On a trip to England she is said to have danced naked in a club for a bet. There she probably had three lovers during her stay. On 30 March 1930 she was found, very drunk, in a hotel room near Central Park with a middle-aged man. They had registered as Joseph and Marie Collins. She was naked, unconscious and had been the subject of a terrible beating. She was taken to Bellevue Hospital.

One thing Stanley Faithfull had said which was correct was that Starr had left home on the Friday. According to the ship's doctor on the liner *Carmania*, on which she had previously sailed, she had come aboard that night and asked him for veronal. She was not seen alive after she left the boat. The options for her death include suicide – she was certainly unstable enough; accidental death – possible if she had taken sufficient drink and drugs to negate her ability as a swimmer; and murder. It is conceivable that the Faithfulls, down on their luck, were starting another spot of blackmail on Peters and that Starr was killed to prevent her giving evidence. It is also suggested, by crime writer Jonathan Goodman, that a bootlegger, Vannie Higgins, had learned of Starr's involvement with Peters and had her kidnapped and beaten to gain further information, with a view to some blackmail himself. She had nothing further to give and so had been taken out in a motor boat and dumped. One of the officers in the case was convinced she had fallen or been thrown overboard from one of the ocean-going liners. He believed she had drowned close to the Ambrose Lightship where the harbour was shallow.

Stanley Faithfull died in 1949. At the time of his stepdaughter's death he had been trying to sell rubber mattresses, and there is no evidence he worked at that for much longer. It must be supposed that he had continued to put pressure on Andrew Peters, who had died eleven years earlier. On the back of Starr's death, her sister, Tucker, had a brief fling with the stage but later married a lawyer. By that time she had changed her name back to Wyman. Vannie Higgins was shot to death in Prospect Park, New York, on 18 June 1932, probably by members of Dutch Schultz's organisation.

Morris Markey, a writer who knew the Faithfulls, offered the somewhat fanciful solution that she had, in fact, been murdered in the following way: whilst planning to commit suicide she had picked up a man, teased him without agreeing to full sex, and in temper he had beaten and then drowned her.

Jonathan Goodman, *The Passing of Starr Faithfull; Murder Casebook*, No. 91

David Faraday

On 20 December 1968 seventeen-year-old David Faraday and his girlfriend, sixteen-year-old Betty Lou Jensen, were shot in Faraday's car while parked in an isolated area of Lake Herman Road, San Francisco. He was killed instantly with a bullet behind his left ear. She was shot as she ran from the car.

Theirs were the first deaths in a nine-month reign of terror carried out by a killer who described himself as Zodiac – because he signed the detailed messages and descriptions of the killings which he sent in cryptogram form to San Francisco newspapers with a cross and a circle.

On 4 July, twenty-two-year-old Darlene Ferrin and nineteen-year-old Michael Renault Mageau were parked in Blue Rock Springs Park, some two miles from Lake Herman. Darlene Ferrin was shot as she sat at the wheel. Mageau was hit in the neck. He survived; she did not. Shortly after midnight the police received a telephone call:

> I want to report a double murder. If you go one mile east on Columbus Parkway to a public park you will find the kids in a brown car. They are shot with a .9mm Luger. I also killed those kids last year. Goodbye.

When Mageau recovered he was able to give a partial description of the killer as 5'8" tall with light brown wavy or curly hair and aged around thirty.

There was no progress in the case until 1 August when the *Vallejo Times-Herald,* the *San Francisco Chronicle* and the *San Francisco Examiner* received identical letters and each one part of a cipher. The letters said that unless they were published the same day the writer would 'go on a rampage', threatening to kill a dozen people. The letters were duly published and the cryptogram was sent to Naval Intelligence on Mare Island Naval Yard. The experts there failed to break the code and this was eventually done by Donald Harden, a schoolmaster and an amateur cryptanalyst. The part sent to the *Vallejo Times-Herald* read:

> I like killing people because it is so much fun it is more fun than killing wild game in the forest because man is the most dangerous animal of all to kill something gives me the most thrilling experience it is even better than getting your rock off with a girl the best part of it is when I die I will be reborn in paradise and all I have killed will become my slaves I will not give you my name because you will try to slow down or stop my collecting slaves for my afterlife.

Nothing more was heard from the man until Saturday, 27 September when he attacked twenty-year-old Bryan Hartnell and twenty-two-year-old Cecilia

Shepard as they sat on a blanket on the shore of Lake Berryessa, about thirteen miles from the scene of the first killing. Initially he demanded money, telling the pair that he was an escapee from Deer Lodge State Prison in Montana, and that he was going to take their car to the Mexican border. He soon changed his tack and this time he stabbed his victims. First Hartnell, at his request, and then, in a frenzy, Cecilia Shepard. Before he left he wrote the dates of the first two attacks on the side of their car in a felt-tipped pen and once more telephoned the police.

> I want to report a murder. No, a double murder. They are two miles north of park headquarters. They were in a white Volkswagen Karmann Ghia. I'm the one that did it.

Again the man survived, leaving the police to speculate that the principal targets were women and that they were the ones who suffered the most savage of the attacks. They were disabused of such a belief when on 11 October 1969 a taxi-driver collected a fare on San Francisco's fashionable Nob Hill by the Fairmont Hotel. The driver, Paul Stine, was shot a quarter of an hour later near the inter-section of Washington Street and Maple Street. The police believed the matter to be a simple robbery until three days later the *San Francisco Chronicle* received a letter from Zodiac saying that he had killed Stine and enclosing a piece of the dead man's shirt to prove it. The letter continued that he rather fancied children as his next targets, threatening to shoot out the tyres of a school bus. It was a threat he never carried out.

On 21 October Zodiac contacted the Oakland Police Department saying that he wished to give himself up but on the condition that he was represented by a celebrated lawyer, either F. Lee Bailey or Melvin Belli. He also wished to appear on Jim Dunbar's breakfast television talk-show.

The next day Belli appeared on breakfast time TV conducting a specially arranged phone-in for the San Francisco audience when, during a commercial break, he heard from a caller who complained of headaches saying, 'I don't want to go to the gas chamber. I have headaches,' and later, 'I've got to kill! I've got to kill!' In all the man made fifteen calls to the studio, a number of which were heard live.

Belli arranged to meet the caller in Daly City, San Francisco, but he did not appear. Two months later he received a letter wishing him a happy Christmas and enclosing another piece of Stine's shirt. Now Zodiac claimed there had been eight victims. There were no further attacks but in 1971 the Los Angeles police and in 1974 the San Francisco police received letters in the same handwriting as that of the killer. By now he claimed thirty-seven victims. The police narrowed the suspects down to two but were never able to find sufficient evidence to make an arrest.

Robert Graysmith, who worked with the *San Francisco Chronicle* throughout the period and later wrote on the killings, believed there were definitely eight victims. The first was Cheri Jo Bates who had been stabbed in Riverside, sixty-two miles south-east of Los Angeles, on 30 October 1966. She had been attacked in her car as she left River City College library. He estimated that there might be as many as forty-one other Zodiac victims, all women.

Robert Graysmith, *Zodiac*

George Fell

On 9 September 1900 the third robbery of the year took place at the Birkenhead Post Office, near Liverpool. George Fell, shoemaker, auxiliary postman and caretaker, failed to answer the gate when the other postmen arrived for the evening shift at about 4.50 p.m. They forced the door and found a pool of blood inside the doorway. Fell was found in the postmaster's room, his face covered with a postbag. A broken poker lay on the floor and a coal shovel had several dents in it. It seemed as though Fell had used it as a shield against the blows from the poker. £19.15.2d had been taken from the safe along with £50 in ten-pound notes and three postal orders. Although details of the notes were circulated and their numbers printed in the national newspapers not one was ever tendered.

Nor was the killer ever found. One theory is that he may have had the gate opened to him by Fell sometime during the day and immediately attacked him, which would account for the blood in the doorway. Another is that he may even have hidden himself in the cellar amongst postal baskets whilst the office was open and was later surprised by Fell.

Fell had a great send-off with the Post Office band playing the Dead March from Saul and a crowd of 10,000 mourners at Flaybrick Cemetery. A trust fund was set up for his widow. The robber was never caught despite enquiries nationwide and, indeed, in Australia. At one time the Birkenhead police fastened on a man in the Grimsby area but that line of enquiry came to nothing.

On the two previous occasions when the Post Office had been robbed the employees were made to make good the loss. Every man had a small amount stopped from his weekly pay until the money had been repaid. This does not seem to have been the case the third time.

Nicola Fellows

On the afternoon of 10 October 1986 Nicola Fellows, aged nine, and Karen Hadaway, aged ten, were found strangled and sexually assaulted. They had been seen the previous evening playing some few hundred yards from their parents' council homes to the north of Brighton, Sussex.

Suspicion fell on ten men who were later eliminated from enquiries. They included Russell Bishop, one of five brothers (who were not suspects). As a child he was found to be partially dyslexic and sent to a Catholic boarding school. He did not settle and was eventually given a private education. At the time of the killings he was twenty and living with Jennie Johnson, but he also had a girl-friend, Marion Stevenson. Such occupation as he had was repairing and reno-vating cars.

On the afternoon of her death Nicola had been rude to Bishop and Marion Stevenson, who had called at her home asking if a friend was there. Her rude-ness was a gesture of solidarity with the pregnant Jennie Johnson. She and Karen were seen playing at about 4.45 p.m. in a garden at Newick Road. The two of them were also seen about 6.20 p.m. eating fish and chips at the entrance to Wild Park. There was probably a sighting of them twenty minutes later on the Lewes Road. They were reported missing shortly after 8.35 that evening.

The next day Bishop and his dog took part in the search. One police officer who had a conversation with him recorded Bishop as saying he was going to stop searching. The officer asked him why since he had a dog. Bishop was said to have replied, 'Well, if I found the girls and if they were done in, I would get the blame. I'd be nicked.' Almost immediately there was a shout that the girls had been found and the officer sent Bishop up ahead to keep people away from the bodies until he himself reached the spot. By the time the scenes-of-crime unit arrived Bishop had been sick on the grass. Later that night a stained blue 'Pinto' sweatshirt was handed in to the police. It had been left on a railing near Moulsecoomb station.

By 9 October attention had focused on Bishop as a suspect. He had already been interviewed and said that he had felt their pulses. He had also described how Nicola's lips had blood-flecked foam. The police did not believe he could have seen this nor that he had been within thirty feet of the bodies. His clothing was taken away for examination and he was arrested in a public house that night and taken for further questioning. Now he said he had not touched the girls but had said so to make himself appear important. He was released from custody on 12 October.

The evidence against Bishop mounted. Witnesses, including Jennie Johnson, said that he had a Pinto sweatshirt. The one found at the railway station was shown to have had blood on it. He was arrested again on 31 October. When questioned he said he had washed his clothes on the night of the murders because he had fallen in dog dirt. He took the police to the spot where, he said, this had happened. They found nothing. He was cautioned by the police at 1.46 p.m. and gave an alibi that he had been at home doing the washing and watching *EastEnders*. He was questioned for a further half hour and provided both intimate (pubic hair) and non-intimate body samples under the Police and Criminal Evidence Act 1984. Bishop was then interviewed again and denied ever owning the Pinto sweatshirt. A year later Jennie Johnson changed her mind about the ownership of the sweatshirt. She said that Russell Bishop had never owned a shirt with the Pinto motif on it. She said the police had forged her signature on the statement of 31 October. Meanwhile Bishop had been released on bail until 4 December.

He surrendered with his solicitor on 3 December and was charged with the murder of both children. This time he was held in custody. The evidence against him was almost entirely forensic coupled with the lies he had undoubtedly told during his questioning. Principally the link was the Pinto sweatshirt. When it came to it, the scientific officer agreed that the Pinto shirt could have been worn by the murderer but not necessarily so. He also agreed it could have been worn by Bishop but again not necessarily so. On 8 December 1987, after a retirement of a little over two hours, the jury brought in a unanimous verdict of not guilty.

On 19 August 1989 a march took place in Brighton demanding that the case be re-opened. Bishop walked alongside the parents of the dead girls. Evidence was later presented by author Christopher Berry-Dee to suggest that another person acting alone or with another might have been responsible for the deaths. On 2 February 1990 the Assistant Chief Constable of the Sussex police wrote to Berry-Dee saying that because the evidence now offered was strongly circumstantial there were insufficient grounds to warrant an arrest.

In April 1990 a seven-year-old girl was abducted on the Whitehawk Estate in

Brighton. She was found an hour and a half later wandering naked. She said she had been partially strangled. Bishop was arrested. There was evidence that red particles on the girl's roller skating boots matched samples taken from Bishop's car. The defence alleged they had been planted, a suggestion which was strongly denied. There was evidence that semen which tested as Bishop's was found on the tracksuit trousers. There was also saliva on them which tested as the girl's. The odds against the saliva being other than that of the victim were put at one in 5.7 million and the semen not being Bishop's were one in 80 million. Bishop, who called an alibi defence, was found guilty after a retirement by the jury of four and a half hours. He was sentenced to life imprisonment. The trial judge had refused to allow evidence to be called for the prosecution that a few days before the attack on the young girl a man driving a red car had followed an eight-year-old girl. The child had written down part of the number plate, TJN 6 something 3 something, and had described the car as a red Ford Cortina. Bishop's car, a red Cortina, had the number plate TJN 673.

In 1994 Bishop brought an action against the Sussex Constabulary alleging perjury. He abandoned the case during the trial.

Christopher Berry-Dee and Robin Odell, *A Question of Evidence*

Rachel Fennick

A forty-one-year-old prostitute, Rachel Fennick was stabbed to death in her second-floor flat in Broadwick Street, Soho, London, on 26 September 1948. She had been savagely attacked with a long-bladed knife. Born Rachel Annie Hatton on 19 August 1907, she had married an American, Herbert Fennick, who had left her almost immediately after the marriage and who had died in Paris. She had been a prostitute for some twenty years. She had eighty-four convictions for soliciting, larceny and brothel keeping.

Fennick had a friend who visited her every weekend and cooked the Sunday lunch. Although he denied it, he was almost certainly her ponce. He was, remarked the police in the official report into the killing, very well dressed for a man who had not worked for a year.

At the time there were a number of prostitute murders and there were stories both that Rachel Fennick was a police informer and that it was a vengeance killing. There was also a story that she had been killed by a man who was a remnant of the Micheletti gang which was still believed to have a foothold in Soho.* The police, however, thought it to be the work of a maniac.

Frederick Herbert Charles Field *see* **Norah Upchurch**

Elizabeth Figg *see* **Jack the Stripper**

Isidor Fink

The thirty-one-year-old Isidor Fink was found shot in the back room of his locked, bolted and barred two-room laundry at 4 East 132nd Street and Fifth Avenue in New York on 9 March 1929. His body was found some thirty feet from the doorway with two bullet holes in the left side of his chest. There was another in his left wrist. It was a classic 'locked room' mystery.

Fink had arrived in America in 1918 and eventually had been able to establish his own small laundry. He seems to have had few friends and certainly no women friends. He lived in a man-made fortress, his front door had the best lock money could buy and the windows were fitted with iron bars set six inches apart.

The motive for the killing does not appear to have been robbery because there was money in both Fink's pocket and the cash register. Suicide was unlikely since there was no gun in the room. As for murder, how could anyone have penetrated the fortress? With the gift of hindsight and the benefit of reading many detective novels, the solution is fairly simple. Fink must have been shot at his door and then run inside, bolting and barring the entrance before he collapsed and died. No one was charged, nor was any motive established.

Richard and Molly Whittington-Egan, *The Bedside Book of Murder*; Ben Hecht, *The Mystery of the Fabulous Laundryman*

---

* *John Bull*, 6 November 1948. The Micheletti gang had been prominent dealers in drugs and women in the Soho of the 1920s. It had more or less collapsed with the death of its titular head at the hands of a rival Juan Castenar. It is quite possible that remnants had lingered on, associating themselves with the Messina brothers who came to prominence in the 1930s and ruled vice in London for the next thirty years.

Mary Fleming *see* **Jack the Stripper**

Evelyn Foster

On 6 January 1931, a bitterly cold night, twenty-nine-year-old Evelyn Foster, who ran a taxi-hire service at Otterburn near Newcastle, was found badly burned at Wolf's Nick, four miles from the village of Kirk Whelpington.

She was still alive when she was found at about 9 p.m. by a bus driver and conductor making the last run of the night. Her car was on fire but nearly burned out. Much of her clothing had been destroyed in the fire and she was suffering from a high percentage of first degree burns. She was taken onto the bus and driven back to her family's home, The Kennels at Otterburn. Apart from asking for water all she said during the journey was 'That awful man.' She was clearly dying when she was interviewed at her parents' home by the police. She was, said the doctor called to treat her, 'quite lucid and sensible in her understanding'.

Earlier in the evening she had driven three passengers in her Hudson Super-Six saloon to Rochester, five miles north of Otterburn, and then picked up another fare at Elishaw, a man who wanted her to drive him to Ponteland, just outside Newcastle.

She said that as they neared Ponteland the man had begun to make advances. She had

Evelyn Foster.

tried to fend him off but he had hit her over the eye and then snatched the steering wheel from her. She had found herself being driven to Wolf's Nick. There the man had attacked her again, and had thrown some liquid over her which he had then ignited. Her last words, shortly before 7.30 a.m., were, 'Mother, I have been murdered.' She had described her attacker as short and dark with a dark coat and a bowler hat. He had spoken with a Tyneside accent and had been a heavy smoker. He said he had missed the Edinburgh to

Newcastle bus and had picked up his previous lift at Jedburgh. Unfortunately her statement had been paraphrased by the police officer and not taken down verbatim.

At Wolf's Nick the police found her purse with the money still in it and an empty petrol can with the cap off. Of the man in the bowler unsurprisingly there was no trace nor, surprisingly, despite nationwide appeals, did the people who had given him lifts come forward. The police began to lean to the theory that she had deliberately set fire to her car for an insurance swindle and had accidently ignited herself.

At the inquest there was medical evidence to disprove the rape theory. Evelyn Foster was a virgin. Perhaps she never made the claim and when she said she had been interfered with it was assumed that this amounted to more than an indecent assault. Although they were never called to give evidence, three villagers did report a suspicious stranger in Otterburn on the evening of Evelyn Foster's death. The jury returned a verdict of wilful murder. The police were not, however, having it and Captain Fullerton James, the Chief Constable, was quoted as saying, 'We are satisfied that the car in which Miss Foster's supposed murderer is said to have travelled from Jedburgh does not exist. We are also satisfied the man she described does not exist.'

The remarks did not please the jurors or the family. A disciplinary tribunal over James's conduct was held in March 1931 but he was not censured.

If the case was an insurance swindle which went wrong then it was for a negligible amount carried out by a girl from a wealthy family, who owned a number of other cars. One suggestion advanced by the crime writer Jonathan Goodman is that Evelyn Foster's killer was none other than Ernest Brown, a groom who shot his employer, Frederick Morton (with whose wife he had been having an affair) on 5 September 1933 and attempted to cremate the body in a blazing garage. Goodman points out that he knew how to drive and that as a groom he wore a bowler hat. He also travelled the North and North-east of England attending agricultural shows. It is said that on the scaffold at Armley Prison on 6 February 1934 he muttered either 'Otterburn' or 'Ought to burn'.

Jonathan Goodman, *The Burning of Evelyn Foster*

Vincent Foster

At about 6 p.m. on 20 July 1993 the body of Vincent Foster, the former Deputy White House counsel and law partner of Hillary Clinton, was found stretched out near a Civil War cannon in Fort Macey Park, McLean, Virginia. He was shot through the head and there was an antique gun in his right hand. The body was discovered by an unidentified man in a white van who told a park worker, Francis Swan, 'There's a dead body by the cannon up in Fort Macey. Will you call the park police?'

Initially the death was thought to be suicide but in the months following the discovery of the body alternative theories have emerged. The park police called neither the local police nor the FBI. Apparently Foster's body was lying perfectly straight, almost as if it had been laid out, but no exit bullet was found. There was no blood underneath his head nor on his shirt or the gun. There is argument whether ballistic tests for powder burns were ever carried out. Some time later a note was found in his briefcase. It expressed concern about the pressures on him in Washington but gave no indication of any suicidal intentions. It had been torn into twenty-six pieces and those who favour a theory other than suicide maintain it could have been planted there after his death. The theories as to his death range across the political spectrum with the right wing seeing a cover-up conspiracy. They include suicide in a Secret Service safe house in Virginia, after which the body was transported to the public park, and a killing in the White House itself.

At the beginning of July 1994 Robert Fiske, the Whitewater special prosecutor, finally quashed speculation that Foster had been murdered. He was, said Fiske, desperately in need of psychiatric help because of the pressures of his position. He felt unable to seek it because it would, he thought, jeopardise his security clearance and so he shot himself at the deserted Civil War site overlooking the Potomac.

Margaret Frame

On 22 October 1978 the body of thirty-six-year-old Margaret Frame was found in Stanmer Wood, Brighton, Sussex, after a massive police search. She had gone missing on 12 October and was last seen taking a short cut through a wood to reach her home at Saunders Hill on the Coldean estate. Her suede jacket was found half-buried near a main road running around the wood. She had been raped and her body buried in a shallow grave near where the bodies of Nicola Fellows and Karen Hadaway (*qv*) were found. No charges were ever brought.

Leo Frank

Hanged by a lynch-mob who dragged him from Milledgeville prison, Georgia, on 17 August 1915, Leo Frank, manager of a local pencil factory in Atlanta, had been convicted of the rape and murder of fourteen-year-old Mary Phagan (*qv*) on 26 April 1913. The evidence against him had mainly been that of a black janitor, James Conley. The illiterate Conley gave evidence that he had seen Frank committing sexual acts with young women and that he had been ordered by Frank to carry the girl's body to the basement. A note had been found by the girl's body which purported to describe her attacker as 'a long, tall, sleam, black negro ... that long tall black negro did buy his self' (*sic*). Conley said Frank, who was sentenced to death, had made him write the note.

After the trial 415,000 signatures were obtained from Chicago alone for a petition to pardon Frank. A fund was set up to finance an investigation by private detective William J. Burns, who exposed a police frame-up to obtain a conviction against Frank. Later, evidence was obtained from a former girlfriend that Conley himself indulged in the acts of which he had accused the factory manager. Frank was reprieved by State Governor John Slaton and his sentence commuted to one of life imprisonment.

The lynching was as a result of anti-Semitic feeling against Frank, a graduate of Cornell University and President of the Atlanta Branch of B'nai B'rith. The local newspaper had already published an editorial: 'Our little girl – ours by the eternal God! – has been pursued to a hideous death by this filthy perverted Jew from New York.' The lynch-mob, naming themselves the Knights of Mary Phagan, drove Frank 175 miles back to the girl's home town. This was probably the first case in the South in which the word of a black man was preferred in evidence to that of a white.

State Farm,
Milledgeville, Ga.,
July 6, 1915.

Mr Sam Minnen,
   Marston, Mo.

Dear Sir:
            Allow me to thank
you for your wire of June 21ˢᵗ
I appreciated your kindly thought
of me so much.

            Now that life is pre-
served, we will work + hope
for that vindication + liberation
which is rightfully mine, even
at this time.

            I am gradually adjusting
myself to my new environment.
My health is now much better
+ I am gaining rapidly in
strength + weight.

            With every good wish, I am,
            Cordially yours

            Leo M. Frank

A letter from Leo Frank, written in prison five weeks before he was lynched.

Dora Freeman

In September 1948 the sixty-year-old prostitute known as Russian Dora was found stabbed to death in her flat in Long Acre, Covent Garden, London. She was thought to have been both a blackmailer and a police informer. Despite the police statements that hers and the killing of Rachel Fennick (*qv*) were the work of a sadistic killer, contrary rumours have persisted, even going so far as to name Teddy Machin (*qv*), a one-time Soho enforcer, as the killer of all three women (Margaret Cook (*qv*) was the third) on a strictly professional basis.

Jesse Edward Fuller *see* **John Coward**

Christine 'Chrissie' Gall

In the early hours of 21 November 1931, Christine Gall was found dead in bed at her home in Glasgow by the man with whom she lived, Peter Queen. According to Sir Sydney Smith, the pathologist who appeared for the defence, the bedclothes were pulled up over her chest:

> Her head was facing to the left; her left arm was at right angles to it, stretched along the pillow outside the bedclothes; her right arm was lying alongside her body under the clothes. A thin rope encircled her neck low down below the Adam's apple. It was tied in a half-knot – the first twist of a reef knot – and the knot was slightly to the right of the middle line. Her tongue was protruding a little; her upper teeth, which were artificial, were in position. She was dressed in her night-clothes with a boudoir cap.

The question was whether she had committed suicide or had been strangled by Queen. The former, said Professors Sydney Smith and the renowned Bernard Spilsbury, on the only occasion in which they appeared on the same side. The latter, said the police and the equally renowned Professors John Glaister (who had in fact examined Smith when he had applied for his Diploma in Public Health in 1913) and Andrew Allison.

Peter Queen, the son of a Glasgow bookmaker, clerked in his father's office. He married at the age of eighteen, but his wife became an alcoholic and was institutionalised. They did not live together again. When Queen was twenty-four his father engaged Christine Gall, then aged twenty-one, as a nursemaid for his younger children. Over the years he began to pay her court even after she had returned home to nurse her own mother. By all accounts Queen was a pleasant, gentle, kind man. Although he does not appear to have had any penchant for drink, he seems to have been attracted to women who did. Christine in turn became an alcoholic. Three years after the death of her mother, Christine left home and Queen arranged for her to have lodgings with a friend of his, James Burns and his wife. She was drunk when she moved in and remained that way. At Christmas 1930 Queen moved in with her. The Burns tried to get her to stop drinking but at times she was suicidal, saying she would 'make a hole in the Clyde'. Once she tried to hang herself from a peg on the kitchen door. One of the reasons for her drinking and depression was that Queen was not, and was not able to be, married to her. She came from a very strict background and her father did not approve of her relationship with Queen.

Christine was very drunk on Thursday, 19 November 1930. Her brother called and she and Queen pretended she did not live there. She appears to have been drunk for most of the next day. Queen was advised to get a doctor to come to see her and he booked one for the following day. But at 3 a.m. Queen had called the police and had been arrested after allegedly saying to them, 'I think I have killed her.' At his trial he told the jury he had said to the police officer, 'Don't think I killed her.' Whatever words he had spoken had not been written down at the time.

Throughout the trial there was a parade of witnesses who testified to the devotion and love Queen had shown to Christine Gall. In his summing up the judge said that the evidence was 'scanty and unconvincing in so far as it supports the theory of homicide by the accused'. There was the question, however, of whether she could have tied the knot herself. Mrs Johnstone, a relation of the Burns who had been in the house and who, with her husband, had been the last to see Christine Gall, said she thought her to be stupid with drink. Mr Johnstone thought that although she was not sober she talked sensibly and could have walked all right. In his closing speech the Advocate Deputy asked if the jury could really believe that the unfortunate woman could get out of bed, take a knife from a drawer, cut the pulley cord from the clothes line, get back into bed, tuck herself in neatly and then strangle herself without Queen, in the next room, hearing or knowing anything.

Smith thought the very worst result for Queen would be a verdict of Not Proven. He was wrong. After a two-hour retirement the jury returned a majority verdict of guilty. Queen was sentenced to death but was reprieved following both a unanimous recommendation for mercy by the jury and a very substantial petition by Members of Parliament and a former Lord Provost. After his release Queen stayed in Glasgow, obtaining another job as a bookmaker's clerk. He died in 1948, well liked and respected by his friends who knew nothing of his past.

Spilsbury, who could be stubborn, remained convinced that Christine Gall had committed suicide. Smith was more cautious. In his book *Mostly Murder* he wrote:

> Did he kill her? Probably not. I would still not be as dogmatic about it as Spilsbury was at the time, but I think that there was insufficient evidence to justify a conviction.

Sydney Smith, *Mostly Murder*; Bill Knox, *Court of Murder*

Barbara Gaul

On 12 January 1977 the estranged wife of property dealer, John Gaul, was shot outside the Black Lion Hotel, Patcham, near Brighton, where she had been visiting her daughter, Samantha. She died eleven weeks later. Strictly speaking the case was solved in that two brothers from London's East End, Roy and Keith Edgeler, were convicted of the killing. The interest is in who arranged the contract. Was it her husband John Gaul, procurer to the rich and with a conviction for living off immoral earnings?

On the basis that when a wife is killed the first person to be questioned is the husband, John Gaul was taken to Cannon Row police station but later released. Almost immediately he fled to Rio de Janeiro. Later that year he was found with a new companion, Angela Pilch, in Switzerland before moving on to Malta.

Originally Gaul had been a property dealer, who diversified into motor trading and then returned to his first love when in 1952 he took over Sun Real Estates, a publicly quoted company which had not paid any dividends for some time. In 1958 it had paid an 8.5 per cent dividend and had a trading profit of £37,000. In 1962 the profit was £122,000 with premises worth £3 million.

On 11 October 1962 Gaul had been fined £25,000 for living off prostitution. Through a firm called Rent and Management he had leased out flats in Soho to prostitutes, charging £20 a week for old squalid properties with poor furniture. Of the £20 only £8.8s was entered in the rent book. Now, in theory, all that was behind him. In practice it was not. His name surfaced in both the Profumo and Lambton vice scandals.

It was not difficult for the police to trace the actual killers. On the way from the killing the shotgun used was dropped from a car window and later the car was traced to a breakers yard in East London.

The brothers were jailed on 24 June 1977. In the witness box Roy said that from his limited knowledge he did not believe it was John Gaul who had arranged the contract for which he was to have been paid £10,000.

On 3 April 1978, Gaul was arrested in Malta where he was living on a boat in the harbour, having defied efforts to have him returned to the UK. There had been troubles with the United Kingdom's extradition treaty with Malta because the Home Secretary had refused to extradite a Maltese woman on a forgery charge. Gaul had high political connections in Malta.

Why should he be involved in the killing, he asked? Barbara had agreed to an undefended divorce claiming neither alimony nor costs and had already relinquished claims to the child, Samantha. There was no reason why he should have had her killed, he argued plausibly.

On 24 April 1978 a blast destroyed a mini-cab office and flats in Hackney Road, owned by Printing House Properties Ltd, a £100 company owned by Gaul. It was thought that a Maltese, John Borg, who had been involved in West End properties over the years and who had been jailed for ten years for gunning down another Maltese outside a Stepney cafe in 1953, had died in the blaze. This turned out to be correct. Borg's body was discovered in the wreckage on 3 May. Curiously no smoke was found to have been in his lungs, a clear indication he had died before the fire. Things were made more complicated when it became known that a Portuguese, Carlos Amazonas, had made a statement to the police that Borg had been approached to kill Mrs Barbara Gaul. This statement had somehow found its way into the Soho Underworld.

By 1981 Gaul was assumed to be safe in Malta because of his political connections. Officially the explanation was that insufficient evidence had been supplied by the British police, but Gaul was now well established – he had built and leased out a 240-room hotel. In March that year he was reported to have had a serious heart attack. On 17 July 1981 a magistrate in Malta said the prosecution case was weak and refused to order extradition.

By April 1984 it was reported the English police had given up. Even if he came back, the passage of time had made witnesses' memories unreliable. Gaul was said to be ill and medical certificates were sent to the Director of Public Prosecutions on whose orders the warrant was dropped. At once Gaul flew to

Switzerland and then came back for his son, Simon's, wedding in September 1984. Gaul died in September 1989 in Italy. He had been reported missing but it was three days before it was realised he had already died in a Milan hospital.

According to *The Sun** Keith Edgeler, then in Ford open prison, named Gaul as the man who had ordered the contract. It was, he said, because Gaul feared Barbara was about to expose shady deals. He said he never received the payment for the murder. Despite offers by the police for a deal he had refused to talk on the basis that if a man could have his wife murdered, his own family was in danger.

James Morton, *Gangland*

Alfred Gerard *see* **Ginger Marks**

Nicholas Gerard

On 27 June 1982 Nicky Gerard, son of the notorious London hit-man Alf Gerard, was shot and beaten to death after leaving his daughter's eleventh birthday party in Peckham, South-east London. His death was one more story in the long and complicated history of London's post-World War II Underworld. Gerard, who was thought to have taken up his father's trade as professional hit man, had been acquitted of the killing of Alfredo 'Italian Tony' Zomparelli at the Golden Goose amusement arcade in Old Compton Street, Soho.

In turn the Zomparelli killing followed the death of David Knight. Knight had been badly beaten in a fight with a Johnny Isaacs in a public house at the Angel, Islington. On 7 May 1970, when David was out of hospital, he was taken to the Latin Quarter nightclub off Leicester Square to see Isaacs, who as it turned out was not there.

However, a fight broke out. Alfredo Zomparelli, run-around man for another of the Underworld's leading figures, Albert Dimes, and bouncer for the Latin Quarter, stabbed David Knight twice in the chest.

Three weeks later Zomparelli, who had fled to Italy, returned and gave

---

* 31 October 1989

himself up. He claimed that he had grabbed a knife to defend himself when two men attacked him. He seems fortunate that he was only convicted of manslaughter for which he received a sentence of four years. The police version of the reason for the fight is that the Latin Quarter had been paying protection to David Knight.

After serving his sentence Zomparelli ran a bucket shop travel agency in Frith Street. Much of his leisure time was spent playing the pinball machines in the Golden Goose. It was in the pinball arcade he was shot dead, by two men wearing dark glasses and moustaches on 4 September, a few months after his release. Appropriately he was playing a game called 'Wild Life'.

As in all these cases, there were a number of theories offered for what was clearly a professional hit. One was that Zomparelli was trying to muscle into the highly profitable amusement arcade business; another that he was taking part in a stolen car racket involving the theft of Lancias and Ferraris in Italy and their resale in London with claims on Italian insurance companies completing the scam, and a third that he was a drug courier.

There the file remained shut, if not closed, until in 1980 Maxie Piggot *aka* George Bradshaw confessed to the murder, turned supergrass and named a club owner as the contractor for the killing and Nicky Gerard as his, Bradshaw's, partner in its execution. On 17 January 1980 Bradshaw received a life sentence for the murder of Zomparelli with a ten-year concurrent sentence for all the rest of his myriad of crimes. In his long confession, in which he admitted to over 100 armed robberies, he named Nicky Gerard as the one who pulled the trigger of a .38 revolver in a contract worth a modest £1,000.

By this time supergrasses were not as fashionable as they had been ten years earlier when there had been a tendency for juries to take their word as gospel truth. Both the club owner and Nicky Gerard were found not guilty of Zomparelli's murder.

Gerard did not last that long after his acquittal. Prior to the Zomparelli trial, in May 1978, Nicky Gerard had been jailed for seven years for an attack on boxer, Michael Gluckstead, at the Norseman Club in Canning Town. He had been found not guilty of the attempted murder of Gluckstead, who, widely regarded as a local bully, had his cheek slit from ear to nose and had been shot twice, as well as being hit about the head and stomped. Gerard would say nothing of his instructions or reasons for the Gluckstead beating.

Whilst he had been in prison Gerard had been sentenced, *in absentia*, by a kangaroo court. His wife, Linda, had received threats and a wreath with the message 'Nicky Gerard, Rest in Peace'.

Now on 27 June 1982, when leaving his daughter's birthday party, he was ambushed by gunmen wearing boiler suits and balaclava helmets at the lock up garage to which he had driven his Oldsmobile. Shots were fired through the windscreen and Gerard was hit in the stomach. He managed to get out of the car and stagger a hundred yards but his attackers followed him, smashing him so hard on the head with a gun that the stock shattered. He was beaten unconscious before the gunmen reloaded and shot him.

Gerard had not been sufficiently careful. Over the previous few days he had known he was being followed but he had thought it was by undercover police.

On 22 November his cousin and 'best friend', Thomas Hole, was arrested and charged with his murder. Hole's criminal career traced back to his friendship with bank robber George Davis and ended on 12 July 1989 at Snaresbrook Crown Court when he acquired a thirteen-year sentence for conspiracy to manufacture drugs, to run concurrently with an eighteen-year sentence for armed robbery.

Now Hole was tried at the Old Bailey in April 1983. He had been picked out on an identification parade by a 'Mr Fisher', the pseudonym given to a protected witness, who said he had seen a man with one rubber washing up glove acting suspiciously. 'But,' he added, 'I am not sure it was the man I had seen that day in June in the car park.' Despite protests by the Crown that there was more evidence it had not been allowed to produce, on 27 April 1983 Thomas Hole was acquitted by direction of the trial judge, Mr Justice French, when he stopped the case at the end of the prosecution evidence.

'This, of course, was an appalling gangland murder, and any right thinking citizen must be dismayed at the thought that no one has been brought to justice for that murder,' said Mr Justice French.

Hole, who left court with his friends, said, 'My head is reeling.'

James Morton, *Gangland*

Marion Gilchrist

On 21 December 1908 the body of Marion Gilchrist, a wealthy eighty-two-year-old, was found in her flat in Queen's Terrace, Glasgow. She was a woman who kept her front door securely bolted and, if her maid was not present, took great care in identifying a caller before unlocking the door. About

7 p.m. on the evening of 21 December she sent out her maid, Helen Lambie, on what the Scots call 'messages'. The girl was not long gone but on her return the downstairs neighbour, a man called Adams, told her that there was an almighty row going on overhead and his ceiling was likely to come down. As they opened the door of Gilchrist's flat a man walked calmly past them and then rushed downstairs. In the dining room they found Marion's body. Post-mortem evidence showed she had been struck sixty times or more, possibly with a chair leg. The flat had been ransacked.

Oscar Slater fell under suspicion first because he was a German Jew; secondly he was a pimp (he called himself a dentist and his detractors suggest that this was a cover for men visiting his home); thirdly because of the first two he was unpopular with the police and fourthly, and incorrectly, they were told that he had pawned a diamond brooch. In fact the piece, a crescent shaped brooch, was not one missing from Miss Gilchrist's, and Slater had pawned it weeks prior to the murder. By the time the police decided to arrest Slater he had sold up and, under his own name, sailed for New York with his mistress on the *Lusitania*.

Marion Gilchrist.

After him went the police together with Helen Lambie and another potential identifying witness, Mary Barrowman, who saw a man in the street after the murder. According to their evidence, they shared a cabin but did not discuss the case during the voyage, which must have been the adventure of their young lives. In New York they duly made the required identification. Slater waived an extradition hearing and stood trial in Edinburgh on 3 May 1909. There was no evidence against him except for the identification. Slater's alibi defence was not helped by a display of hostility by Alexander Ure, the Lord Advocate, who prosecuted him. 'I say without hesitation that the man in the dock is capable of having committed this dastardly outrage.' Slater was convicted by a majority decision – nine guilty, five not proven and one not guilty. His death sentence was commuted to one of life imprisonment by Lord Pentland, the Scottish Secretary.

Over the years public support for Slater grew. Mary Barrowman said she had been bullied and coached until her evidence tallied with what was required of her. Helen Lambie was alleged by a Glasgow detective, John Thompson Trench, to have gone to Miss Birrell, Marion Gilchrist's niece, to say she knew who the attacker really was. The first review of Slater's case was in 1914. It was held behind closed doors. Trench gave evidence that he had gone to Miss Birrell's house and obtained a statement from her that Lambie had given the name of the man in Miss Gilchrist's flat. This was denied by Miss Birrell but Trench had made a note of it in his diary. She had said, 'Oh, Miss Birrell, I think it was A.B. I am sure it was A.B.' Miss Birrell had replied, 'My God, Nellie, don't say that… unless you are very sure of it.' He was supported by a Glasgow lawyer, David Cook. Later the *Solicitors Journal* put it quaintly: 'For this conduct both Trench and Cook suffered severely.' Both were arrested on a trumped up receiving charge and, although they were acquitted on the direction of the judge, both were ruined. Neither lived long after the case. The enquiry seems to have muddied the waters by throwing up the name of another potential suspect, A.B., later identified as Dr Francis Charteris, the nephew of Miss Gilchrist. Slater was not released.

It was not until 1925 that Slater managed to get a note smuggled out by another inmate, on his release, to Sir Arthur Conan Doyle who had always been interested in Slater's problems and who again took up the cause. In 1927 he wrote the introduction to the book by the crusading journalist William Park, *The Truth About Oscar Slater*. This was reviewed by the *Solicitors Journal*: 'What is stated above, however, would seem sufficient to show the reasonableness of the demand that a new and thorough investigation into the whole matter should even now be made.' On 5 November, Mary Barrowman wrote in *The Daily News* that she had been told what to say in her evidence by the Procurator-Fiscal of Lanarkshire, James Hart. It has been alleged that she was nowhere near Queen's Terrace at the time of the murder.

Slater was paroled and now a fight began for an appeal hearing, financed by Conan Doyle. Helen Lambie had married and was living in America. She refused to return for the hearing but a New York detective came to give evidence that Slater had been pointed out to her before she made her identification. The appeal was allowed, not on the grounds that the verdict was unsafe but on the grounds that Lord Guthrie, the trial judge, had gone too far and had not been corrected in his denunciation of Slater. His remarks had included, 'A man of that kind has not the presumption of innocence in his favour which is a reality in the case of the ordinary man,' and, 'He had maintained himself by the ruin of men and on the ruin of women ... living in a way that many blackguards would scorn to live.' In fact although Slater's mistress, Andree Junio Antoine, worked as a prostitute under the name Madame Junio, there is little evidence he actually lived off her earnings. Their's was a long-term relationship: in 1908 they had lived together in New York under the name of George. Prior to his trial for murder he had only one conviction, when he was fined £1 after a fight.

Slater received £6,000 *ex gratia* payment, not including the cost of the appeal. The local Jewish community collected £700 and Conan Doyle paid the balance. Sadly, Slater does not seem to have been at all grateful to his patron and saviour. Each cordially disliked the other. He donated £250 to the £1,350 Conan Doyle had spent on his campaign. On the other hand he sent a gift of £200 to William Park, who died shortly afterwards embittered that he had not received the credit he deserved in establishing Slater's innocence.

Slater died in early 1948. In 1936, then aged sixty-four, he had married the thirty-four-year-old Lina Wilhelmina Schad. He was interned as an enemy alien during World War II, then lived the remainder of his life in Ayr on the West Coast of Scotland. William Merrilees, later Chief Constable of The Lothians and Peebles Constabulary, wrote in his memoirs *The Short Arm of the Law*, 'As a boy I knew Slater. I used to see him drive down to the Old Ship Hotel on the front at Leith with his "old bun" [prostitute] with him in a carriage and pair.'

It had been suggested that the killer of Miss Gilchrist was her nephew Dr Francis Charteris. He later achieved a position of high respectability, retiring in 1948 as Professor of Materia Medica and the Dean of the Faculty of Medicine at St Andrews' University. He died in 1964 at the age of eighty-eight. A theory advanced by Jack House suggests that Charteris was assisted by Austin Birrell, another relative of Miss Birrell, and they were looking for Miss Gilchrist's will. The argument runs that whilst rummaging through the premises Birrell was confronted by Miss Gilchrist, who promptly had an epileptic fit during which he attacked her. This would account for the visit by Helen Lambie to Miss Birrell, if not for the amazing hostility towards Slater. This latter can, in part, be because he ran a prostitute but, even before the police chased after him, Slater was out of the jurisdiction and therefore no trouble to them any more. In fact House had it wrong. There was no such person as Austin Birrell.

William Roughhead (ed), *Notable Scottish Trials*; William Park, *The Truth About Oscar Slater*; Peter Hunt, *Oscar Slater: The Great Suspect*; Jack House, *The Square Mile of Murder*; Thomas Toughill, *Oscar Slater: The Mystery Solved*

Beatrice Gold

On 8 September 1975, forty-seven-year-old fashion designer Beatrice Gold was found shot dead at point-blank range in her dress factory in Islington, North London. Bert 'Battles' Rossi, once jailed for seven years for his part in the 1955 attack on gangster Jack Spot, and Errol Heibner appeared at the Old Bailey charged with her murder. The prosecution was unable to suggest any motive and said that the person behind the killing was not in the dock with them. The allegation was that Rossi was the contact man who had set up the murder and provided a weapon and that Heibner was the hit man for a fee of £8,000.

Mrs Gold, who was due to leave, with her husband Eric, to celebrate their silver wedding in America, had written two unpublished novels on sex. Both she and her husband frequented gay parties although he stated in the witness box that he was not homosexual. His wife found gay men 'amusing and entertaining', the parties 'good fun'.

It was alleged that hours before the killing Rossi handed Heibner the gun wrapped in a package at a meeting near the Strand Palace Hotel. In his evidence Rossi said that he believed the package contained jewellery. He went on to say that he had heard from a Soho porn dealer, Bernie Silver, that Mrs Gold was 'deeply involved with pornography' and that she was in possession of documents which could be used for blackmail. A meeting had taken place to discuss the documents at which other leading Soho figures, Tony Zomparelli and Frankie Albert, had been present.* He told the court that anyone who became involved with Mrs Gold's affairs was 'playing with dynamite'. Rossi was acquitted. Heibner, who denied his part in the murder, was convicted.

Apparently there were some fifty sets of keys to the dress factory premises in existence, not all of which could be accounted for. There was no difficulty therefore in Heibner getting access but one of the problems of the case was how he could have known when Mrs Gold would be on her own. Eric Gold was obliged to bring a claim in the High Court against an insurance company to obtain the monies payable on her death. He was successful.

For some years after the murder a television producer endeavoured to put together a programme showing the involvement of a London solicitor in the case. The programme was never made.

James Morton, *Gangland*

---

* Zomparelli was shot dead in a Soho pinball arcade (*see Nicky Gerard*) and Frankie Albert fell to his death from a roof during a police raid before the trial of Rossi and Heibner.

Rita Green

Rita Green (also known as Driver), a prostitute nicknamed Black Rita because of her dark hair, was found shot dead on the first floor landing of a house in Rupert Street, Central London, on 8 September 1947. She was a striking six-foot woman, the daughter of a former police officer who had been stationed at Bow Street. According to Duncan Webb, the crime reporter, the Bobbed-hair Bandit* told them she had seen a man of the student type with Green shortly before her death. She was also known to have had a new boyfriend and one report says that she had been told he carried a revolver. Like so many other street women, Green was suspected of being a police informer and may have been killed for that reason. It was also suggested that she had refused to co-operate with the Messina brothers and was made an example of for others. Certainly that was a story which lingered on amongst old Soho hands even into the 1990s. The police, however, decided her killer had never seen her before and her death was thought eventually to be a random killing by a man with a dislike of prostitutes. Generally speaking, however, that type of man does not usually carry a gun.

Green River Murders *see* **Deborah Lynn Bonner**

Michael Gregsten

On 23 August 1961 Michael Gregsten was shot and killed at Deadman's Hill on the A6 in Bedfordshire, England. A married man, he had been out with his girlfriend Valerie Storey. They were either courting or planning a motor rally in a field in Dorney Reach near Maidenhead when they were surprised by a gunman. There followed a nightmare drive over the Home Counties with

---

* The Bobbed-haired Bandit was Lilian Goldstein, a long-time associate of members of the Underworld. She was the first woman involved in smash and grab raids in the United Kingdom and she assisted the notorious robber and prison escaper Ruby Sparkes in his escapes from prison. A watch was kept on her during a period of probation after Sparkes's escape from Dartmoor in 1942 but she seemed to have hung up her boots. Clearly she was still keeping an eye of the denizens of Soho.

Michael Gregsten.

Gregsten at the wheel and the gunman in the back giving away clues and snippets of his life. His hair seemed to have been dyed and he said 'fink' for 'think', by no means an uncommon characteristic of London speech. He had been through the penal mill and one thing he let slip was that he had 'done the lot' – criminal slang at the time for having done a full term of corrective training without remission.

During the drive Gregsten desperately tried to attract attention by flashing his lights. He left the car to pay for petrol and was deliberately slow, hoping the attendant would notice something. At about 3 a.m. he was ordered to stop the car and was shot dead. The murderer then made Valerie Storey drag the body from the car and raped her. She was then shot, causing partial paralysis. Some four hours later she was found by a farm worker. She was able to say the killer had deep-set brown eyes.

There was an uproar at the time. Landladies were advised to report on any odd behaviour of their guests. The public was alerted to a 'crazed gunman' and a Miss Perkins became worried about the behaviour of a man staying at the Alexandra Court Hotel in Finsbury Park, North London. He paced up and down his room and did not join the other guests for meals. Could he be the A6 killer? Over the years many people have tried to establish that he was.

He was Peter Alphon, certainly an odd man with Fascist leanings, a knowledge of greyhounds and a wanderer. He gave a voluntary statement to the police of his whereabouts on the night of the murder saying he stayed in the Vienna Hotel, Maida Vale. He had been out with his mother earlier in the evening and had then returned to the hotel. By this time the gun used to kill Gregsten had been found poked down the back of a London bus and cartridges were found at the Vienna Hotel on 11 September. Another guest at the hotel was a James Ryan, alias James Hanratty.

The police broke the first part of Alphon's alibi with no difficulty. Mrs Alphon had not seen her son for some time. A criminal named Nudds (also known as Baker, Bartlett, Beaumont, Itter and Knight) made a damaging statement saying that Alphon had not been in his room on the night of the murder. The equivalent of an APB went out, with the press using the euphemism that the police wished to see Alphon to help with their enquiries. The daily papers prepared articles anticipating the arrest of this 'misfit' and an announcement was made over the tannoy at Slough Greyhound Stadium, a track near Maidenhead which Alphon was known to use. Alphon duly walked into Cannon Row police station, was put on an identification parade by Superintendent Bob Alcott but was not picked out by Valerie Storey, who made a wrong identification.

Alphon was then charged with an assault on a woman in Wimbledon who claimed she had been attacked by a man saying, 'I am the A6 rapist.' He produced an alibi that he had been in a wholesale firm at the time of the attack. No evidence was offered and he was discharged and awarded costs. Nudds made two more statements, the latter saying that his previous ones had been wrong and he had only made them to curry favour with the police. Valerie Storey then changed her statement to say that her attacker had ice-blue eyes.

The focus switched away from Alphon, and Hanratty, who had been mentioned in Nudd's first statement, telephoned Alcott. On 11 October he was arrested in Blackpool and was identified by a man who had seen a figure near Gregsten's car the day after the killing. At an identification parade held the following day at Stoke Mandeville Hospital he was identified by Valerie Storey.

What was the sum total of the evidence against him? The identification by Valerie Storey, who had been wrong before and had changed an important detail in her evidence; his pronunciation of the word 'think'; the cartridges that had been found in the room he used at the Vienna Hotel albeit three weeks after he left; that he had told another petty criminal, Charles 'Dixie' France, that a good place to get rid of unwanted stolen jewellery was down the back seat of a bus; and that Dixie's daughter, Carol, had dyed his hair. It was not strong evidence and there were good grounds for thinking the magistrates might refuse to commit him for trial.

In the event they did and the prosecution case was bolstered by two additional

James Hanratty, who was hanged for Gregsten's murder on 4 April 1962.

witnesses: a prisoner named Langdale who said Hanratty had confessed to him and a Mrs Anderson who said she had bought stolen jewellery from him. There was also some evidence the gunman referred to himself as 'Jim'.

From the start Hanratty had given an alibi. He said he had been in Liverpool and had visited a sweetshop in the Scotland Road. Most importantly he said that at the time of the murder he had been with four men whom he refused to name. Despite this refusal, a private investigator found one of the men who said he had not seen Hanratty for some years. Worse was to come for the defence counsel Michael Sherrard. Hanratty changed a crucial part of his alibi: now he said he had not been in Liverpool in the evening but had travelled to Rhyl on the North Wales coast to see a friend.

The defence found both the friend and the landlady in Rhyl, a Mrs Jones, in whose guesthouse Hanratty said he had stayed. She was effectively destroyed in cross-examination by Graham Swannick QC, leading for the Crown. After ten hours of deliberation – in those days a lengthy time – the jury returned a verdict of guilty.

After the trial the defence found some further witnesses. An actor said he had seen Hanratty on the train to Liverpool and a Mrs Walker identified him as a man looking for a room on the night of the murder. Once again, as was the fashion in those days (*Olive Balchin qv*), the Court of Appeal declined to hear the witnesses. The Home Secretary refused a reprieve and Hanratty was hanged at Bedford Prison on 4 April 1962.

By now, however, Alphon had reappeared. He was befriended by another odd man, Jean Justice, who wrote a book based on Alphon's oblique confession to him. A parliamentary debate was arranged with a call for a public enquiry. The Labour MP Fenner Brockway appeared on television and claimed a 'Mr X' had committed the murder. Alphon replies with a writ for libel saying he was 'Mr X'.

Paul Foot, the journalist, began researching the case and interviewed Alphon on a number of occasions during which he made a series of admissions. For his book *Who Killed Hanratty?* Foot meticulously researched the Liverpool and Rhyl alibis and concluded the latter was true. Of Alphon, he wrote in 1971 'either he had been leading all of us, and me in particular, a fantastic dance' or he was the murderer. In the 1990s Alphon appeared on television to make what was billed as a confession. In the event he seemed confused and disorientated as he wandered up and down a railway platform. Certainly nothing he said could be interpreted as a confession.

Hanratty is a clear example of a defendant not convicted on the strength of the evidence against him but because he was caught lying. Since his death his family has worked tirelessly but, so far, unsuccessfully to obtain a pardon for him. A number of other books have been written proving or disproving that Hanratty was the killer. At least one of the authors, Louis Blom-Cooper, has changed his mind and now comes down in favour of his innocence.

Paul Foot, *Who Killed Hanratty?*; L. Blom-Cooper, *The A6 Murder*

Richard Griffin

On 24 March 1946, twenty-four-year-old salesman Richard Griffin and his nineteen-year-old girlfriend, Polly Anne Moore, were killed after they parked their car near Texarcana, Texas. He was shot through the head and she was shot twice and then mutilated and assaulted. The medical evidence was that he had been killed some two hours before the girl. Just over a month before the killings took place there had been an attack on a young couple, also in a parked car, in the same town. On this occasion the man had been hit on the head with a revolver and the girl, who had also been struck, had been raped. Six men were arrested but released.

At the place of the Griffin-Moore killing, tyre-tracks were found which proved identical to the ones found at the site of the earlier attack. Once again the usual suspects were rounded up and released.

On 13 April of the same year fifteen-year-old Betty Jo Booker and her seventeen-year-old boyfriend were attacked and killed. Again the boy had been shot first whilst she had been tortured and raped for some hours before also being shot. Similar tyre-marks to those at the other killings were found.

On 3 May a local farmer, Virgil Starks, was reading a newspaper at his home when he was shot dead. His wife rushed into the room and was also shot. However she staggered to the house of a neighbour to give the alarm. Once again similar tyre-tracks were found and it was noted that, as in all the other cases, the attack had occurred about the time of the full moon. Once again the usual suspects, this time in their hundreds, were questioned and released.

Shortly after the death of Starks a man died after jumping from a train near Texarcana. His identity was never established but a car was found on fire in a wooded area nearby. Because of the fire it was impossible to link the tyres with the tracks found near the killings. There were, however, no further similar killings in the area. The identity of the man was never discovered.

The cases had similarities to, though they cannot possibly be connected with, the Wilson (*qv*) and the Kelly Watson (*qv*) killings.

Colin Wilson and Patricia Pitman, *The Encyclopaedia of Murder*

Mary Speir Gunn

On Saturday 18 October 1913 the still handsome Mary Gunn was shot dead in Northbank Cottage at Portencross, Perthshire. She was forty-eight and in her youth had been regarded as 'the beauty of Beith'.

She, together with her elder sister and Alexander MacLaren, her brother-in-law, had gone to live at the cottage some six months earlier. According to the information given to the police by MacLaren (and supported by his wife), on the night of the murder he had been reading out loud a short story by W.W. Jacobs when a gun was poked through the window of the cottage and shots were fired. He received a broken finger, his wife was shot and seriously injured but Mary Gunn died from wounds to the chest. MacLaren ran to the local Laird for help.

Various theories were advanced by the police, including robbery (but nothing was taken), a deranged man (but none was found), and a previous and jealous lover of Mary Gunn (but he was traced to Saskachewan where he had certainly been on the night of the murder).

The search moved to Glasgow and the newspapers announced imminent arrests. None followed. On 4 December 1914 an action was filed against MacLaren in the Kilmarnock Sheriff Court by a Mrs Gibson. She claimed that 'the defender falsely and calumniously made statements to the effect that she had participated in or had guilty knowledge of the murder of the defender's sister-in-law, Miss Mary Gunn, at Portencross on October 18th last year.' She claimed £1,000 damages saying her husband's business had been badly affected by the lies. A year and a half later she withdrew the action, paying MacLaren's costs. Alexander Gibson had, it appears, been interviewed by the police during their visit to Glasgow.

No arrests were ever made and the murder remains unsolved. Jack House puts forward the theory that MacLaren was having an affair with his sister-in-law and intended to shoot his wife but instead killed his inamorata. He had left the room and fired the shots, deliberately injuring himself with the last one. House surmises that, with her rival dead, Mrs MacLaren did not wish further disruption in her life and went along with her husband's story.

Jack House, *Murder Not Proven?*

Karen Hadaway *see* **Nicola Fellows**

Hagley Wood

In April 1943 three boys out birdnesting found the remains of a body wedged in a tree at Hagley Wood in Warwickshire, England, on the estate of Lord Cobham. The shock was so much for one of them that he died shortly afterwards. The skeleton was that of a woman identified as being between twenty-five and forty, about five feet tall with mousey hair. She had probably been suffocated to death because the post-mortem showed that clothing had been pushed in the cavity of the mouth. The pathologist Professor Webster gave his opinion that the body had been stuffed into the tree before *rigor mortis* had set in. The body, which had been there for some eighteen months, was never identified and there were a number of suggestions on offer about the death, including one that she had been murdered in a ritual killing. There was a certain amount of early graffiti chalked on walls in the neighbourhood asking, 'Who put Bella [sometimes Luebella] down the Wych Elm?' Both names are diminutives of Elizabeth, itself a name associated with witchcraft. Dr Margaret Murray, the cen-

The tree in Hagley Wood in which the remains of a woman were discovered in 1943.

tenarian anthropologist, believed this to be the case, suggesting that the woman was 'another victim of the devil-worshippers'. A local vicar was, however, more prosaic. He suggested the woman was a gypsy and had been tried and condemned at a Romany court.

Suggestions have been made that the body was that of a murdered prostitute or even a German spy. In 1953 the *Wolverhampton Express & Star* ran a series of articles linking this murder with that of Charles Walton (*qv*). Following them, a woman who signed herself Anna wrote that the woman was Dutch and the person responsible had died insane in 1942. Anna was interviewed by the police but her details were never disclosed.

The belief that she was foreign has some backing in that neither maker nor seller of her shoes, an unusual crepe-soled variety, was ever traced and, more significantly, neither was her dentist. Some two hundred women missing at the time answered the description of the remains and all but twelve were finally traced. Donald McCormick concluded that the woman may have been a Dutch agent named Clara who was parachuted into the Kidderminster area in mid-1941 and who subsequently disappeared.

Donald McCormick, *Murder by Witchcraft*; Robert Fabian, *Fabian of the Yard*

The Reverend Edward Wheeler Hall

On the night of 14 September 1929 the forty-one-year-old Reverend Edward Wheeler Hall and his mistress, twenty-four-year-old Mrs Eleanor Mills, were killed in a lovers' lane in New Brunswick, New Jersey, where he was the minister of the Episcopalian Church of St John the Evangelist and she sang in the choir. He had been shot once in the head and she three times before her throat was cut. The surrounding area was littered with their love letters.

Their affair had not been a well kept secret. James Mills, eleven years older than his wife and the janitor at St John's, knew she kept company with the Reverend Edward but said he thought it was a platonic friendship. He was to give evidence that as she went out at about 7.30 p.m. he asked where she was going and received the reply, 'Why don't you follow me and find out?' The bodies were found two days later by a courting couple.

Favourites for the killing were the Hall family. There was a witness who had seen Mrs Hall and her brother, the eccentric Willie Stevens, leave their home in the middle of the night. She denied this, saying she had spent a sleepless night awaiting her husband's return after he had left saying he was going out to see Mrs Mills who had had an operation paid for by the Halls. It was not, said Mrs Hall, until she met Mr Mills at church the next day that she heard Mrs Mills was also absent without leave. There was some evidence from a Mrs Jane Gibson, who raised hogs, and was consequently known in the case as the Pig-Woman, that she had seen the killing of Hall and Mills. Her evidence was confused and, despite questioning Willie Stevens and Mrs Hall for some hours, the Grand Jury refused to return a Bill of Indictment. The investigation, said one New Jersey lawyer, was one of 'bungling stupidity'. Part of the trouble was that the police had allowed dozens of people to trample over the area thereby ruining any possibility of obtaining footprints.

Nothing more happened for four years until the case cropped up again when Arthur Geist sued his wife Louise for an annulment of their marriage. She had been a maid in the Hall household at the time of the killing and, so he said, had been paid $5,000 to hold her tongue. The story was picked up by the New Jersey *Daily Mirror* and continued until the State Governor appointed Alexander Simpson as special prosecutor. Mrs Hall, Willie Stevens and a cousin, Henry de la Bruyere, were arrested and charged.

The trial was one of the more sensational in a country where sensational trials are the order of the day. Mrs Gibson told her story once more to the Grand Jury. About 9 p.m. on 14 September she had been riding in her wagon near her farm when she heard noises. Over the past weeks thieves had been stealing her corn and so she unhitched and saddled her mare, Jenny, and set off after them. In the headlight of an automobile she saw a woman with white hair and a man who looked like a coloured man. She identified them as Mrs Hall and Willie Stevens. She said she saw three people (later increased by one as her testimony progressed). She then heard shots and a woman moan, 'Oh, Henry.' She rode off home, losing a moccasin on the way. Three hours later she retraced her steps trying to find it. There she saw Mrs Hall weeping in the lane. She saw no bodies. This time the Grand Jury believed her and committed Mrs Hall, Stevens and de la Bruyere for trial. The case was simple. If the trial jury believed the Pig-Woman was right then Mrs Hall and the others would have to explain just what they were doing that night.

Simpson and the Press believed that the trial would turn on the credibility of Willie Stevens. Simpson had privately said he intended to 'flay' the defendant. Stevens was probably what could be described as a wise fool. He had been allowed only a trust fund rather than the full inheritance from his parents and much of it he spent on and with the local fire-brigade, with whose members he could generally be found. When it came to it, however, he was more than a match for Simpson, who could not shake him in his story that he had gone to his room after dinner to smoke and then had been awakened by his sister who asked him to go with her to look for her husband. Simpson tried to shake his alibi, asking how he could establish the truth of his statement that from 8 or 9 p.m. he was in his room. 'Why,' replied Stevens, 'if a person sees me go upstairs and does not see me come downstairs, isn't that a conclusion that I was in my room.' It is the kind of flawed logic which defeats an opponent and Simpson was reduced to saying 'Absolutely.' It had not been a good trial for him. Throughout the evidence the Pig-Woman had been constantly barracked by her mother who called out 'Liar' at crucial and regular intervals. The defence had also made considerable inroads into her testimony. The unfortunate woman was suffering from cancer and was brought into court on a stretcher. Under cross-examination she could not recall when she had married, whether she had re-married and the names of various men.

The jury retired for five hours before acquitting all the defendants. The Halls sued the *Mirror* for $3 million and settled out of court. Various suggestions have been made as to the killer. One variant is that the Pig-Woman, thinking her crop was being stolen, shot them. If this is the case, since no one suspected her at all, why should she make up the story? Another is that the Klu Klux Klan, those 'guardians of morality' who did not only operate in the South but were apparently active in New Jersey at the time, put a stop to the extra-matrimonial activities of the pastor. Neither is a very likely solution. On balance it must surely have been a domestic killing.

James Thurber, *My World and Welcome To It*

Patricia Hall

The body of the mother of two young boys who disappeared from her home in Pudsey, Yorkshire, in January 1992 has not been traced. On 10 March 1994 her husband Keith was acquitted of her murder at Leeds Crown Court. The prosecution case was that Hall, who ran a mobile grocery, had confessed to an undercover policewoman, 'Liz', that he had strangled his wife and then incinerated the body. The policewoman had been planted on Hall after he replied to a lonely hearts advertisement in his local paper. All their meetings and telephone calls had been tape-recorded and when Liz was discussing marriage and expressed a worry that Patricia might return, Hall was alleged to have said, 'I was sleeping downstairs, then I woke up. I strangled her. It wasn't as simple as that, there were voices in my head telling me to do it. I'm sorry. Does that change anything? Do you still want me?' At the trial the judge, Mr Justice Waterhouse, refused to allow the jury to hear the tape, saying that the questioning by the policewoman had driven a coach and horses through the Police and Criminal Evidence Act 1984 which was designed to protect suspects in interviews. After the verdict he did, however, allow the publication of the contents of the tape. Hall had maintained his wife, who had had psychiatric treatment, had simply walked out on him after the marriage had deteriorated. He appealed to her to return so their relationship could be renewed.

Thomas Charles Hall

On 8 July 1948 the body of Thomas Charles Hall was found under the floorboards of 1805-20 Avenue N.W., Calgary, Alberta. Next to the body was an envelope addressed to Hall and postmarked 1929. It was from his brother, Wallace.

The cause of death was a fracture of the skull caused by at least two blows or shots. The discovery had come to light because the daughters of the new owners of the property were complaining of ghosts in the room and Alfred Peace, their father, had decided to investigate why the floorboards were springy.

Hall, who had married for the second time in 1908, had three sons. He was described as cold, overbearing and bullying and his wife, Camilla, left him in 1923. Fred, his eldest son, had already left the home and only Charles and the youngest John, born in 1914, remained. In early 1929 Charles left the house and John stayed with his father. In March 1929 Thomas Hall disappeared. In June 1929, by which time Hall was two-quarters in arrears with his rent, his landlords sent an agent to the house only to find it unlocked and deserted. It does not appear any of the family was particularly disturbed by his disappearance. John, apparently a talented carpenter, had stayed in the Calgary area along with his brother Charles. He later served in World War II where he became a Flight Lieutenant and, after the war, a test pilot.

Once the body was discovered, on the Sunday, John was invited to identify it. He failed to do so, remarking only that it 'was similar' to that of his father. Fred, who had been in Quebec, was however to make a positive identification. On Monday 10 July, John Hall was badly injured in a plane which crashed shortly after take-off. He had severe facial and head injuries but survived. His wife attended her father-in-law's funeral, as did Camilla. Fred and Hall's brother Wallace did not do so.

One theory for the murder was robbery. It was rumoured that Hall had made substantial money on the stock exchange and from his activities as a Teamster but he had no insurance and no verification of assets seems to have been made.

Several years later Wallace Hall was killed in a gun shop robbery.

Gary Hanlon *see* **Susan Blatchford**

Gladys Hanrahan

Just after 10 p.m. on 2 October 1948 thirty-five-year-old bookkeeper Gladys Hanrahan, who lived in St Ervan's Road, North Kensington, London, was found strangled on Cumberland Green in Regent's Park. A man's handkerchief, embroidered with a large letter A, had been forced into the corner of her mouth. There was no question of robbery, for her handbag with £5 in it was under her body and she was still wearing a valuable ring. Nor had she been sexually assaulted.

Enquiries were led by Detective Chief Inspector Jock Jamieson. He traced the handkerchief to a neighbour of Hanrahan's, a local grocer, who said he had lost it some time before. She had been drinking with him on the morning of her death in the Golden Cross public house in the Portobello Road and they had been observed rowing on previous occasions. At the inquest, at which he was represented by F. Elwyn Jones, who later became Lord Chancellor, the grocer gave an alibi that after drinking with Gladys Hanrahan he had had a couple more drinks in the Metropolitan public house and then on impulse gone to Brighton for the afternoon. He had stayed there two hours and had then returned to London, wandering about World's End between Chelsea and Fulham before going back to the Metropolitan for a final drink. He had returned home at about 10.45 p.m. This alibi was at least partly broken by witnesses who said he had been in London. The coroner told the jury that even if they disbelieved the man there was still nothing to connect him to Miss Hanrahan's death, and a verdict of murder by person(s) unknown was returned.

Later, John Allen, the so-called Mad Parson, who had escaped from Broadmoor a year earlier where he had been detained following the murder of a child before World War II and who was recaptured in the St John's Wood area, was a prime suspect for a number of murders which had occurred locally. In addition to that of Gladys Hanrahan, these included the prostitute Russian Dora Freedman (*qv*), and the frail, bespectacled sixty-nine-year-old Emily Armstrong (*qv*), beaten to death in a St John's Wood cleaners, allegations which he vigorously denied. The thinking ran that he had killed these women whilst in a mental blackout. The day after his re-arrest he was placed on identification parades and was not picked out. He was returned to Broadmoor and was released a year later.

Leonard Read, *Nipper*; John Allen, *Inside Broadmoor*; Peter Beveridge, *Inside the CID**

Harley Street

On 3 June 1880 the body of a woman aged between forty and forty-five, height around 4'9", was found in the basement of 139 Harley Street, London, covered with empty bottles. The discovery was brought about by the return of a particularly unpleasant smell which had been present about eighteen months earlier. At that time it had been thought to be bad drainage and extensive work had been carried out. The woman, who the police determined 'came from a lowly station in life', had been stabbed in the left breast.

At the subsequent inquest, a serving soldier, Henry Smith, gave evidence that he had been the butler at number 139 some two years earlier. He had been sacked for excessive drinking. He said he was married and that his wife 'is alive but I do not live with her'. He agreed he had asked a man named Green to dig a hole in the cellar so he could get rid of an excess of stale bread. Green denied this was the reason for the digging and the cook at 139 denied there was ever

---

* The version of the case given in Peter Beveridge's book does not quite tie in with the report of the inquest in *The Times*. He says that the grocer had satisfied him that he had nothing to do with the death. It is clear from the remarks of the coroner that this was not the case.

any waste in the household. Various members of the staff gave evidence that there was no smell before 1877. The jury returned a verdict of murder of an unknown woman by person or persons unknown. Curiously no one seems to have made any real enquiries as to the whereabouts of Mrs Smith.

Late in his life at a medical lecture, following a discussion of the case, Sir Bernard Spilsbury thought that, given the locality, the death might have been as a result of an abortion following which the woman had died. He suggested that the stab wound in the breast might have been made to deceive the authorities.

Rose Harsent

In the case known as the Peasenhall Mystery, William Gardiner was charged with the murder of the twenty-three-year-old serving- and choir-girl, Rose Harsent. On 1 June 1902 the girl's father was taking some linen to his daughter in the village of Peasenhall, Suffolk, when, on opening the back door of the house where she worked, he found her half-naked body with her throat cut. There had been deep cuts made to her shoulders. Her nightdress had been torn and partly burned. A broken medicine bottle, which had contained paraffin, was found on the floor nearby. In her room were three letters signed by William Gardiner, father of six and a devout Methodist Sunday School teacher. One of them invited her to meet him at midnight.

Peasenhall was a small village and everyone knew of the on-going relationship between Gardiner and Rose Harsent, who was pregnant at the time of her death. Some time prior to her death, two youths had passed the little old seventeenth-century building known as the Doctor's Chapel and had heard a rustling of clothing and a girl calling 'oh, oh'. There had then been a discussion about Onan spilling his seed. Gossip seeped around the village.

The local Methodist minister, the Reverend John Grey, had conducted an enquiry in which Gardiner had denied the boys' story saying that the reason he had been with Rose was to help her move a stiff door. Grey had equivocated, letting Gardiner off with a warning, but the affair had continued. When questioned Gardiner denied the signature or the writing on the letters was his. This was difficult for him to explain since the envelope was identical to a batch which came from Gardiner's building firm. He was arrested.

The evidence against him was formidable and he was perhaps fortunate that, since his clasp knife was stained, forensic evidence had not then developed in England to the extent that animal and human blood could be distinguished. There were no bloodstained clothes but neighbours said there had been a large fire burning at Gardiner's house. His loyal wife explained that this was their usual June fire. His defence was that of an alibi – he had been in bed with his wife all night. In the days when there had to be a unanimous verdict one member held out for an acquittal. In the re-trial there was also a disagreement. In accordance with tradition the prosecution offered no evidence for a third case. Gardiner and his wife left Suffolk and opened a shop, under their own names, in London.

However black it may look against Gardiner there were some other possible, if unlikely, candidates for the role of killer. Certainly there had been some indecent poems written by the boy next door, who was in love with Rose, and there was more than suspicion in the village that she had other lovers who might not have been all that keen she should go through with her pregnancy. Other commentators have taken the view that Rose Harsent may have committed suicide.

William Henderson (ed), *Notable British Trials*

Richard Hart

Dicky Hart, a minor associate of the Kray Twins, was shot to death in an affray at Mr Smith and the Witchdoctor's nightclub in Peckham, South-east London, on 7 March 1966. It is not completely clear exactly what caused the affray which led to the shooting but it is most likely that it was over the protection of the club by rival South-east London factions. The Richardsons were proposing to take over control from the Hayward brothers and their friends the Hennesseys. By some accounts the Richardsons had been appointed to control the club by the owners who had unfortunately failed to inform the Haywards they were being dispossessed. Another account is that the fight began over a domestic dispute.

There is no dispute that during the evening the rival factions chatted and drank or that Dicky Hart went out and armed himself with a shotgun. During the fighting Hart was shot. Frank Fraser, a close friend of Eddie Richardson, was charged with the murder, mainly on the evidence of Henry Botton who said he saw Fraser shoot Hart.*

Ron Kray claimed that the Twins had an interest in Mr Smith's Club and that the killing by him three nights later of George Cornell in the Blind Beggar in the Mile End Road was in revenge for the death of Hart.

Reg and Ron Kray, *Our Story;* Frank Fraser, *Mad Frank*

Edwin Richard 'Teddy' Haskell

On the night of Saturday, 31 October 1908, between 10.20 and 10.30 p.m., twelve-year-old Teddy Haskell had his throat cut whilst in bed in his home at 40 Meadow Road, Fisherton, Salisbury, Wiltshire, where he lived in a two-storey cottage with his thirty-four-year-old mother. The knife stroke was through the jugular vein and below the vocal cords. Teddy could not have made a sound. He was an enormously popular child in the neighbourhood. His father had died some four years previously of consumption at about the time that Teddy had had his right leg amputated below the knee as a result of a bone disease. He was, nevertheless, an active child, playing football and running with his crutches. By all accounts Flora Fanny Haskell was a devoted mother. 'She was all a mother could be,' said one witness at the trial.

Her movements at the time of the killing can be timed up to 10.20 p.m. and then after 10.30 p.m. She worked as a laundress and that evening did her shopping in Salisbury, came home at about 8.30 p.m., went and collected Teddy from his uncle's next door, took him to buy a comic and was back indoors by 8.45. She said that after that she had given Teddy his supper, a footbath for his good leg and put him to bed.

At 10.05 p.m. a delivery boy, John Wyatt, was sent with a package to number 42, could not get a reply and so knocked on Mrs Haskell's door and she took it in for her neighbour. He was to say that she appeared absolutely normal and

---

* Botton was himself sentenced to five years' imprisonment for his part in the affray. He was shot to death in July 1983 at his home in Shooter's Hill Road, Greenwich, probably over a dispute involving antiques. Two men were convicted of his murder. Fraser, who himself was shot in the thigh, was acquitted at the Old Bailey when the trial judge ruled he had no case to answer. No one else was ever charged with the killing.

the time was 10.20 p.m. Ten minutes later Percy Haskell, Flora Haskell's nephew, called round at the back door and, when he found it fastened, knocked. Mrs Haskell called 'all right' and he heard first what he thought was the sound of a kitchen chair scraping. Then he heard what he later described as a jump, the sound someone would make if they leaped the last few stairs. There was a scream and Mrs Haskell came to the back door shouting, 'Go and stop that man! He has killed my poor Teddy! Go for a doctor quick.'

Percy Haskell could see no one in the street; nor could Walter Steer, a neighbour who had heard Mrs Haskell's cries and came running to help. The only two men in the locality were one whom Steer recognised who was talking to another who had been relieving himself in the yard of the local public house. Another neighbour, a Mrs Chivers, went back to the house with Mrs Haskell and was asked by her to go to the bedroom. At the foot of the stairs was a bloodstained knife. Mrs Haskell then said, 'There is the knife. I fancied I heard footsteps upstairs. Someone came down the stairs and threw the knife at me. Look there is blood on my sleeve.' There were some small bloodstains on her blouse.

Dr H. L. E. Wilks said that the call for his assistance had come at 10.30 p.m. and so the time of the murder can be fairly accurately pinned down to those ten minutes. Wilks found that the force of the knife thrust was such that a spurt of blood had sprayed a chest of drawers near the bed. It is difficult to see, therefore, how Mrs Haskell if, as was said, she was the killer, could have avoided being covered in blood. She had no time to clean up and change.

Search parties for the man who had jumped down the last few stairs were organised and indeed a police description shows that a man of 5'6" or 5'7" dressed in a dark suit but with no collar was being sought. Mrs Haskell seems to have been questioned throughout the night and somewhere around 3.30 a.m. asked a police sergeant whether 'the money' was all right. This was a reference to money kept in Teddy's room. He had been saving to buy an artificial cork leg and had put together eight pounds in gold and two shillings. When the sergeant checked, only three sovereigns and a half sovereign remained.

There is no doubt whatsoever that the investigation was thoroughly mishandled. At about 6 a.m. Mrs Haskell's mother, Mrs Carter, decided, and was allowed, to scrub the bloodstain from the bottom of the stairs where the knife had been found. The bedding had also been re-arranged and Teddy Haskell's body was washed. The all-night search was fruitless and the Chief Constable called in Scotland Yard in the shape of Chief Inspector Dew, who had been involved

in the hunt for Jack the Ripper and who, two years later, would achieve a kind
of immortality as the man who caught Crippen.*

In a search of the house he found some newly washed men's clothing and
when questioning Mrs Haskell she said that on the night of the murder a man
had called asking for lodgings. She had turned him away. Asked about the
clothing and the local rumour that she was planning a re-marriage, she said that
the clothing belonged to an Alfred Mold who was a steward on the liner the
Adriatic. He slept in the house whilst on shore and she did his laundry in his
absence. Dew also found eight sovereigns in Mrs Haskell's purse. She said she
was keeping them for her mother, who confirmed the story. The money was
returned.

On Tuesday, 3 November 1909, Mrs Haskell was charged with her son's murder and remanded to Devizes prison. A defence fund was set up by neighbours
to pay her legal costs. A coroner's jury returned a verdict of wilful murder
against her and the magistrates committed her for trial. Clearly, Mrs Haskell had
the time and the opportunity to kill her son. The only motive which could be
advanced by the prosecution was that she was contemplating marrying Alfred
Mold and that Teddy was an impediment to the union. That, at least, had been
the line which counsel for the police had taken during the inquest and committal proceedings. When it came to the Devizes Assizes, J. Alderson Foote for the
Crown, threw this overboard: 'The only theory which the Crown are able to
present is that this woman committed this act in one of those abnormal conditions of mind which overtake human beings sometimes, and which it is impossible for medical men or legal experts to give any adequate explanation of.
During her stay in prison, the accused has been under the observation of the
prison doctor, and he is of the opinion that she is perfectly sane.' Translated into
lay language – she snapped.

Flora Haskell was represented by the up and coming barrister, Rayner
Goddard, who would later become the Lord Chief Justice. Mr Justice Ridley
summed up against her but the jury, after a three-hour retirement – a lengthy
one in those days, when the jury in the Steinie Morrison case took just twenty-
eight minutes – disagreed. The next hearing was before Mr Justice Darling, who
was by no means any more sympathetic to Mrs Haskell. 'Although the defence
argue that there is no motive for the woman's guilt, it is altogether difficult to
see why a man should have come to the house to murder the boy. It has not

---

* It is curious that in his memoirs of his life as a police officer, *I Caught Crippen*, Dew barely
mentions the Haskell case. His proud boast, however, was that the Ripper case was the only
one he was unable to solve.

been shown that there is a man who had any ill will against the lad.' Goddard had not called Mrs Haskell to give evidence and Mr Justice Darling was not happy that the jury had not heard an explanation for the bloodstains on her clothing. The jury retired for only ten minutes before returning a verdict which sounded extremely like the Scottish Not Proven. 'We find her not guilty on the ground of insufficient evidence.' The public gallery erupted in applause. Goddard never defended another murder case of any note.

One outcome of the case was that a directive was issued to provincial police forces that, if the assistance of Scotland Yard was required in a case, steps should be taken to preserve rather than to destroy the evidence.

The general view of commentators is that Mrs Haskell did kill her son. But is it not possible that it was indeed a burglary which went wrong and that a man was surprised by the sparky Teddy who was killed to silence him?

Fenton Bresler, *Lord Goddard*; Tom Tullett, *Murder Squad*

Josslyn Victor Hay
(22nd Earl of Erroll)

At 3 a.m. on 24 January 1941 the driver of a milk truck on the road outside Nairobi in Kenya stopped to investigate what appeared to be a car accident. On closer inspection the driver was clearly dead and the man went for help. The driver was the 22nd Earl of Erroll, forty-year-old Josslyn Victor Hay. At first it was thought that he had been been killed by his head striking the dashboard in the crash. It was soon discovered that he had been shot in the head. The inside of the car reeked of perfume and the armstraps had been torn off.

Kenya in the late 1930s and early 1940s was awash with adultery and society scandal, with the handsome if impoverished Erroll an outstanding player of the game. His latest and, but for the shooting, possibly lasting love had been the twenty-two-year-old Diana Caldwell, formerly the wife of the second piano player in the Savoy Orpheans and now the wife of the arrogant and also somewhat impoverished Sir Henry Jock Delves Broughton. Diana Caldwell, accepted as a fine horsewoman but described disparagingly by Nairobi society as 'a trifle Aldershot', had known Broughton for five years, during part of which time she had run a cocktail bar, The Blue Goose in Bruton Street, London. Before the

Diana Caldwell and the Earl of Erroll in Nairobi.

marriage, which took place on 5 November 1940, he had arranged with her that
if she fell in love he would not oppose a divorce and would pay her £5,000 a year
for three years. He cannot have expected the marriage to end so quickly. Her
affair with Erroll began when they met at the Caledonian Ball held at the
Muthaiga Club in Nairobi on 30 November 1940.

It was early in January, after the loving pair had spent a weekend at the home
of June Carberry, that Diana told Broughton she was going to leave him. He
appears to have taken the news very badly and to have begun to drink heavily,
talking of trying to start over again in Ceylon. Then his attitude seems to have
changed. On the night of 23 January he held a dinner for them and June Carberry at the Muthaiga Club at which he proposed a toast to the couple, hoping
they would be blessed with an heir. Erroll and Diana went dancing after the
dinner with Erroll agreeing to bring her home before 3 a.m. In the event he
brought her back half an hour earlier.

When the police learned that Broughton had been having shooting lessons,
had reported the theft of a pair of .32 Colt revolvers before the killing and
burned a pair of plimsolls afterwards, they looked no further for a culprit.
Broughton certainly had bad fortune with thefts. Shortly before he left England
there had been two burglaries at his homes in which valuable paintings and
objets had been taken. Now the reconstruction of the killing was that when

Erroll returned Diana, Broughton had crept out of the bathroom window and hidden in the back of Erroll's car. He had shot him during the drive back to Nairobi and, with the car out of control, had torn the armstraps whilst trying to keep his balance before he could steer the car into the ditch. That would account for the torn straps, and Diana's earlier presence would account for the smell of scent. The police were also convinced that Broughton had been trying to set up an alibi: twice he had visited June Carberry, who was staying in the house, to enquire if she was all right.

His trial began on 26 May with Harry H. Morris KC, recruited by the loyal Diana from South Africa for a fee of £5,000, leading the defence. Unfortunately for the Crown they had no gun against which to match the bullets found in Erroll and on the firing range where Broughton had practised. Broughton also had an arthritic arm and a dragging leg which, said Morris, would have effectively disabled him. The jury acquitted him on 1 July 1941.

He now found himself something of a social outcast in Kenyan society. He had not helped himself by renting Erroll's house the next year, in which his marriage to Diana finally ended. He returned to England where he was arrested over the burglaries he had suffered there. The insurers claimed they were fraudulent, and there does seem to be evidence that such was the case. He was released without charge and checked into the Adelphi Hotel in Liverpool where he was found dead on 5 December 1942. He had injected himself with Medinal.

In 1979 June Carberry's daughter, Juanita, who had been fifteen at the time of the murder, made a statement that Broughton had told her he had killed Erroll.

James Fox, *White Mischief*

Eamon Helly

An Irishman who taught at a British Aerospace School in Saudi Arabia, Helly was killed in his hotel room whilst on holiday in Goa, India, on 7 November 1991. Efforts had been made to poison him as well as strangle him using nunchakas, a martial arts weapon. His throat had also been cut. Although his passport, Visa card, travellers cheques and a camera had been taken from his room, neither the card nor cheques were ever used or cashed. The local police were convinced Helly had been murdered by a contract killer, probably a foreign one.

His body was not discovered for three days. It was said the staff did not have time to clean the room because they were overworked during the Diwali festival. A number of motives have been advanced, from simple robbery or a homosexual killing to a murder involving a local gangster group, the Goa Protectors, possibly over drugs. Helly's brother, a London policeman, travelled to Goa to investigate the murder enquiry and to try to galvanise the local police into further action. One local man was questioned at length but he was released and no charges have been preferred.

Tim McGirk, 'Blood Brothers', *The Independent Magazine*, 18 December 1993

Kathleen Higgins

The body of an elderly woman was found in the grounds of Winfield House, Regent's Park, London, about 7.30 on the morning of 12 March 1949. She was shabbily clothed and had only a few stumps for teeth. Her knickers lay over the lower part of her legs and thighs. There had been an attempt at sexual intercourse. She had been strangled with a scarf.

For some days she was not identified. Various people suggested names and one man thought it might be his mother. She, however, turned out to be alive and well at her home in Camden Town. One lady wrote in saying she had dreamed about the murder. On 15 March the body was identified as that of Kathleen Higgins, a seventy-six-year-old woman known as Irish Kit and who, amazingly, was still an active prostitute. She had lived in what were described as filthy conditions with John Murphy, a sixty-year-old builder's labourer. At the time of her death he was in hospital with stomach ulcers. After her death some rotting kippers were found on the table of her home and, as part of trying to trace her movements prior to her death, a good deal of police time was spent trying to ascertain when and from which shop they had come.

She was believed to have left the British Flag public house, Newcourt Street, St John's Wood at about 7.30 p.m. on 11 March. Her purse, thought to contain less than a £1, was never found. Over 400 people were interviewed, including a large number of RAF and WRAF personnel who were billeted at Viceroy Court, Prince Albert Road, the direction Kathleen Higgins had walked from the public house. On the round-up of the usual suspects principle, John Allen (*Emily Armstrong qv*) was placed on an identification parade but was not picked out.

In September 1950, for a few moments the police must have believed that they had a lead when a man was brought into the police station by another who said he had confessed to the murder of Irish Kit. He had been drinking and was eliminated from the enquiry.

When John Haskayne appeared on remand on 26 May 1953 charged with the murder of Grace Melina Darrington by strangulation, he was interviewed over the killing. He denied involvement in the matter and, as he did not fit the description of a man circulated in the *Police Gazette*, he too was eliminated.

After his arrest in 1958, Adam Ogilvie (see page 5) was briefly suspected for the killing. He was eliminated because at the time he was serving a sentence of three years' penal servitude for wounding with intent, passed at the Exeter Assizes on 21 June 1948 and had not been released until 16 June 1950.

From then on no further arrests were made.

Leonard Read, *Nipper*; John Allen, *Inside Broadmoor*

Joe Hill *see* John and Alving Morrison

Vera Hilda Emma Hoad

On 25 February 1924 the body of eleven-year-old Vera Hoad was found in a field near the mental hospital at Greylingwell near Chichester, Sussex. She had been raped with considerable bruising to the vagina but no signs of internal semen. There was, however, 'an abundant amount on her bloomers'.

At first the police had a variety of suspects, including one youth described as sickly and effeminate who had an obsession with obtaining a photograph of Vera and so came under suspicion. He was eliminated when his parents gave him an alibi. There was a theory that Vera knew her assailant. There had been no signs of a struggle until she had reached the field and her music case was still with her. There was vague speculation that at first she might have been agreeable to some form of sexual activity – her right hand was ungloved – but that ultimately she had been raped and then strangled to prevent her identifying her attacker. There were barracks close by and it was then thought that a soldier may have committed the crime. In any event the police believed the man's penis might have been damaged in the attack. One hundred and fifty men were paraded and their clothes inspected without success. In all more than 1,200 statements were taken from men living in Chichester. There were no charges brought.

The probability is that she was killed by Earl(e) Leonard Nelson, also known as Earle Ferrell and Virgil Wilson, who was hanged in Winnipeg, Canada, on 13 January 1928. He was suspected of the deaths of over twenty women in the United States and Canada in cities as far apart as San Francisco, Detroit, Kansas City, Philadelphia, Buffalo and Portland. One of his *modus operandi* was to gain entry into their homes on the pretext of looking for lodgings and then rape and strangle them. He was finally arrested after killing Emily Patterson in Winnipeg on 9 June 1927. Among his possessions were clippings of the killing of Vera Hoad and also of a girl, Nancy Clarke, in similar circumstances in Birkenhead. It was known that he had been in England between 1919 and 1925 and that he had been in the Sussex area. The death of Nellie Clarke occurred at a time when Nelson was in Liverpool waiting a passage back to America.

Nelson, a man with a receding forehead, protruding lips and huge hands, was nicknamed the Gorilla Murderer. He was born in Philadelphia in 1892 or 1897 (dates vary). His mother contracted venereal disease from his father when Nelson was a baby and he was brought up by a religious aunt who hoped her nephew would train for the Baptist ministry. His first conviction was in 1918 when he was sent to the Napa State Hospital for the Insane for attempted rape. He escaped and commenced his killing spree. Although he normally killed older women he had killed a fourteen-year-old flower seller, Lola Cowan, the day before he strangled Mrs Patterson. Lola Cowan had called at his lodgings and had been 'strangled, stripped and raped'. He was convicted for the latter killing after an unsuccessful plea of insanity was offered on his behalf.

The British authorities hoped that there might be a stay of execution to enable him to be questioned over the English murders but none was given. On the scaffold he is reported to have said, 'I am innocent. I stand innocent before God and man. I forgive those who have wronged me and ask forgiveness for those I have injured. God have mercy!'

He had baffled the police with the facility with which he had made his escapes in his killing spree and the Chief of the Winnipeg Police, C. H. Newton, wrote of him:

> Nothing in the history of crime known on this continent seemingly parallels the number of his killings or the atrocious acts he is alleged to have committed. His cunning in escaping from the scene, the frequency with which he changed his

clothing and the speed attained by him in travelling from place to place, stamp him as an altogether abnormal person.

Brian Lane and Wilfred Gregg, *The Encyclopedia of Serial Killers*; Jay Robert Nash, *World Encyclopedia of 20th Century Murder*

James Riddle Hoffa

Sixty-two-year-old Jimmy Hoffa, a one-time leader of the powerful Teamsters Union, disappeared on the afternoon of 30 June 1975. He had, he told his wife Josephine, a two o'clock appointment with union members as well as leading Underworld figures including Tony Jack Giacalone and, possibly, Tony Provenzano in the Manchus Red Fox restaurant in Detroit. He had been nervous before the meeting but his wife apparently thought nothing of it. Giacalone had visited the Hoffa household within the previous week and their children had grown up together. On the way to the meeting Hoffa stopped at an airport limousine service, in which he was a sleeping and hidden partner with Louis Linteau, who had, at Giacalone's request, arranged the meeting. Hoffa telephoned his wife at 2.20 p.m. to say that no one had arrived. He was seen in the parking lot of the restaurant getting into a car at about 2.45 p.m. and was never seen again. Louis Linteau said he had a call from Hoffa at 3.30 p.m. but his employees thought it was probably an hour earlier. Giacalone was able to produce a cast-iron alibi. First he had been to a barber who remembered him well and then he had been with his lawyers. Provenzano had been playing kalooki at his union hall in New Jersey. Both men denied there was to be a meeting with Hoffa at the Manchus Red Fox.

Hoffa had begun life as a stockboy in a department store in Detroit but, by the time of his death, he was estimated to be worth about $12 million. He had been a union organiser all his adult life and, as such, had been the subject of the attentions of Robert Kennedy when he was Attorney-General. In his book, *The Enemy Within*, Kennedy described the Teamsters as a 'conspiracy of evil' and had suggested their leadership was mixed up in fraud, extortion and killing. Over the years Hoffa had been charged with a number of offences but it was only in 1962 that he was successfully brought to trial in Nashville, charged with extortion. The result was a hung jury but he was found guilty of the attempted bribery of a juror and sentenced to eight years' imprisonment. Later, in Chicago, he was found guilty of misappropriating Teamster Union funds and sentenced to another five years. Down with him went almost a hundred Teamster officials and friends, including Tony Provenzano. Hoffa was pardoned by President Richard Nixon after serving four years. Part of the release package had been that Hoffa was banned from taking part in Teamster activities until 1981, a decision which, at the time of his death, he was still contesting.

The reason for Hoffa's death was almost certainly to do with union politicking. One version is that he was murdered to stop him regaining power, something which his Mafia friends could not countenance; a second is that he was killed to prevent him blowing the whistle on the control organised crime figures still had in the union. Another line of thought is that he died because he had too much knowledge of the John F. Kennedy assassination (*qv*) (after the president's death, Hoffa was reported to have said that now his persecutor, Robert, was now just another lawyer) and of CIA plots against Castro.

As to the death itself, there is speculation that he was garotted in the car in which he left the restaurant. Bits of Hoffa's hair and some blood could be traced to the back seat. Various methods of disposal have been suggested including the use of a fat-rendering plant and subsequent burial in concrete in the New York Giants football stadium in East Rutherford, New Jersey. A mob executioner, Charles Allen, said that Hoffa had indeed been garotted by Salvatore Briguglio, one of Provenzano's men, but that the killing had taken place in a syndicate hide-out. Hoffa's body had then been processed at a meat-grinding plant and the pieces thrown into a swamp in Florida. A further version is that his body was dumped in the Gulf of Mexico in a fifty-five-gallon drum filled with wet concrete. At a senate hearing in 1988 the then FBI director, William Sessions, said that he believed the men responsible for Hoffa's death were now in prison after being sentenced for other crimes.* Hoffa was legally declared dead in 1982.

Jay Robert Nash, *World Encyclopedia of Organised Crime;* Martin Short, *Crime Inc;* Kirk Wilson, *Investigating Murder*

---

* Tony Jack Giacalone was later sentenced to ten years for tax fraud. Tony Provenzano died whilst serving a life sentence for the murder of Anthony Castellito in 1961. He had been convicted in 1978. Briguglio was shot to death outside a New York restaurant in 1978.

David Holden

The fifty-three-year-old chief foreign correspondent of *The Sunday Times* was shot dead through the back near Cairo airport around 5 a.m. on Wednesday, 7 December 1977. He had arrived in Cairo from Amman about midnight. On the flight he had sat next to an American woman from Ohio on a group tour and he had not been seen talking to anyone after passing through immigration. He had apparently ignored a line of licensed cabs which commuted between the airport and Cairo hotels. His body was found in the Cairo suburb of Nasr City on the fringe of the desert at about 8.30 a.m. and the post-mortem showed he had been dead about three hours. There were no papers, luggage or money on the body which delayed identification, but the newspaper *Al-Ahram* said that his portable typewriter and notebook had been found in a white Fiat car without plates in a side-street in Dokki. Two men and a girl were immediately arrested, not as suspects, the police said, but to help with enquiries.

Holden had been a regular visitor to Cairo for the previous twenty years and his newspaper did not believe that he could have become lost so near the airport and then strayed into a situation where he was robbed.

By early January the police became convinced that he had been killed by an intelligence team and that the murder had been planned at least twenty-four hours, and possibly up to two weeks, in advance. The car in which Holden had been shot was owned by a director of the Nile Agricultural Export Company, and had been stolen on 18 November on the West Bank. This was the day on which Holden had made definite plans to go to Cairo. It was found after the killing at Tanta, with a 9 mm short cartridge bullet of the same kind which killed Holden, under the seat. There were spots of blood between the front seats. The car contained two headrests which had come from the white Fiat car in which Holden's luggage was found. This had been stolen on 24 December just twenty-four hours before Holden first arrived in Cairo from Jerusalem. His cameras, tapes, and most of his papers were missing. A third car, a green Fiat, also appears to have been involved. A letter found in the White Fiat was addressed to the owner of the green Fiat, a prominent sportsman who was not considered to be a suspect. His car had also been stolen the same night as the white Fiat. He had lent it to his sister who shared it with a family friend, Walid al-Ahmad, who had reported it stolen on 6 December. Walid al-Ahmad's brother had been deported from Cairo for political activities two weeks before Holden's death and for a time the authorities thought there might be some connection. Walid had an alibi and all three were released.

The Egyptian police, bereft of ideas as to the identity of the killers, turned over part of the enquiry to a three-person *Sunday Times Insight* team. They were not helped when it appeared that two months later papers from the Holden file had been stolen from *The Sunday Times*. At that stage the theory was that Holden had been killed by either a Palestinian commando group, the Saudi Arabians or even the Israelis. He had been working on a book about Saudi Arabia at the time of his death.

Three years later the best theory on offer was that he had been murdered by an Arab terrorist group in an effort to disrupt the meeting of President Sadat with Israel's Prime Minister Begin for peace talks.

When asked whether Holden was a British intelligence agent Harold Evans, then editor of *The Sunday Times*, replied:

> News to me. It is totally against our policy for a member of our staff to work for any intelligence outfit. There is a standing instruction that there should be instant dismissal if this should happen. We can never be dogmatic, of course, that no one has ever worked for intelligence, as *The Observer* has discovered.*

The Sunday Times established an award in Holden's memory for the Best Contribution to International Understanding.

Kate Jackson

On 4 February 1929 the fifty-year-old Kate Jackson was attacked outside her bungalow, Kenilworth, at the Limeslade Bungalow Colony, Mumbles, Swansea. She was found unconscious and it was thought that the attacker drove away in a waiting car.

A neighbour, Mrs Dimmock, told the police that on the night of the attack she and Mrs Jackson had been to the cinema and returned home at about 10 p.m. They parked at the gates and Mrs Dimmock had just got indoors when she heard a scream. She had rushed out and found Kate Jackson by her back door, unconscious and bleeding. Mr Jackson had then joined them but there was no sign of the attacker. The only noise was of a car starting up and driving off on a nearby road. She saw it had no lights on. The police waited by Mrs Jackson's bedside in the hope she would regain consciousness.

---

* John Knight in the *Sunday Mirror*, 14 October 1979. The reference to *The Observer* relates to Kim Philby who worked as their Middle-East correspondent before defecting to Russia.

Then Mrs Jackson's background began to emerge. She had been a witness in what was described as a 'sensational case in London' in 1927 as a result of which William George Harrison was sentenced to five years penal servitude for embezzling the funds of the National Association of Coopers of which he was both secretary and treasurer. Referred to as Madame X throughout the trial, Mrs Jackson had admitted that she had received between £8,000 and £9,000 from Harrison whom she had met in London in 1914 when she was married and known as Madame Le Grys.

So where did Mr Jackson fit into the picture? Thomas Jackson, a fish dealer, had apparently met Madame Le Grys in London in a teashop and, after a period of friendship, had married her in 1922. He was able to tell the *Western Mail and South Wales News:**

> She was eight years older than me and was very well connected and well educated. She speaks several languages. We were very happy together until the embezzlement case. Occasionally she received anonymous letters. She never told me the contents of them. They used to frighten her and she was nervous when she saw a stranger near the place.

He went on to describe his movements on the night of the killing. He was in bed, half asleep, when he heard a scream and a dog bark. He went to the door and found his wife on the ground but raised up as if trying to open the door. He said she seemed to have crawled about seven feet and was bleeding from the head. A Dr Taylor was called and she was taken to hospital. He said the doctor had told him he'd seen a car was driving away fast without lights. Dr Taylor claimed the lights were on.

As the days went on and Mrs Jackson recovered consciousness she had nothing to say about the attack. Mr Jackson, however, was able to fill in her background. She had, she had told him, been born in India and called herself Mollie Le Grys. When she married him she had called herself Kate Atkinson from Lancaster. She had told him that she had bought the identity of a girl who went to Australia and, on another occasion, said that she was the youngest daughter of a Duke.

> As time went on I became convinced that my wife had married me because she wanted me to protect her from someone. She never told me her real secrets and I do not know today who she really is.

By Friday, 8 February, Mrs Jackson had recovered sufficiently to say, 'They hit

---

* 7 February 1929.

me hard.' A broken flagon lying near the site of her attack was taken away for fingerprinting. The police were not convinced that the first blow was struck with the flagon and dug over the Jacksons's back garden. Questioned by the police, she said that her attackers (plural) were after her adopted daughter, Betty, whom Jackson believed was of titled birth.

She died on Sunday, 10 February without making the hoped for dying declaration. The police now regarded the car as irrelevant and concentrated on Mr Jackson as the attacker. He, said Mrs Morgan, a local woman, was the son of her dearest friends and in a change of tack said that she believed Betty was Mrs Jackson's own child. The Jacksons had stayed with Mrs Morgan and 'curious things had happened', including letters arriving for Mrs Jackson in at least four different names, and her claims that she was a romantic novelist and the only journalist at the Siege of Sydney Street. Most of the letters contained postal orders or Treasury notes and on one occasion Mrs Jackson had thrown a handful in the air saying, 'That is what comes of being clever.'

Mrs Jackson had told Mrs Morgan of her life, which was considerably different from the working class existence in Lancashire. She was born in India, daughter of a famous Scottish family. They had left the country when she was six because of a stabbing – a bad scar on her leg had been caused by an Indian servant who had attacked her. Back in England she had fallen in love with the family's butler at their house in Portman Square and had eloped with him.

The police had a different story and confirmed Madame Le Grys/Jackson as Kate Atkinson, the daughter of a Lancashire labourer. There could be no doubt – a deformed thumb was proof. It was, however, correct that she had also operated under a wide variety of names: Mary Kathleen Hamilton, Mrs Hamilton, Mrs Amber, Mme Humber, Mrs Gordon Irwin and Molly Ingram. In the village of Frimley, near Ash Vale, neighbours, no doubt encouraged by Mrs Jackson, had thought she was Ethel M. Dell, the famous woman romantic novelist of the time. (Mrs Dell denied any knowledge of, or connection with, Mrs Jackson. She had never, she said, employed the woman as her literary agent.)

Mr Jackson then ventured to describe their first meeting. He had been buying some fish in Lyons Corner House in Piccadilly in 1919 when his future wife approached him, saying he reminded her of a friend, Lord Carroll. She had told him that he was too ill to eat cold fish and had bought him an expensive meal. They spent the afternoon together and married shortly afterwards. This was later amended to a marriage in Cardiff in February 1922.

The inquest was opened on 15 February and it appeared that at least the mystery of Mrs Jackson's identity was solved. Her birth certificate was produced and showed she had been born in Wray, Lancashire, on 26 July 1885.

On 18 February the police removed the back door from Kenilworth and on Saturday, 23 February they arrested Jackson and charged him with Kate Jackson's murder.

The case for the prosecution was that Mrs Jackson had been beaten with a tyre lever after she had taken off her coat which was then thrown over her head to deaden her screams. The blows were struck in the scullery inside the bungalow and Mrs Jackson then staggered outside to try to escape. The significance of the back door was that there was blood on it which the police said had been caused by Mrs Jackson's head touching it. The prosecution were also able to show that Jackson had behaved in an odd fashion that night. When the doctor had arrived Jackson had chatted about the state of the roads and high taxation. It was the doctor who had called the hospital. On the way back from the hospital where his wife had been detained Jackson had made no comment to the police about the incident. To further confuse matters, a Nathaniel Rees came to court to say that he had married Marthe Louise Gordon Ingram in January 1917 in Newport. He had last seen Jackson at his home in 1918 when he was staying with a 'Mrs Jones'. In the room they shared had been a marriage certificate which showed Marthe's prior marriage to Harry Gordon Ingram. It disappeared when Jackson and 'Mrs Jones' left and it was assumed Jackson had stolen it to give credibility to her claim to the name Ingram. Jackson was committed for trial to the Glamorgan Assizes.

He appeared there on 1 July. The allegation basically remained the same: he had killed her inside the house because he had a violent temper and was tired of supporting her. The prosecution's case was that the money stolen by Harrison from the National Association of Coopers had been repaid by the Jacksons selling their rather larger home and moving to the bungalow. Now they were able to show two marriages between the Jacksons, the first, which the Crown alleged, was at her instigation when, as Kate Atkinson, she had married him as Captain Gordon Ingram. There was conflicting evidence about his attitude when he had found his wife attacked. Mrs Dimmock said he had told her to go to bed, but other witnesses had said he appeared to be upset. The worst piece of evidence against him was that there was a tyre lever under what was described as the dunny seat. Jackson's explanation, and it never improved, was that, despite the fact that he already had one, his wife might have left it there as a present. When later, in a most hostile summing-up, Mr Justice Wright described Jackson as quick-witted, he was probably putting his intelligence too highly. He would have done better to say his wife had the tyre lever there for her protection.

For that was one of the highlights of his case. Both defence and prosecution witnesses alike said that Kate Jackson was a frightened woman, particularly when a strange car drew up. She had kept two revolvers in the house and on one occasion when she had heard a car she had run naked from the bathroom onto the veranda. She had also received hate mail from miners describing her as a 'robber of miners' money' and another which specifically put the case against her: 'How many more men have you blackmailed until they have to pinch money until they shut you up?' The prosecution suggested that Jackson himself had written these letters.

Jackson was also helped by the evidence of a young girl, Gertrude Owen, who said that about the time of the attack she saw a man near the bungalow run away and cross a stream. Nothing of Jackson's case appealed to the judge, who dismissed the stories about Mrs Jackson, saying there were no mysteries about her after 1910: 'Since then all her movements have been known.' He added that the possibility of someone killing her and slipping off was 'very bare': 'Where there is sufficient evidence of fact other directions [such as] the question of motive ought not to be important.'

The jury would have none of it. On 7 July they retired for only thirty minutes before returning a verdict of not guilty, something which was greeted with 'cheering and clapping' both inside and outside the court.

Amelia 'Millie' Jeffs *see* Elizabeth Carter

Helen Jerome

On 27 August 1958 the body of the fifty-year-old British stage actress, Helen Jerome, was found in the ground-floor apartment at the residential hotel on North Las Palmas Avenue, Los Angeles, in which she lived. Her seventy-year-old estranged husband Edwin, himself a Broadway and Hollywood character actor – he had recently appeared in *Gigi* – with whom she remained on good terms, had telephoned her a number of times and, getting a constant engaged signal, had gone round to see if she was all right. At first sight it appeared she might have had a heart attack. It was then thought that, as her comeback as a film star in Hollywood had not exactly taken off and there were a number of bottles of sleeping pills in her bathroom and at the bedside, she might have committed suicide. Her problem was alcoholism coupled with a vile temper and an inability to appear on the set on time. Detectives then noticed a bruise on the side of her neck.

As the investigation continued it became clear that Helen Jerome had been in the habit of picking up young men in late-night bars and clubs and taking them back to her apartment. The investigation now switched to the theory that she was another victim of a Hollywood strangler who had attacked a number of lone women about that time.

A number of arrests were made, including the night manager of the hotel, who had boasted that he had been one of Helen Jerome's lovers. He was cleared. The most promising candidate was a Latin American looking man whom the hotel staff said had been with her the night she had died. A young car valet from Texas was arrested and, after some initial denials, he admitted he had been with her in a bar. He said he had walked home after she had told him she was not feeling well. After lie-detector and fingerprint tests he was released. In October a coroner's jury returned an open verdict. Edwin Jerome died a year later of natural causes.

John Austin, *Hollywood's Unsolved Murders*

Brian Jones

On 3 July 1969 ex-Rolling Stones guitarist, Brian Jones, was found dead in his swimming pool at his eleven-acre estate, Cotchford Farm in Sussex. High levels of drugs and alcohol were found in the body and at the inquest a verdict of death by misadventure was returned. Jones had been sacked by the band following a long period of rivalry with Mick Jagger. From then on his career had spiralled downhill. At the time of his death he was some £160,000 in debt.

Over the years there have been rumours that Jones's death was not an accident. In 1994 two rival books were published in which it was claimed that he had been deliberately drowned during a late-night swim by Frank Thorogood, a London builder who was working on Jones's property. The killing was said to

Brian Jones.

have two motives: the first was straight-forward theft – after Jones died substantial sums of cash disappeared from his house. The second was to prevent the uncovering of a long-running fraud which, it is argued, Thorogood was operating against Jones. The claim, based on tape recordings of a witness, is that Thorogood and an unnamed assistant held Jones underwater. The analysis of the drugs and alcohol in the body is misleading, says Geoffrey Giuliano, one of the rival authors. He maintains that the quantity in the body would not have affected Jones's ability to swim.

Conveniently Thorogood died in November 1993 and so a libel action cannot be brought, which is why he has now been named. His daughter, Janis Bell, has denied the allegations telling the *Mail on Sunday* (3 April 1994), 'I know my father was not capable of murder. Dad was not an aggressive man. I never saw him lose his temper and he thought the world of Brian. People have said he was jealous of Brian and didn't get on with him, but that's nonsense.' (The name of the book by Terry Rawlings derives from the fact that a previous owner of Cotchford Farm was the author A. A. Milne who wrote the *Winnie the Pooh* books.)

Geoffrey Guiliano, *Paint it Black: The Murder of Brian Jones*; Terry Rawlings, *Who Killed Christopher Robin?*

Christine Jones

On 1 September 1977 seventeen-year-old Christine Jones, who lived with her parents in Boulder Heights, Colorado, told them she was going to wash her car. She left the house at 9.30 a.m. and when she had not returned by noon a search was instigated. Her body was found at Lefthand Creek, about one and a half miles above Buckingham Park. She had been shot with a .38 gun and sexually assaulted. Although latent fingerprints were discovered they were never matched. It was thought she had been lured into a van and then taken to the creek road and dumped 50 feet from a busy road. Until the fingerprints can be matched no charges will ever be made.

Diane Jones

On 23 July 1983 Diane Jones, left the Woolpack public house, Coggeshall, Essex, after a row with her doctor husband Robert. She was two months pregnant. Things had not been going well between the doctor and his wife and he said they were on the point of splitting up. On 2 August he reported her missing but it was not until 21 October that her body was found by members of a shooting party in woods at Brightwell near the Suffolk Police headquarters. On 14 November Dr Jones was questioned intensively by the police. The interrogation lasted on and off for fifty-five hours until his solicitors applied for and were granted a writ of *habeus corpus* to prevent further questioning. He was released on police bail and returned to Ipswich police station on 9 February 1984 when he was again released and told the papers in the case would be sent to the Director of Public Prosecutions. On 5 April of that year the DPP announced that no charges would be brought against him. In March 1990 a new witness came forward and the investigation was re-opened but no progress was made. No charges have ever been preferred.

Violette Kaye *see* **Brighton Trunk Murders**

John Fitzgerald Kennedy

On Friday, 21 November 1963 John Fitzgerald Kennedy, the President of the United States of America, was shot to death as he drove in a motorcade through Dallas, Texas. He was there to heal what were seen to be political difficulties between the rival wings of the Democratic party before the primaries began in February for the 1964 elections. Dallas was by no means receptive to the President. There was an extreme right-wing element present and there had been physical hostility displayed to Lyndon and Lady Bird Johnson during the 1960 campaign. Before the drive through the city, pamphlets with the President's photograph in the form of a 'Wanted' poster were being handed out. Much of the citizenry, backed by the *Dallas Morning News,* believed that the President was selling out to communism throughout the world.

Kennedy, his wife Jacqueline and Governor John Connally and his wife Nellie were in a Lincoln convertible with security guards in the front. At 12.30 p.m., as they drove from Houston onto Elm, they passed the Texas School Book Depository. A shot, followed by two others, was fired. One bullet hit the President in the neck. A second shot took off the top right-hand side of his head and Connally was hit with a bullet which entered his back, spun round through his chest, breaking a rib, exiting through his wrist and stopping in his thigh. The official line is that it was the same bullet which killed the President.

Both men were rushed to hospital and, at 1.45 p.m., a bullet fell from a stretcher pad. It was believed that this bullet had passed through Kennedy and then entered the Governor. This was the beginning of the lone gunman theory. At 1.16 p.m. a police officer, J. D. Tippett, was shot dead in the Oak Cliff section of Dallas and some witnesses said the killer matched the description of the assassin. At 1.51 a man was seen to run into the Texas Theatre. He was chased by officers, disarmed when he pulled a .38 Smith & Wesson and was arrested. That man was Lee Harvey Oswald who worked at the Book Depository. He was taken to Dallas City jail where, when questioned, he denied he had been involved in either killing and called out to reporters that he was just a patsy.

The police interviewed some 266 witnesses. Thirty-two believed the shots came from the Book Depository; fifty-one had heard shots from a grassy knoll towards which the motorcade was travelling; some heard shots from both directions. Now the alternatives to the lone gunman theory sprang up.

On Sunday morning, watched by millions of television viewers, Oswald, who still denied his guilt, was being moved to the county jail when he was shot by Jack Ruby, a Dallas stripclub and bar owner. Oswald died an hour and a half later whilst undergoing surgery. Ruby told Tom Howard, the first lawyer to represent him, that he was acting alone to spare Mrs Kennedy the pain and suffering of returning to the city for Oswald's trial. He denied receiving any help from the Dallas police. He was represented at his trial by the celebrated F. Lee Bailey who pleaded 'psychomotor variant epilepsy' on his behalf, the effect of which was to suggest that Ruby was not responsible for his actions. This ingenious defence failed to convince the court and Ruby was sentenced to die in the electric chair. He appealed the conviction and was granted a re-trial which he was awaiting when he died on 3 January 1966 of a blood clot on his lung. The previous month he had been diagnosed as having cancer.

Within a week of taking office President Lyndon Johnson had ordered the Chief Justice, Earl Warren, to hold a Commission to determine the facts surrounding the assassination. The Commission failed to keep to its reporting deadline of 30 June but reached its conclusion at the end of September. The findings of the Commission were simple: it was sad, but true, that both men were mad men acting independently. It is also a sad fact that within three years of the assassination some eighteen key witnesses died – six were shot, three died in car accidents, three had heart attacks, two committed suicide, one was given a karate chop to the neck, one suffered a throat slashing and two died of natural causes.

The verdict of the Warren Commission was challenged fourteen years later when, in December 1978, the House Select Committee on Assassinations concluded that Kennedy 'was probably assassinated as a result of a conspiracy'. Since a conspiracy need only be between two people, that does not take things very much further. The Committee did clarify their position and specifically excluded from blame and involvement the Soviet Union, Cuba, Organised Crime, and anti-Castro groups, and, on the side of law and order, the CIA, the FBI and the Secret Service. It is difficult to see just who was left.

Who were Oswald and Ruby? Oswald was a communist sympathiser who had lived in Russia, returning in 1963 to espouse the causes of Fair Play for Cuba and the politically opposite China Lobby. He certainly had links with the FBI, one of whose offices he had threatened to burn down. He may, or may not, have been directly involved with all or any of the CIA, the FBI or Soviet intelligence. He may simply have been mad. Ruby was possibly an informer for the FBI. He certainly had links with organised crime – as the owner of a stripclub it would have been almost impossible for him not to. Efforts have been made to establish links between Oswald and Ruby but they have not been successful.

After the Warren report, the conspiracy theories began to proliferate with Jim Garrison, District Attorney of New Orleans, leading the way. It is possible to make out a case for most of those factions eliminated by the Warren Commission to have been involved. It is really a question of paying one's money and making one's choice.

Mark Lane, *Rush to Judgment;* Anthony Sampson, *Official and Confidential;* Kirk Wilson, *Investigating Murder*

Dot King

On 15 March 1923 twenty-nine-year-old playgirl Dot King was found dead in her New York bedroom apparently of an overdose of chloroform. An inspection of the body by the celebrated coroner, Charles Norris, showed that one arm had been twisted behind her back, that there were scratches on her face and some burn marks. The police now became more interested in a murder theory. There was no shortage of suspects.

Dot King had been born Anna Marie Keenan into a poor Irish family. She married a chauffeur before she was eighteen but, as her modelling career progressed, she discarded him and her given name. Now she was Dot King. She became a fashionable hostess in a speakeasy where she met an older man named Marshall who, in the year of their association, gave her money and presents totalling something in the region of $30,000. Marshall's yellow pyjamas were found on a chair and he was known to have spent part of the night of 14 March with her.

Dot King also had a Latin lover, a small time gigolo, Alberto Santos Guimares. Theirs was a difficult relationship – she paid for him; he beat her. He was, however, able to provide an alibi. Dot was not the only woman to benefit from his favours. At the time of her death he had been with another and more socially acceptable woman, Aurelia Dreyfus, who backed his story.

Mr Marshall was traced and identified as J. Kearsley Marshall, the wealthy son-in-law of a Philadelphia millionaire. Was it possible she was blackmailing Marshall who, for a man with a socialite wife and three children, had written some indiscreet letters?

> Darling Dottie: Only two days before I will be in your arms. I want to see you, O so much, and to kiss your pretty pink toes.

As to his movements at the time of the murder, he claimed he had left Dot King in the early hours of 15 March. The police eventually solved the case by saying that Dot King had died in a robbery gone wrong. They theorised that she had opened the door to 'delivery men' who had administered too much chloroform.

A year later Aurelia Dreyfus fell to her death from a window in her hotel suite. Papers were discovered which indicated she had lied to protect Guimares, who was now arrested over her death. He was released without charge.

Kingsbury Run *see* **Edward Andrassy**

Wendy Knell

Shortly after 11 p.m. on 22 June 1987 Wendy Knell left her boyfriend and went to her flat in Guildford Road, Tunbridge Wells, Kent. The next day she did not arrive for her job at Supasnaps in the town and colleagues asked her friend if he knew where she was. In turn he went to the flat and after climbing in through an open window found her body on her bed. She had been strangled, beaten about the head and sexually assaulted.

The Kent police linked the case to the killing later that year of twenty-year-old Caroline Pierce who was taken to her flat by taxi on the night of 24 November. She did not turn up for work the next day at Buster Brown's restaurant in Camden Road. Three weeks later her body was found in a field off Chittenden Lane in St Mary in the Marsh, some forty miles from Tunbridge Wells. One link was that both girls had distinctive keyrings, and each of which was taken. In both cases a car was seen outside their flats. In the case of Wendy Knell it was a light blue Talbot Horizon; in the case of Caroline Pierce possibly a Vauxhall Carlton. No one was charged with either killing.

Suzy Lamplugh

Estate agent Suzy Lamplugh disappeared on 25 July 1986 after leaving her office to show a client, noted on her blotter as Mr Kipper, a property in Shorrolds Road, Fulham, South-west London. She had left her handbag on her desk and when she had not returned by the late afternoon a massive search was organised. Her car was found parked in Stevenage Road, a mile from Shorrolds Road and further away from her office than the property to which she was taking the client. A number of witnesses said they had seen her carrying what appeared to be a bottle of champagne. Enquiries were made both in the United Kingdom and the Continent during which a Mr Kuyper was traced. He was a wholly innocent Belgian whose car was found abandoned in England.

There were suggestions that Mr Kipper was Cockney rhyming slang for Jack the Ripper. Another unproved suggestion was that her murderer was rapist

John Cannan who, the following year, was convicted of the murder of Shirley Banks who had disappeared whilst shopping in Bristol. Cannan had only been released from prison three days before the death of Suzy Lamplugh. In prison he had been known as 'Kipper' because of his love of 'kipper' or very wide ties.

A very similar case was that of Canadian realtor, MaryAnn Plett (*qv*).

John Lane
(aka Gobba)

In late November 1990 John Lane, alias John Gobba, was found shot by a single bullet in the back. His body had been buried under a pile of rubble on a building site in Limehouse, East London. He had a curious tie-in with a case which had been heard at Southwark Crown Court earlier in the month when high-living Peruvian, Rene Black – he had wanted to be both a top class racing driver and show jumper – who had planned to flood the market with cocaine, earned a fifteen-year sentence and the stripping of his £1.5 million fortune. His slightly reduced sentence was an acknowledgement that he had turned Queen's Evidence. His distribution partner, James Laming, was jailed for eleven years and stripped of £23,950 of his profits. Patrick Fraser, the son of Frankie Fraser, a former member of the Richardson gang, was jailed for eight years.

Former car dealer Laming's defence had been an ingenious one. He had not been dealing with Black over cocaine at all, about which he knew nothing, rather he was attempting to organise horseracing coups. He had, he said, invented an ultrasonic stun gun which could bring down a horse at three furlongs' distance. All you had to do was point and shoot. Laming tested this at Royal Ascot in 1988 when jockey Greville Starkey was brought down on Ile de Chypre while leading the field in the King's Stand Stakes. Very sportingly, Starkey allowed the defence to test out the machine again, this time in the peace of the paddock. But the jury would have none of it. Laming was found guilty on two charges to supply cocaine and one of conspiracy to supply. Lane had been arrested along with Laming at his Holborn flat but had been released when no drugs were found on him. He was a close associate of Lionel Webb (*qv*), ostensibly an estate agent but one who, when his body was found in January 1988, also shot, had a substantial quantity of drugs in his safe.

Florence Little *see* **Freda Burnell**

Charles Lindbergh Jnr

On 1 March 1932 Charlie, the twenty-month-old son of Charles Lindbergh, the first man to fly the Atlantic solo, and Anne Morrow, a poet and writer, daughter of the United States Ambassador to Mexico, was kidnapped from the family home near Hopewell, New Jersey. Charlie had a bad cold and was wrapped up in bed with the window left open. The usual nightlight had been extinguished and the room had faulty shutters. A ladder had been placed against the house and, it appeared, entry had been effected that way.

A ransom of $50,000, later increased to $70,000, was demanded and paid on 2 April. Lindbergh was told in a note that the child would be found safe and well:

> the boy is on Boad Nelly
> it is a small Boad 28 feet
> long, two person are on the
> Boad, the are innosent.
> you will find the Boad between
> Horseneck Beach and gay Head
> near Elizabeth Island

Charlie's body was discovered on 12 May in woods near Hopewell. The first of the bills paid over on the ransom came to light on 4 April, and on 16 September a gold certificate bill presented by Richard 'Bruno' Hauptmann, a carpenter who lived with his wife and young son, Mannfred, in the Bronx, was recognised as being part of the ransom money. He was arrested three days later and, indicted for extortion, was sent to Flemington, New Jersey, to await his trial.

The hard evidence against him ran basically that he was found in possession of $14,000 in gold certificate bills of which only $100 could legally be held at a time (which he certainly was), that the ladder left propped against the Lindbergh house had been repaired and that he was a carpenter (again correct), that the note had probably been written by a German (which he certainly was). There was also rather more dubious evidence, some of which, according to later writers on the case, was fabricated.

After the disappearance of little Charlie Lindbergh, his father took a leading part in negotiations with the kidnappers. At first members of the Underworld were recruited, but their efforts came to nothing except to say that they were sure it was not a professional matter. Following that a seventy-two-year-old teacher at Fordham University, Dr John Condon, wrote to the editor of the *Bronx Home News*, to which he was a contributor, volunteering his services as negotiator if they cared to contact him. The letter was published in full. Surprisingly the kidnappers did contact him, and it was his evidence which would later go a long way to convicting Hauptmann. A preliminary meeting was set up on 12 March in the Woodlawn cemetery in the Bronx where, according to Condon, he met Cemetery John whom he later identified as Hauptmann. On 2 April he was driven by Lindbergh to St Raymond's cemetery, also in the Bronx, where the money was handed over and where Lindbergh heard a voice, which a year and a half later he testified as Hauptmann's, calling, 'Hey, Doc!'

After Hauptmann had handed over the gold certificate bill his car number was taken and traced. He was an illegal immigrant to the States with convictions in Germany for theft and robbery, something he blamed on the privations fol-

lowing World War I. What was clear, however, was that he had worked hard during his time in America and, a skilled carpenter, had made a good life for himself and his family amongst the German community in the Bronx. It is now that versions of the case begin to differ.

The prosecution's case was that he was working singlehandedly in both the kidnap and the subsequent negotiations. Those who defend Hauptmann argue with some force that he could not possibly have been working alone. There must have been more than one kidnapper – apart from anything else there were two pairs of footprints outside the Lindbergh house – and almost certainly it was an inside job.

Charles Lindberg Jnr.

There is little doubt that Hauptmann was railroaded. Condon, who would later appear on the vaudeville circuit rather as Monson did, was threatened with being charged as an accomplice if he did not identity Hauptmann as Cemetery John. It is difficult to believe that Hauptmann would make such a botched job of the work on the ladder, a rung of which was identified as coming from wood at his home. There was evidence that he had written the ransom note.

He was not well defended – his senior counsel, Edward Reilly, was drinking heavily and within a few years was confined in a hospital for a syphillitic condition. Even so he had a great problem to overcome – what was a little under a quarter of the ransom money doing in his home? Hauptmann's story was that he had been in business with a part-time fur dealer and whole-time German con-man, Isidor Fisch, who had swindled him out of $7,000. Fisch, whom he still trusted at the time, had left a box with him before returning for a holiday in Germany where he had died. Hauptmann had opened the box, seen the money and kept it all. There was no one to support the account, but it is obvious why Fisch could not have banked it. Another problem was that Lindbergh was a national hero and the kidnapping of his child was rightly regarded as an outrage. When Lindbergh identified Hauptmann's voice as the man in the cemetery, he was done for. Worse, Hauptmann had initially denied having the $14,000. He was caught lying, he was a robber and an illegal immigrant.

Nevertheless there were a number of people who were by no means convinced of his guilt, including the Governor of New Jersey, Harold Hoffman, who saw Hauptmann in prison, called for the papers and effectively re-opened the case. He argued loud and hard for a reprieve, but on 11 January 1936 the New Jersey Court of Pardons confirmed the death sentence. Hoffmann once more granted a stay of execution, but on 3 April Hauptmann was executed. Throughout he had refused to confess to the crime, although he had been offered a term of life imprisonment in exchange for the story of how he had committed the crime, and a New York newspaper had promised his wife the considerable sum of $90,000 following a confession.

What has become clear over the years is that much evidence which would have gone at the very least to raise considerable doubt in the jury's mind was suppressed or doctored. Hauptmann had an alibi for the day of the kidnapping. He had been working but, it is argued forcefully by Ludovic Kennedy in his book *The Airman and the Carpenter*, the records were tampered with. Kennedy's assessment of the case against Hauptmann has come under considerable fire from, amongst others, Jonathan Goodman.

It is difficult to see how it cannot have been an inside job. The Lindberghs had decided only that day to remain another night in their new home. How could Hauptmann, or indeed anyone, have known in which room the baby would be sleeping without inside help? Suspicion at the time fell on an English parlour-maid, Violet Sharpe, who was said to have had an affair with the Lindberghs' drunken butler, Septimus Banks. When questioned about her movements on the night of the kidnapping, she said at first that she had been at the cinema and then that she had been in a road-house with a man. She was re-interviewed on

21 May and was in a state almost amounting to collapse. During which time, however, when she did speak, she made further contradictory statements. She was due to be interviewed yet again on 10 June when she killed herself by drinking crystals of cyanide chloride dissolved in water. The crystals were more usually used for polishing silver.

The police were convinced she had been involved. 'The suicide of Violet Sharpe strongly tends to confirm the suspicions of the investigating authorities concerning her guilty knowledge of the crime against Charles Augustus Lindbergh,' said Norman Schwartzkopf, the officer initially in charge of the case. Inspector Walsh, who interviewed her, said, 'I am convinced that Violet Sharpe deceived us and that she did so deliberately. I am convinced that she was the informant and agent for the kidnappers.' Kennedy believes that active participation was beyond Sharpe, but that she might have inadvertently passed on information which was subsequently used in the crime. There is no evidence that she ever came into contact with Hauptmann.

Jonathan Goodman, *The Modern Murder Yearbook*; Ludovic Kennedy, *The Airman and the Carpenter*; Anthony Scaduto, *Scapegoat*; Frank Wilson and B. Day, *Special Agent*

Dora Alicia Lloyd

The body of prostitute Dora Lloyd, who had described herself to her landlady as an actress, was found on 21 February 1932 after the police had received a message from a man to say that a woman had been found dead in a house in Maida Vale, London. She had been beaten and strangled.

The previous evening she had been working in the West End where she had been seen to pick up a client and leave with him in a taxi. He was described as young, slim, clean-shaven and wearing horn-rimmed glasses. Although there were others in the house to which Mrs Lloyd took her client, only one appeared to have heard anything. He told the police he had noticed a queer gurgling noise, as if someone was being strangled, coming from the room below his. He then heard a door bang and went down to investigate. He saw Mrs Lloyd's body on the bed and it was he who had called the police.

Two days later a girl was picked up by a man at Piccadilly Circus. As they got into a taxi a number of girls gathered round and told the driver the man was the murderer. The man stopped the driver in the Strand and got out. Later the driver found the man, this time off Leicester Square. They spoke and the man said this was not the first time he had been identified. The taxi driver's description of the man did not tally with the one who had gone off with Dora Lloyd.

There were at least a dozen murders of prostitutes in the West End during that period, and in one year alone four were strangled. The name of Frederick Field, who was acquitted of the murder of Nora Upchurch (*qv*) and convicted of that of Beatrice Sutton, is often linked to the crimes.

George Cornish, *Cornish of the Yard*

Irene Lockwood *see* **Hannah Tailford**

Caroline Mary Luard

On 24 August 1908 the 58-year-old Caroline Mary Luard, the handsome wife of Major-General Charles Luard, was found shot dead in a summerhouse near their home in Ightham Knoll, Kent. They had gone out together at about 2.30 that afternoon. The General went to collect his golf clubs from the nearby Godden Green club whilst his wife went walking in the country. Luard refused a lift home from a friend and whilst having tea with a Mrs Stuart at around 4.30 speculated as to where his wife might be. In the evening he went looking for his wife and found her body. Four valuable rings had been taken from her fingers. The time of death was fixed at 3.15 p.m. when a farmer heard shots.

Neither Luard nor his wife had apparent enemies and for no very clear reason he became the chief suspect at the inquest. At the second inquest he established an alibi. He was seen on the 18th green at 3.30 p.m. and the club members and secretary saw nothing amiss in his demeanour. A verdict of murder by persons unknown was returned, but the general suffered a mental collapse and threw himself under a train at West Farleigh leaving a note: 'I have gone to her I love. Goodbye. Something has snapped'.

One suspect of the killing has been John Dickman, a bookmaker who was hanged for the robbery/murder of John Nisbet in July 1910. He was out of his area at the time of the Luard killing and was known to be short of money. There was some evidence that he had forged a cheque sent by Mrs Luard as a response to an advertisement for financial help.

Colin Wilson and Patricia Pitman, *Encyclopaedia of Murder*; Julian Symonds, *A Reasonable Doubt*

Countess Teresa Lubinska

O n 24 May 1957 the seventy-three-year-old Polish countess, who had survived imprisonment in Ravensbruck, was stabbed through the heart in London on the platform of Gloucester Road tube station. She had been known as the Angel of Ravensbruck because of her bravery and the efforts she had made to comfort her fellow prisoners.

Countess Teresa Lubinska.

That day she had attended a Polish-Catholic name-day celebration at the home of friends in Ealing and had been in the company of a priest, Father Kazimeirz, until he got off one stop earlier at Earls Court. At 10.19 p.m. she alighted and three minutes later she collapsed in the lift saying, 'Bandits, bandits.' She died before reaching hospital. Her last words were, 'I was on the platform and I was stabbed.' She had, in fact, been stabbed five times in the chest with a knife whose blade was about two inches long.

Escape for the killers was simple – the lift shaft at Gloucester Road is not deep and a fit man could run up the emergency stairs in forty-five seconds. In those days the lift took fifty-eight seconds. Motive was more of a problem. Robbery could be excluded because the Countess still had on a silver brooch and her handbag with her. A politically motivated killing was then suggested: she was opposed to the post-war Polish government, whom she castigated both volubly and at length. She was also the chairwoman of various Free Polish organisations throughout Britain. The Polish community believed it could have been an attack by ex-Nazis as an act of reprisal against her railings against that regime. The more prosaic explanation is that probably she criticised the behaviour of some Teddy boys who attacked her or that the killing was a robbery but that she held onto her handbag so denying her attackers. Over a period of four years a team of detectives led by some of Scotland Yard's top men of the time – John du Rose and Ted Greeno amongst them – questioned over 20,000 people. No arrests were made. The Countess was posthumously awarded the Golden Cross of Merit with Swords by General Anders, Commander of the Polish Forces in World War II.

Lord Lucan *see* **Sandra Rivett**

Alice Mackenzie (aka Clay Pipe Alice) *see* **Mary Anne 'Polly' Nicholls**

Joseph Maggio

On 24 May 1918 Joseph Maggio, an Italian grocer living in New Orleans, and his wife were attacked in their room in the house they shared with his brothers, Jake and Andrew. Jake Maggio had heard noises and together with his brother had gone to Joe's room to find Mrs Maggio lying in a pool of blood with her head almost severed and Joe with his throat cut. Entry to the house had been gained by removing a panel in the back door. The safe door in Joe Maggio's room was open but he had been sleeping with a quantity of money beneath his pillow which was untouched. The police were inclined to believe that the safe door had been opened to fool them into believing the motive was robbery. A bloodstained axe was on the steps to the backyard, as was a cut-throat razor. Both surviving brothers were arrested but later released.

Seven years earlier, in 1911, there had been a spate of axe murders of Italian grocers, including Tony Schiambra and his wife. Now chalked on the pavement near Maggio's shop were the words, 'Mrs Maggio is going to sit up tonight, just like Mrs Toney [sic].' It was thought that the 1911 killings had been protection money murders by members of the Italian Black Hand who had had a strong presence in New Orleans for the previous forty years.*

On 28 June 1918 another grocery shop owner, Louis Besumer, was found by a delivery man. He had been attacked, as had the *soi-disant* Mrs Besumer, Harriet Lowe. This time both survived, she to accuse Besumer whom, for good measure, she alleged was a German spy. He was arrested but she then withdrew her allegations. Later, in hospital and seriously ill, she accused Besumer once more and then died. He was charged with her murder.

---

* On 15 October 1890 Police Chief David Hennessy was murdered by Mafia connections in the city. He had been investigating a feud between the Mafia and the Camorra. On 14 March 1891, under the leadership of W. S. Parkerson, a New Orleans lawyer, they stormed the jail lynching and shooting the Sicilians on remand there. If anything, this outrage seemed to strengthen the position of the Mafia which tightened its hold on the city.

It was fortunate for him that the same night the Axeman struck again. Edward Sneider returned home to his pregnant wife to find her covered in blood. She had been asleep, she said, and had awoken to find a man with an axe standing over her. Attacks came swiftly after this. The next victim was a barber, Joseph Romano. His nieces, who slept in the next room, heard noises and saw a dark man, tall and heavy-set with a hat, standing by Romano's bed holding an axe. Again a panel on the back door had been cut to provide access. The last attack that year was on 30 August when a Nick Asunto scared off a man he described as heavily built and with an axe.

Operations were recommenced by the Axeman when, on 10 March 1919, sixty-nine-year-old Iorlando Jordano heard screams from the Cortimiglia household across the street. He and his son went over to find Rosie Cortimiglia holding Mary, her two-year-old daughter, dead in her arms. She had also been hit and her husband, Charles, lay on the floor. For their pains she accused Jordano and his son Frank of being the attackers, even though before he died Charles Cortimiglia said they were nothing like the men.

In the middle of Lent that year the *Times-Picayune* received a letter purportedly from the Axeman saying that he proposed to pay another visit to New Orleans on St Joseph's Night but would spare any household where jazz was being played.

In April 1919 Louis Besumer was acquitted of killing Harriet Lowe. The Jordanos were not so fortunate – against all odds they were convicted. Frank was sentenced to death and his father to life imprisonment.

On 10 August there was another attack and there were subsequent ones at the beginning of September. Although the victims were injured they survived.

On 27 October another grocer, Mike Pepitone, was killed in his bedroom. His wife, who had been sleeping in an adjoining room, heard noises and had run in to find his blood splashed on the wall. Again there had been an entry by the removal of a door panel and a bloodstained axe was on the back porch. It was the last of the killings.*

Meanwhile the Jordanos kept up their appeals against their convictions until, on 7 December 1920, Rosie Cortimiglia went to the offices of the *Times-Picayune* to confess that she had made up her story against the Jordanos because she had hated them. They were released. Shortly before this there had been an incident in Los Angeles when the widow of Mike Pepitone shot and killed Joseph

---

* In 1909 Pepitone's father, Pietro, had refused to pay protection to Paul di Cristina who operated Black Hand activities in New Orleans and shot and killed him. He was released after serving six years of a twenty-year sentence for manslaughter.

Mumfre, whom she alleged was the Axeman. The dates fitted because when there had been a lull in the killings Mumfre had been in prison, but there was no other evidence against him.

Mrs Pepitone pleaded justifiable homicide but was sentenced to ten years' imprisonment. She was released after three. It has been suggested that both the 1911 killings and those at the end of World War I were Mafia operations, but, against this proposition, not all were carried out on Italians. It has also been suggested that there was more than one Axeman.

John Canning (ed), *Unsolved Murders and Mysteries*

Ghislaine Marchal

At 8 p.m. on 24 June 1991 the body of the widow Ghislaine Marchal, owner of La Chamade, a villa on a street the locals called Paradise Row at Mougins near Cannes, France, was discovered by gendarmes who had been alerted by a neighbour. She had been stabbed thirteen times and struck on the head. A widow in her mid-sixties, who drove a white Rolls-Royce, she died in her cellar, apparently after trying to write the name of her killer in her own blood on the wall. She had written, 'Omar m'a tuer,' a reference, the police said, to her Moroccan-born gardener, thirty-one-year-old Omar Raddad. She had clearly struggled with her killer.

Robbery was suggested as a motive and possibly a video recorder was taken. If so it was never traced to Raddad. Mme Marchal was said to have 3,000 francs in her handbag but again this was never found. Raddad's movements on the day of the killing could be traced except for an unfortunate gap of around thirty minutes: he had been working in the garden during the day, observed by the eighty-year-old next-door neighbour Mme Pascal. At noon he had left on his moped and bought a baguette at about 12.20 p.m. He had then returned to his apartment. At ten to one he had set off for work again and had stopped to make a telephone call to his wife who was staying with her sister in Toulon awaiting the birth of a second child. The owner of the next door villa gave him an ice-cream at about 1.30 p.m. and did not notice any injuries on him or anything strange in his behaviour. The first two medical reports failed to state a definite time of death and after what was intended as the definitive autopsy, the time of death was stated to be a day later than originally indicated. This was then passed off as a clerical error.

Raddad always protested his innocence and at one stage of his detention embarked on a forty-day hunger strike. At his trial in Nice the prosecution did its best to destroy Raddad's character – they had trawled the prostitutes in the Cote d'Azur without finding one whom Raddad had patronised. So far as gambling the best they could do was show he played the five-franc slot machines in the casino in Cannes. He was behind with his rent and he had been asking his employers for loans. On the other hand his residence papers were in order and he lived quietly in a two-room flat in Cannes with his wife and two children. He was described as polite and timid. He spoke little French and was barely literate. There was evidence that he had worked honestly and well for Mme Marchal and others in the neighbourhood who trusted him.

But Nice was not a good venue for his trial. The townspeople there were not on the whole favourable to North Africans who were looked on as a generally predatory race. He faced a hostile judge. When evidence was given that Raddad 'wouldn't hurt a fly', the judge remarked, 'No, but he would cut a sheep's throat.'

On 2 February 1994 Omar Raddad was convicted of the murder and sentenced to eighteen years imprisonment. It was a decision which displeased a number of people, including Jean-Marie Rouart, literary editor of *Le Figaro*, who describes the conduct of the police as 'irretrievable negligence'. Raddad's supporters point to the appalling grammar displayed by the dying woman when she wrote on the wall. It should read, 'Omar m'a tuee,' something which would be known to school children. They asked whether Ghislaine Marchal, by making such an elementary error, was trying to alert the police to the fact that she was writing under duress or whether the murderer, himself with no command of French grammar, was trying to implicate Raddad. Unfortunately no fingerprints of Marchal were taken and the body was cremated at an early stage in the investigation. Those who seek to uphold the conviction suggest that the grammatical error was an understandable error by a dying woman.

Mme Pascal, who obtained some fame in the press as a sort of French Mrs Marples, suggested that Mme Marchal had been very secretive about her bank accounts in Switzerland and that the police would do well to check out that end of matters. On the day of her death a car with Swiss plates had been seen near La Chamade.

Georgi Markov

On 7 September 1979 at around 6 p.m. Georgi Markov was walking in the Strand, London, when he was stabbed in the right thigh with the point of an umbrella. A refugee from Bulgaria who had been living in Britain for ten years, Markov was on his way to broadcast a World Service news bulletin to Bulgaria. The man who had seemingly merely touched him, apologised and then hailed a passing cab. By the end of the evening Markov's leg was stiff and he felt feverish. His wife took him to hospital the next day but the doctors were unable to explain the mark on his leg. He died on 11 September. In the post-mortem a miniscule hollowed out pellet, made from an alloy of platinum and iridium, was found in his thigh. He had been poisoned with ricin, a derivative of castor oil seeds.

The tiny pellet, in a glass case, that contained enough poison to kill Georgi Markov. It measures just 1.53mm in diameter.

Another Bulgarian defector had been attacked in a similar way. On 24 August 1978 Vladimir Kostov was shot in a Paris street but on this occasion the pellet did not contain sufficient poison and he had felt nothing more than a stinging sensation in his back. Although never proved, it is reasonable to assume that both attacks were the work of the Bulgarian secret police, the Dazjavna Sigurnost.

Ginger Marks

On 2 January 1965 Marks, a small-time London criminal, simply disappeared. At once there sprang up a whole series of rumours about him and his whereabouts. First there was a story that he had been involved in the 'Jack the Stripper' nude murders (*Hannah Tailford qv*). Almost immediately petrol bombs were thrown into the office of a suburban newspaper after it had run a story linking those murders to Marks.

From a chip found in the wall in Cheshire Street in the East End, the police believed he had been shot in the stomach. A dig took place on a local bomb site but there was no trace of the body. Three weeks later no one was any nearer a solution. Now came a suggestion in the *Daily Sketch* that his body had been thrown in the Thames in concrete. Next the police thought the killing had a link with the Great Train Robbery.* So the *News of the World* offered a reward of £5,000 for information leading to the recovery of Marks or his body. A couple of days later the paper was on the right track.

'It is accepted that he was the unintended victim of a "crime of passion" feud between two South London gangs,' wrote their major crime reporter Peter Earle.

It was ten years before George Evans, known as Jimmy, a hard and quick-tempered Welshman, was arrested for the attempted murder of George Foreman, who at one time ran a club with Buster Edwards and whose brother Freddie was a close friend of the Kray Twins. The prosecution's case was that on 17 December 1964 George Foreman was shot by Evans because he had suspected his wife was carrying on with another man. By hiding out in the boot of her car he had discovered that man to be George Foreman. He borrowed a single-barrelled twelve-bore shotgun but returned it because it was not powerful enough. He then borrowed a double-barrelled shotgun which he shortened.

On 11 April Evans was acquitted of shooting Foreman and having a shotgun and triumphantly gave an interview to the *News of the World*. He claimed he was continually being framed by police because he would not talk about the disappearance of Marks.

'Think what happens when a car breaker compresses a car into a cube box of metal no bigger than a cornflake box,' said Evans in the witness box, going on to deny that he and Ginger had been up to no good on the night of the latter's disappearance.

On 10 January 1975 the police arrested Jeremiah Callaghan, Alf Gerard and Ronald James Everett. By now Evans, serving a seven-year sentence for manslaughter, was prepared to give evidence. He said that he, Marks and three others had been involved in a night raid on a jewellers. When they failed to get in they noticed a red car of the 1100 type following them near the Carpenters Arms in Cheshire Street, Bethnal Green.

The car drew up beside them and a voice called out, 'Jimmy come here.' Marks thought it was 'Ginge' and he stepped forward. Three shots rang out and

---

* In one version of the Great Train Robbery story, Marks was the man engaged to burn down Leatherslade farm, but failed to do so.

Ginger fell. He was another who just happened to be in the wrong place at the wrong time. Evans ran round the corner and climbed under a lorry, clinging to the transmission link. Marks's body was bundled into a car and driven away. Evans named the attackers as Alf Gerard, Ronald James Everett, Jeremiah Callaghan and Frederick Foreman.

On 30 October 1975 Gerard, Callaghan and Foreman were acquitted by Mr Justice Donaldson. 'The problems with identification are very real. This crime is ten years old. The first time Mr Evans condescended to say it was these three men who were in the car was last year,' said the trial judge. Ronald Everett had been acquitted earlier in the trial.

Outside the Old Bailey, Alfred Gerard commented, 'This is the end of a nightmare for us. Justice has been done at last.'*

Over the years various suggestions have been made as to Mark's last resting place, including a funeral parlour in South London said to be used for the victims of Gangland killings. It is more probable that his body was fed to pigs on a Hampshire farm.

In August 1981 Gerard was found dead in a flat in Brighton, the year his son Nicky (*qv*) was put on trial for the killing of Zomparelli. An inquest showed he had died of cirrhosis of the liver. The preferred version, more in keeping with his lifestyle and culinary artistry, is that he choked over a lobster.

James Morton, *Gangland*

Marius Martin

O n the night of 5–6 December 1894, the French-born thirty-nine-year-old Martin, a night porter at the Cafe Royal in Regent Street, London, was found unconscious in the exit to Glasshouse Street. He had four wounds to the head and was taken to the Charing Cross Hospital where he died at 3.45 a.m. It is possible that the motive was robbery but, according to Martin Fido, his killer lay in wait for him, hiding in the men's lavatory. Martin was not popular with

---

* Marks's wife, Anne, remarried but did not tell her son Philip of his father's career. He obtained seven O levels and won a medal for encouraging children to help the police. On 10 February 1987 Philip, then aged twenty, was sentenced to twelve years' imprisonment for masterminding a security van ambush in Limehouse, East London, in 1986. His twenty-two-year-old step-brother Robert Judd received ten years for the same offence.

the other staff whom he regularly reported for taking home left-over food. No one was ever charged.

Martin Fido, *The Chronicle of Crime*

Paul Martin *see* Richard Griffin

Pat McAdam

This seventeen-year-old girl disappeared on 19 February 1967 after accepting a lift, along with her friend Hazel Campbell, from a lorry driver. They were going back to Dumfries after a night out in Glasgow. Her friend was dropped off but Pat McAdam was never seen again. Three years after her disappearance a journalist from the Scottish *Daily Record* approached a Dutch psychic, Gerald Croiset, about the case. Croiset became convinced that she had been murdered, and though he unsuccessfully endeavoured to identify the place of her death he was able to describe a bridge.

In 1968 the decomposed body of a young woman, Frances Barker, was discovered at Glenboig. She had disappeared on 10 June. A lorry driver, Thomas Young, was traced through a teenage girl who said she had been raped repeatedly by him after calling at his house looking for a friend. A search of his house at 71 Ashley Street, Glasgow, turned up Frances Baker's powder compact. He was convicted of her murder. During police enquiries he admitted he had given a lift to Pat McAdam but said he had dropped her off at a lay-by near the bridge described by the psychic Croiset after he had had sex with her. He admitted to the police that he had had sex with over 200 women in his lorry, some of whom he had raped when they would not consent. Pat McAdam's body has never been found.

Andrew Boot, *Psychic Murder Hunters*

Jemima McDonald *see* **Patricia Docker**

Marion McDowell

On 6 December 1953, seventeen-year-old Marion McDowell went for a drive with James Wilson, a nineteen-year-old scaffolding rigger. They had been out together a few times in the preceding weeks. According to Wilson, at about 7.40 p.m. they parked in an area for courting couples in Scarborough, a suburb of Toronto. Whilst they were necking, the passenger side door was opened and a flashlight was pointed into the car. They were told, said Wilson, 'This is a stick-up.' He identified the attacker as being about 5'8" tall with a narrow face and, he said, carrying a handgun, either a Walther .38 or a Luger. Wilson was told to hand over his wallet, which he did. He was then hit on the back of the head with two blows and later required seventeen stitches.

Wilson's recollections of the subsequent events were, unsurprisingly, vague. He recalled being in the back of his own car with Marion's body across him, then being alone and of the bandit getting into a second car and driving off. Of Marion there was no sign. He got into the driver's seat and went back to his father who took him to the police. Wilson directed them to the yard where he had woken and there the police found broken locks and a chain. They also found a bar of laundry soap. The back seat of his car was covered in blood, some Wilson's and the rest was believed to be Marion's. His wallet was found back in Scarborough.

There was considerable discussion as to the significance of the soap. There were street suggestions of a botched abortion rather than a robbery but there was anecdotal evidence that McDowell had suffered menstrual pains the previous month. As the last person seen with her, Wilson was under considerable suspicion but although regarded as none too bright, he held firm under lengthy interrogation and came through a lie-detector test with flying colours.

In the late summer of 1954 Robert Fabian of Scotland Yard was brought into the case by the Toronto *Telegram*. He was on a lecture tour in America promoting his latest book and, apart from an effort to solve the mystery, was roped in to boost circulation during a slack period. He was unable to throw light on the case and returned to America to continue his signing tour. The body of Marion McDowell was never found.

The case has interesting comparisons with the Brown-Watson case in Boulder, Colorado (*qv*).

Derrick Murdoch, *Disappearances*

Ken Rex McElroy

On 10 July 1981, Ken Rex McElroy was shot to death in his home town of Skidmore, Missouri. The local town bully, he had effectively terrorised its inhabitants for some years.

His death came as a result of his shooting and wounding a local shopkeeper, Ernest Bowenkamp, who had told one of McElroy's eleven children to return a sweet if she was not paying for it. McElroy had followed the much older Bowenkamp, challenged him to a fight and, when he refused, shot him in the shoulder and neck. He was convicted but released on bail for sentencing hearings.

On 10 July, after he had been drinking at the D&G inn, he was shot dead as he got into his pick-up truck. The shooting was watched by a large crowd, not one of whom was prepared to give evidence. T-shirts appeared in the town with the legend, 'Who killed KR?' on the front and 'Who gives a damn?' on the back.

Margaret McGowan *see* **Hannah Tailford**

Joseph McKinstry *see* **Peggy Richards**

Ernest Clifford Melville

The body of the thirty-five-year-old Ernest Melville, a known homosexual, was found by some children about seventy-five yards from the Full Moon public house on waste ground near Croft Street in the Swansea dock area, on the afternoon of 22 January 1949. It was thought he had been killed around 11 p.m. the previous evening.

Melville was of slight build and about 5'5" in height, one of a family of three sons and three daughters. He had always been regarded as a girlish individual. During that evening, he had been importuning men and indeed had made an indecent assault on one man.

He had been seen in various public houses in the company of two seamen, probably from the merchant navy, in their early twenties and wearing dark blue gaberdine raincoats and dark blue peak caps. One was thought to have some gold insignia on the badge. There were severe injuries to Melville's head, including fractures of his skull; there was evidence of gripping of the throat and the scrotum. The body was fully clothed and the trousers had been ripped down the inside seams from crotch to turn-ups. Some of the fly buttons were undone. Near the body was a plain brass brooch-type tie-pin and an artifical tooth, as well as a white and two black buttons. None of these belonged to Melville.

Dr A. F. Sladden, who conducted the post-mortem, believed the sequence of events had probably been that first Melville's testicles had been squeezed, then he had been throttled into at least helplessness if not unconsciousness. He had then been struck several blows under the chin and to the face, either with a fist or a stone.

The Master of the *SS Killurin*, which had docked at 10.40 p.m. on the evening of the killing, made a statement that to his knowledge none of his men left the ship that night but, if they did, it was certainly not before 11 p.m. The police then turned their attention to other ships which had docked but with no positive result.

The Swansea police then called in Scotland Yard in the form of Detective Inspector Reginal Spooner, who conducted a trawl of men in the locality with any form of sexual conviction, but with no great success. He encountered considerable difficulties in his investigation and wrote to his wife:

> Don't know how long we shall be here – it's a very sticky job, one of the worst I've had. Not very much to go on and all sorts of unreliable information and rumours – and a dock area full of strange people and strangers. Apparently, they have never cleaned up a murder down here, so this may be the one! But we have not had any lucky breaks so far, so am looking forward to one or two, which might make all the difference.

He did not get the breaks. No charges were made. Spooner, whose report on the killing is a model of its kind and can be found in the Public Record Office,

believed he had narrowed the suspects to two but that they were being sheltered by members of the community.*

Iain Adamson, *The Great Detective*

Eleanor Mills *see* **Edward Hall**

Freddie Mills

On 24 July 1965 the former world light-heavyweight boxing champion
Freddie Mills was found dead in his car in an alleyway outside a nightclub
he owned at the top end of the Charing Cross Road, London. He had been shot
through the right eye with a gun owned by, and borrowed from, a woman
friend from the days when he had worked in a boxing booth on fairgrounds. A
coroner's verdict that he had committed suicide was not accepted by his wife,
Chrissie, nor by many members of the boxing community and by many others
who knew him casually. It was rumoured that the Krays, who were regular
visitors to his club, had been involved. In the course of his investigation into the
Twins, the officer in charge, Leonard 'Nipper' Read, re-opened the enquiry.

The most usual version of the rumours had been that a gang operating a
protection racket had been rebuffed when they had approached Freddie. Sometime later one of the other small club owners in the West End had been warned
to keep up his payments or else. He had been told that something would soon
happen in the West End which would underline the warning. The 'something'
was Mills's death.

In his career lasting fourteen years, Mills had had just short of 100 contests
and innumerable bouts in fairground booths. Two of his contests for the world
title were with Gus Lesnevitch at the old Harringay Arena and in the first on 14
May 1946 he took a terrible beating. After these contests he began to suffer from
terrible headaches. On his retirement he became a club-owner and television
personality.

Read recalls that:

* MEPO/3/3125.

The murder theory ran as follows. The Krays had been known to take over clubs. The Krays frequented Mills's club. There was money missing from Freddie's estate – something like £12,000 which was big money in the 1950s. There had been an unsuccessful arson attack on the club. There was the story that some weeks before Freddie's death small operators were told something big was going to happen. Freddie had obtained a gun to protect himself and he had left the club saying he was going to an appointment. Usually Chrissie went with him to the club but on that night she had been delayed and he had gone on alone. Therefore, so the theory ran, it all fell into place and Freddie had been killed to get hold of his club.

In the end Read could find no evidence to support the theory that the Krays were involved in the death. Apart from anything else, the Twins revered him as the boxer they would like to have been. Read also found the club was not doing well. Trade had fallen off disastrously and it wasn't worth taking over – even for free. Read found Mills to have been a terrible businessman, a gambler and, as with so many other sporting celebrities, his star was fading. Others younger were coming to take his place on the programmes. A great friend, singer Michael Holliday, who had appeared with him on the *6.5 Special* show, had killed himself and he, Freddie, had been turned down as a member of a panel set up to discuss the Clay-Liston fight on television. There were also allegations that the club was being frequented by prostitutes posing as hostesses and that a round of drinks and a plate of sandwiches had cost £19 – a fortune at the time. There was no suggestion that either Mills or Andy Ho, his partner, had been involved and clearly the villain was one of the waiters, but it did nothing for his image. Mills issued a writ for libel but this was dropped when the newspaper produced proof of the allegations. He had also had a bad dose of 'flu, almost pneumonia, and had asked whether he could have a 'few quiet words' with his doctor. Andy Ho thought he was depressed.

In the July he went to an old fairground acquaintance, May Ronaldson, who ran a shooting stall at Battersea Pleasure Gardens, a hangover from the Festival of Britain. He told her he was opening a fête in Esher the next week and was going dressed as a cowboy. He asked to borrow a rifle, brought it back but, a week or so later, came to borrow it again. In the meantime he and Andy Ho had been summoned for supplying drink to customers who were not taking a proper meal and for having an illegal fruit machine on the premises. The magistrates had fined them each £50.

During his second visit to Ronaldson's there were some of those rifle range bullets which had a soft head to eliminate ricochet on the mantelpiece. May Ronaldson left him alone for a few moments to make a cup of tea and, Read believes, it was then he took a bullet. It was with this rifle that he was killed.

In Bill Bavin's book he has an argument against suicide because the bullet actually entered Mills's eye. 'No one,' he declares, 'would choose the eye as a suitable location. It could also be argued with equal vehemence that the eye is not the usual target of an assailant. There is no doubt that the eye as the site of injury is most unusual. There is something repugnant, in most people's minds, about putting a bullet through one's eye. Certainly the temple or mouth is the more usual target.'

Read disagrees. 'I am sure, however, that the eye was not chosen as the site. I believe he chose to shoot himself in the forehead and, at the moment of pulling the trigger, jerked the weapon causing the bullet to be deflected into the eye. Keith Simpson, the very senior Home Office pathologist, who was also an expert in the use of firearms, was quite satisfied the wound was self-inflicted.

'One more thing was suggested as being peculiar and that was there was no suicide note,' wrote Read. 'In my experience, and I have dealt with scores of similar cases, the majority of suicides do not leave notes. There is the additional possibility that even had he left one, it was removed from the car.'

In a subsequent book Tony Van den Bergh advances the relatively unsupported theory that Mills had been killed by a group of Triads who wanted his restaurant.

Leonard Read, *Nipper*; Bill Bavin, *The Strange Death of Freddie Mills*; Jack Birtley, *Freddie Mills*; Tony Van den Bergh, *Who Killed Freddie Mills?*

Frank Mitchell

K nown as the 'Mad Axeman', Mitchell had an unhappy life. His disappearance, shortly before Christmas 1966, came about because he was a pawn in the game being played between the Kray Twins who controlled the East End, and the Richardson brothers who had interests in South-east London. From the age of eight Mitchell had been in special schools – he was sent to Borstal at seventeen, and was in prison three months later. From then on it was downhill all the way, starting with a flogging for an assault on a prison officer. In 1955 he was sent to Rampton, certified as a mental defective. In January 1957 he escaped and whilst on the run hit the occupant of a house he burgled over the head with an iron bar. This time he received nine years. Back inside he was sent to Broadmoor, escaped and attacked another householder and his wife. On his arrest he said, 'I want to prove I am sane and know what I am doing.' He received ten years' imprisonment. Involved in the 1962 Hull prison riots, he was birched and transferred to Dartmoor.

His behaviour improved and by July 1963 he was removed from the escape list. In May 1964 he was allowed to work outside the prison walls on the Quarry party, a small and well-supervised group. In September of that year he was transferred to the Honour party, a more loosely supervised group, and now, financed by the Krays, he abused his relative freedom no end. Instead of working he was more or less free to do what he liked. He became a regular in a local pub. Once he took a taxi to Tavistock where he bought a budgerigar. Women were provided by the Twins to while away his afternoons. As one warder said, 'I just could not afford to have Mitchell troublesome.'

For the Krays, Mitchell became a special 'away' – a member of the Firm who was away in prison. Their reputation was on the slide in the East End; some members of the Firm were now disrespectfully referring to them as Gert and Daisy, after Ethel and Doris Walters, the cockney music hall act. Some thought they were becoming too dangerous for their own good. Their financial adviser, Leslie Payne, was gone. With the Richardsons in general, and Frankie Fraser in particular, in custody, there was no need for any more strongmen on the Firm. So Mitchell was to be a rehabilitation, or at least a damage-limitation exercise, showing the East End both how their Twins cared for people and, if they put their minds to it, what they could actually do. On one occasion Mitchell had also protected Reggie Kray against a screw prison officer, so something of a debt was owed. They would arrange the release of the 'Mad Axeman'.

Mitchell was becoming querulous about getting a date for his release and the plan was evolved that he would escape from a working party on the Moor and then a campaign would begin to bring pressure for his release. To this end, friendly MPs such as Tom Driberg could be relied on for help. On 12 December 1966 Mitchell went to work at Bagga Tor. The weather that day was too bad for work and the party stayed in a hut playing cards. At 3.30 p.m. he asked if he could feed some ponies. Fifty minutes later, when the prison officers took the remainder of the party to the bus pick-up point, there was no sign of him. By 4.40 p.m. when the police were notified, Mitchell was well on his way to London. When the hue and cry really went up Mitchell was rather grumpily eating bacon and eggs cooked for him in Whitechapel at the flat of a small-time porn merchant and gang hanger-on, Lennie 'Books' Dunn, so named because of the bookstalls he ran in the Whitechapel Road. Mitchell had, it seems, been expecting something more in the way of a red carpet.

When, next morning, his clothing was found in a lay-by some thirty miles from Tavistock it was 'assumed he had made good his escape'. The next and really the last thing the outside world heard of Mitchell was from the newspapers. He wrote to *The Times* and the *Daily Mirror*. Each letter, actually written by Dunn, bore a thumbprint impression to confirm its authenticity and each asked for a release date. At first the Home Secretary agreed to meet with Mitchell but amended this by imposing the pre-condition of his surrender. The letters dried up.

For a few days Mitchell lived in relative comfort. The problem for the Twins was how to keep him happy. A hostess, Lisa, was more or less kidnapped from Winston's nightclub to provide him with sex and there is little doubt that she became fond of this semi-moron, who exercised by lifting up members of the Firm two at a time in displays of strength.

The problem was that Mitchell had exchanged one prison cell for another. Without his surrender he was no nearer obtaining a release date and without doubt surrender meant loss of privileges and very probably loss of remission and further time to be served. He began to say he would never be captured alive. And the more he said such things the more of a liability he became to the Twins. He wanted to go and see his mother and sister at the family house in Bow and was told a meeting would be arranged, but nothing came of it. He began to rave about going to look for the Twins, both at their home in Vallance Road and 'all around the clubs'.

On 24 December Mitchell was told by Albert Donaghue, one of his minders, that he was being moved to a new address in Kent. He protested at being separated from Lisa but was told she would be following on. He was never seen again, although, rather like those in the Lord Lucan case, there were reports that he had been seen in Scotland, Ireland, Germany and, indeed, in most other countries throughout the world. At the trial of the Krays for the murder of Mitchell, Donaghue gave evidence that the Axeman had been shot just as the van left the Barking Road, by Freddie Foreman (Ginger Marks (*qv*)) and Alf Gerard, the more or less freelance hitman who died in 1981 in Brighton. The Firm, said Donaghue, had a series of codes: 'The dog has won' meant a successful operation had been carried out; 'The dog has lost' meant the reverse. According to Lisa, Donaghue returned to the flat and said, 'The dog is dead.' There was no corroboration of Donaghue's evidence. He himself had been arrested and, in a plea bargain, had given evidence for the Crown. The Krays were acquitted along with Freddie Foreman. Alfie Gerard, who was in Australia at the time of the trial, was never charged. In 1994 Donaghue repeated his version of events in graphic and chilling detail on the BBC's programme *Underworld*.

Leonard Read, *Nipper*

Andre Mizelas

The forty-eight-year-old royal hairdresser was shot to death in London as he drove in Mayfair traffic on 9 November 1970. He was a partner in the fashionable Andre Bernard chain, part-owning twenty salons employing 400 staff. A woman cyclist found his body sprawled over the steering wheel – he had been shot twice in the head with a .25 gun. The police were unable to find anyone who would have benefited from his death and one theory was that he was shot at random by a person who had flagged him down. Another was that he had rebuffed a client who had taken revenge. And another might well be that he had tried to end an affair and been shot by the woman or by a jealous husband.

Sophia Money

On Sunday, 24 September 1905 this young woman, who worked for a local dairy, left her home at 245 Lavender Hill, Clapham, London saying she was going for a 'little walk'. She called in at a local confectionary shop at around 7 p.m. and remarked that she was on her way to Victoria. Some four hours later her badly damaged body was found in the Merstham Tunnel on the London to Brighton line. There was little evidence about her death. A guard on the 9.33 p.m. train from London Bridge said that he had seen a young woman who corresponded to Miss Money's description in company with a man at East Croydon. A signalman at Purley Oaks said that he had seen a couple struggling in a carriage as the train passed. His evidence was rather pooh-poohed by the coroner, who said that the struggle cannot have impressed him at the time and it was possible in thinking over the evidence he had thought he had seen more than he did. At the inquest her former employer, Arthur Bridger, was under some scrutiny. He was asked if he had given her presents, something he denied.

There was also evidence that he had been seen with Miss Money on a day trip to Bognor.

The police theory was that she had met a man who had lured her onto the train under the pretext either that they should go for a ride or that he would see her home. She was then pushed, or fell, from the train. Three years later the police were still receiving information they were following up. An Albert Cooper wrote to them saying that he thought a William Wakeman was their man. His evidence was slender. On the day before the Money killing Cooper had tried to borrow Wakeman's walking stick. He had been turned down on the basis that Wakeman was going to meet a 'very special Tart'. After the death Wakeman had some minor injuries and had kept to the basement for some six weeks, coming out only after dark and then with his hat pulled well down. Cooper and he had quarrelled and Cooper had said, 'I know something which could hang you.' Wakeman had, according to Cooper, turned pale. Nothing came of this or any other information.

The case had a curious sequel. Sophie's brother, Robert Henry Money, a dairy farmer, had affairs with two sisters. He had two children by one and another child by the other whom he married. In 1912 he took the whole entourage to Eastbourne and shot them all. He then shot himself. One of the women survived. There have been suggestions that it was he who killed his sister but there is no evidence – other than coincidence if that can ever be evidence – to support the theory.

H. L. Adam, *Murder by Persons Unknown*

Marilyn Monroe

At about 3.30 on the morning of Sunday, 4 August 1962, the body of Marilyn Monroe, born Norma Jean Rae, one of Hollywood's most gifted comediennes and possibly the greatest sex symbol of the twentieth century, was found in her bungalow apartment in Hollywood. A housekeeper, Eunice Murray, obtained by Monroe's psychiatrist, Dr Ralph Greenson, later told the police that she had seen a light under the bedroom door at midnight and again at 3.30 a.m. This time she walked around to the outside and saw the actress lying in bed on her stomach holding a telephone. She called the psychiatrist and then Monroe's doctor. The actress had been dead between four to six hours and the police listed her death as between 8 p.m. and 3.25 a.m. The coroner's report was that she had died of 'acute barbiturate poisoning due to ingestion of overdose'. He suggested it was 'probably' suicide.

It was put about that the reason for her suicide was that she was in financial difficulties and that she was having professional problems. Neither appears to have been correct.

In the days before her death she had made telephone calls to someone, who for a long time was coyly described as a high government personage. That person was Robert Kennedy, brother of John. Marilyn Monroe had been linked with the brothers for a long period. She had been sleeping with the President-elect during his campaign of 1960 and the affair continued until, according to actor Peter Lawford, Robert Kennedy's brother-in-law, John tried to disentangle himself and sent Robert to 'cool her off'. Lawford maintained she had begun an affair with Robert, now finding it difficult to distinguish between the brothers.

Whatever the cause of Marilyn Monroe's death, a major cover-up resulted. The housekeeper and a publicist girlfriend both took extended holidays. All traces of contact between Monroe and the Kennedys were eliminated, including telephone records which showed she had been trying to reach them. It was a favour which temporarily tightened the grasp of the FBI on the White House.

There seems to be some evidence that Monroe was intending, or at least threatening, to call a press conference on 5 August to explain to the world at large just what treatment she had suffered at the hands of the Kennedy brothers. As a result there had been a major row with Robert Kennedy and her psychiatrist had been called to quieten her down. Shortly afterward she had declined a dinner invitation with Peter Lawford and his wife.

In 1982 Chuck Giancana claimed that his half-brother, Sam, had had Monroe murdered in the hope that her affair with Bobby Kennedy would be exposed and that he would be politically ruined. Other theories of her death are that the overdose was injected, possibly rectally.

John Austin, *Hollywood's Unsolved Mysteries*; Donald Spoto, *Marilyn Monroe: The Biography*; Anthony Summers, *Official and Confidential*

Wilma Montesi

On 9 April 1953 Maria Montesi and her daughter Wanda, who lived in the Via Tagliamento, a working and lower middle-class suburb in the north-east of Rome, went to the cinema. Her younger daughter, twenty-one-year-old Wilma, declined to go, saying she did not fancy the film. Her carpenter father was working a few blocks away. When they returned there was no trace of Wilma who, according to the concierge, had gone out by herself. She had left behind her money, jewels and the photograph of her fiance, a policeman, which she normally carried.

On the morning of 11 April Wilma's body was found, seemingly drowned on a lonely beath at Tor Vaianica about fifteen miles from Rome. Her shoes, stockings and suspender belt were missing. So began one of the great Italian scandals of the period.

At first it was suggested that she had gone to the beach at Ostia, some ten miles up the coast, to bathe her heels which were sore and which she had been painting with iodine. Although she was a good swimmer it was suggested she was menstruating and had fainted whilst paddling and drowned, with her body then being swept down to Tor Vaianica. A woman who had recognised her photograph in the newspapers had seen her on the 5.30 p.m. train from Rome to Ostia.

The problems for the Government started when a satirical magazine suggested that the missing suspender belt had been brought by carrier pigeon into the police headquarters in Rome and there had been destroyed. The play on words was clear to the magazine's readers. The Italian for 'carrier pigeons' is *piccioni viaggianti*. The Foreign Minister at the time was Attilio Piccioni. Next came a suggestion that one of this sons, Piero, had been involved in the death. The gossip was almost enough to lose the Christian Democrats the next election but, severely weakened, they held on.

The troubles returned when in January 1954 Silvano Muto, who edited a weekly magazine *Attualita*, wrote that next to the beach at Tor Vaianica was a hunting reserve, Capocotta, belonging to a syndicate. There, said Muto, drug taking and orgies were commonplace. Could they have had anything to do with the death of Wilma Montesi? Was it possible she had died at a sex party after taking drugs? Muto was charged with publishing falsehoods likely to disturb the public peace. His trial began in Rome on 28 January 1954. His defence was that there was a good deal of drug and cigarette smuggling in the area at the time and he had reliable information from an Adriana Bisaccia and an Anna

Maria Caglio that Montesi's death was not an accident. Somehow it was linked with Ugo Montagna, a Sicilian, Knight of the Holy Sepulchre and Marquis of San Bartolomeo, one of the administrators of the shoot. At the time he was declaring his income for tax purposes at around £400 a year. Called to the witness box Caglio claimed she had been Montagna's mistress, suggested that she had seen Wilma Montesi with Montagna and implied that she herself had been poisoned by him. Later she claimed that Ugo Montagna was head of a gang of drug traffickers and was responsible for the disappearance of many women. She named Wilma Montesi's killer as Piero Piccioni.

Her evidence, at least about the drug trafficking and Wilma Montesi's involvement, was supported by a number of witnesses. The body was exhumed and a new post-mortem carried out. She had been buried in the great cemetery in Rome with an inscription:

> Pure creature of rare beauty, the sea of Ostia claimed you and carried you to the beach of Tor Vaianica. You seemed to be resting in the sleep of the Lord, as lovely as an angel. Your mother and your father, your sister and your brother, are near you in their great love and terrible grief.

The family then announced it was to make a film of the events. They were to play themselves. Jazz musician Piccioni, Montagna and Saverio Polito, the former head of the Rome police, were arrested. Polito had resigned during the Muto case. The allegation was that Montesi had died from a drug overdose and that there had been a conspiracy to cover up the death.

The trial began in Venice in January 1957. The experts disagreed on the cause of death, whether Montesi was pregnant at the time, and on how long the body had been in the water. Montesi's uncle, Giuseppe, came under suspicion of being involved with his niece, calling an alibi which was demonstrably false and later being charged with criminal libel for saying his colleagues had lied about him. Finally it was decided that Montesi was a virgin at the time of her death and that she had drowned. Piccioni produced an alibi which held up and was acquitted 'for not having committed the crime'. It followed that Montagna and Polito had to be found not guilty on the basis that once Piccioni had been acquitted there was no crime for them to cover up. Bisaccia was given the equivalent of ten months' suspended sentence for perjury. The film with the remaining members of the Montesi family duly appeared.

Wayland Young, *The Montesi Scandal*

James Alfred Moody

On 1 June 1993 James Moody was shot dead in a contract killing in the Royal Hotel, Hackney, East London. Moody had always been a shadowy figure in the London Underworld. Known as a hard man, his first conviction in 1967 was for the manslaughter of a young man, merchant navy steward William Day, at a South London party, and, along with Moody's brother, Richard, he received a six-year sentence. It was his last conviction but by no means his last involvement in crime. In 1965 he helped carry the wounded Frankie Fraser to comparative safety after the shooting of Dickie Hart (*qv*) at Mr Smith's Club in Peckham, which led to the smashing of the Richardson gang. Moody was tried for his part in the affray that night and was acquitted.

At school in Hackney he was said to be a mother's boy but, later, a committed body-builder, he was enormously fit and strong. He became an invaluable member of the Thursday Gang of the late 1970s, which specialised in hi-jacking, often with considerable violence, security vans in the London area. On one occasion Moody, dressed as a policeman, jumped out of a car in the Blackwall Tunnel and forced a security van to stop. To prevent the alarm being given he took the keys from a number of nearby motorists. Wanted for a series of armed robberies he hid out in a lock-up garage which he furnished with books, food, body-building equipment and a chemical toilet. He was caught when he visited his son's flat in Brixton. He was charged with raids totalling £930,000 and sent to Brixton prison to await trial. In the 1980s it was still possible for remand prisoners to have food, wine and beer brought in by friends and relatives. Moody's brother Richard brought, with the Sunday lunches, hacksaw blades, drill bits and other tools.*

Moody had noticed that outside his cell was a flat roof and it was to this that he and cell mates, Gerard Tuite, a Provisional IRA bomb-maker and Stanley Thompson, veteran of the Parkhurst prison riot of 1969 and now charged with armed robbery, cut through the brickwork. Every morning the rubble was removed in their chamber pots at slopping out time. On 16 December 1980 they pushed out the loosened brickwork of their cell, stepped onto the roof where a ladder had been left by roofers and were away.

Thompson need not have bothered. The escape took place whilst the jury was out in his trial at St Albans and, in his absence, they found him not guilty. Tuite

---

* There is a full account of Moody's life and death in Cal McCrystal's *The Hit at the Royal Hotel* in *The Independent on Sunday*, 8 August 1993.

was later arrested in Dublin, becoming the first person to be charged in Ireland with criminal offences committed in England. He received ten years. Richard received two years for the help he had given his brother.

And James Moody? He simply vanished. Some Underworld faces say they received irregular Christmas cards from him but, apart from that and an unsuccessful raid on a flat in West London where his fingerprints and nothing else were found, of Jim there was no sign at all for the next thirteen years.

Then on the night of 1 June 1993, whilst drinking at the bar of the Royal Hotel, Hackney, where he was known as Mick, he was shot dead by a man described as in his early forties and wearing a leather jacket. The man had ordered a pint of Foster's lager and put two coins down on the bar to pay for it. Then he had moved towards Moody and fired three shots. As Moody slumped to the floor, a fourth was fired into his back before the man was driven away in a stolen white Ford Fiesta XR2.

Where had he been and why was he shot? As to the first there were suggestions he had been hidden out by the Provisionals, but clearly he had returned to England some years earlier, if indeed he had ever left. At the time of his death he had been living in Wadeson Street, a back alley off Mare Street in Hackney. As to why, one theory was that it was a killing done on behalf of a cuckolded husband, for Moody was very much a ladies' man – he is said to have required the services of a different woman each evening. A second version is that it was part of the long drawn out struggle for power between the Arif family and other South London interests and that it was in revenge for the killing of David Brindle (*qv*) in the Bell public house in Walworth in August 1991.

Now that he is dead the most convenient name in the frame for the killing of David Brindle is that of Moody, who is also fancied for the killings of Terry Gooderham and his girlfriend Maxine Arnold (*qv*) in Epping Forest in December 1989, and antique and cocaine dealer Peter Raisini (*qv*) in Palmers Green in March 1991. There is also speculation that he carried out the killing of Peter and Gwenda Dixon (*qv*). Attributing all these deaths to Moody may, however, be just another way of clearing up crimes or, in the Underworld, diverting suspicion.

There is, however, another theory over David Brindle's death which fits the facts but has nothing to do with the over-all game plan of the South London warlords. It was probably simply a personal matter. Says Frank Fraser, his one-time beneficiary:

> It now turns out that Jimmy Moody was working in a pub at the back of Walworth under the name Tom. He'd been in the area for ten years. He wasn't an out and

out nightclubber so he could have been there and very, very few people would know who he was. He'd done quite a bit of bird and now he took it as a personal thing to keep out. It was a personal challenge for him. There's a lot of other guys been in that position and they've been out nightclubbing it and soon got caught. Jim did have that determination and single-mindedness to keep that low profile and trust no one. He could be stubborn and obstinate, a good man but a loner. He'd be content to do his work and watch the telly knowing that every day was a winner. That's how he would look at it. I think David had had a row with the publican and Jimmy had crept behind him and done him with a baseball bat. David was badly knocked about and told Jimmy it wouldn't be forgotten. Next night or a couple of nights later Moody and another man went into the Bell in East Street and shot David and a bystander. Immediately afterwards he went over to the East End.

Much as I knew Jim well, I can understand the feelings about David's death and that it was one that had to be done. I suppose if someone who knew it was going off had really pleaded for him it might have made some difference but I doubt it.

Once Moody had been traced to Hackney it became common knowledge in South-east London that reprisals were to be taken and Fraser absented himself from London on the night of the killing.

Frankie Fraser, *Mad Frank*; James Morton, *Gangland 2*

Polly Anne Moore *see* **Richard Griffin**

Philomena Morgan *see* **Linda Agostini**

Alving and John Morrison

On 10 November 1914 in Salt Lake City, Utah, John Morrison and his seventeen-year-old son Alving were shot by two gunmen in their grocery store. A second brother, fourteen-year-old Merlin, survived. John Morrison, a former policeman, had been threatened on a number of occasions in industrial disputes with the Industrial Workers of the World (The Wobblies), one of America's earliest forms of trade union. No money was stolen.

The man arrested and tried for the murders was the great Wobbly poet and songwriter, Joe Hill. On the night of the killings, when he was treated for gunshot wounds by a Dr Frank McHugh, he explained that he had been shot in a fight over a married woman whom he refused to name. McHugh later gave evidence that he saw a revolver in a shoulder holster in Hill's possession but when he was arrested Hill was unarmed. The murder weapon was never found.

So far as the evidence against Hill was concerned there was no identification and also the bullet that injured Hill had passed through his body. Morrison's gun only fired lead bullets. None was found at the store. It was suspected that the second gunman was a roommate of Hill's, Otto Applequist, who disappeared on the morning after the murder. The motive was said to be revenge for the killing of a Wobbly by Morrison, whilst he was a policeman.

Perhaps the most telling piece of evidence against Hill was that he was a member of the hated Wobblies. There is also some evidence that Hill was indeed in love at the time of the murder but the identity of the woman has never been made known.

The trial was, it seems, by no means an unfair one. Defence objections to evidence were upheld and Hill's lawyers were perfectly competent. Halfway through the trial, however, he discharged them and the IWW then recruited a sixty-seven-year-old labour lawyer, Judge O. N. Hilton, to act for Hill.

Hill was convicted but, at his appearance before the Utah Pardon Board, he maintained his silence over the identity of the woman. Hilton was apparently genuinely dumbfounded, first by the conviction on such slender evidence and then by the refusal of a reprieve. Despite worldwide mass protest meetings, including one of 30,000 Australian workers who petitioned for clemency, he was executed by a firing squad in Utah on 19 November 1915. He exercised his right not to be blindfolded. His last words are said to have been 'Don't waste time in mourning. Organize.' He is also said to have told his followers 'Don't let the sun in Utah set on my body'. He is remembered in the folk songs 'Long Black Veil' and 'I Dreamed I Saw Joe Hill Last Night'. The victims of the shooting which led to his execution are not similarly remembered.

Patrick Renshaw, *The Wobblies*

Steinie Morrison *see* **Leon Beron**

Henry Treise Morshead

On 17 May 1931 Lt Col Henry Morshead DSO was shot dead in the Burmese Jungle. The short-tempered Morshead, who had been an explorer and mountaineer of note, had lost several fingers from frostbite on the 1925 abortive climb of Mount Everest when he had reached 22,000 feet. At the time of his death he was director of the Survey of India's Burma Circle. Married with four children he lived at Upperfold some two miles from Maymyo, with his sister Ruth acting as housekeeper. His wife and family had returned to England because of the outbreak of anti-British disturbances led by Saya San the previous year. On the morning of 17 May he wrote a letter to his wife and then, at about 7 a.m., rode through the jungle. He was seen at Elephant Point near the village of Inlya.

Two hours later his riderless pony appeared at the Manor House owned by a local businessman, Syed Ali, with whom Morshead was not on good terms. There was blood on the saddle. A search party was organised but it was not until early the next day that his body was found some two and a half miles from Inlya. He had been killed with a shot to the chest fired at close range. There was a second slight wound on the left shoulder-blade.

A month later the *Rangoon Gazette* reported that a Gurka had admitted the killing, saying it was an accident. The man was released when it became clear that the confession could not be an accurate one. In September a short five page report was published by the Government. There had been Saya San rebels in the area at the time saying that 'they were forced to the conclusion that the identity of the assailant must remain a mystery'. There were a number of other possibilities – dacoits or a dismissed employee. Morshead could easily have acted harshly in his treatment of staff.

In 1980 Morshead's eldest son, Ian, travelled to Burma to enquire into the circumstances of his father's death. There he was told that the assassination had been carried out on behalf of Syed Ali, then the Worshipful Master of a Masonic lodge. The disagreement between Ali and Morshead was probably over Ali's relationship with Ruth Morshead. Her brother objected to her going out riding with Ali. Shortly after Morshead's death Ali handed over his business interests to his brother and left the area. Morshead's widow received only a small pension on the grounds that her husband had not been killed on active service.

Ian Morshead, *The Life and Murder of Henry Morshead*

Jonathan Moyle

The twenty-eight-year-old editor of *Defence Helicopter World* and a former RAF helicopter pilot was found hanging in his room at the Hotel Carrera, Santiago, Chile, on 31 March 1990. His 5'8" body was found hanging by one of his shirts from a clothes' rail only five feet from the ground. His head was covered in a pillow case and he was wearing an incontinence pad. It appeared that at one time his legs had also been bound. The cupboard door was shut. He had been in Chile at an international airspace fair and was due to leave for La Paz to join a CIA drugs mission to Bolivia.

At first it was announced that he had hanged himself during a sexual experiment, an opinion which the British authorities in Chile appear not to have contested, but it was not one which appealed either to Moyle's fiancée and family or to the media. An alternative theory was that Moyle had been investigating a story of the sale of helicopters, which could be used as attack weapons, to Iraq. *Channel 4 News* ran a story on the case and was immediately threatened with libel proceedings by Carlos Cadoen, the manufacturer of the helicopter.

Miss Catherine Royle, of the British Embassy in Santiago, said, 'We do not know how Mr Moyle died and are awaiting the judge's report which could take several more weeks. He is very keen to do a thorough investigation. Suggestions have been made that the Iraqis were responsible, but nobody has any hard facts. Experts tell us that it was quite possible for him to have committed suicide, and there is no evidence of a motive for murder, but we are not in a position to judge.'*

Because of what he described as 'loose ends' the examining magistrate, Judge Alejandro Solis, had ordered the investigation to be taken over by SO-7, the criminal intelligence unit and the suicide theory was exposed when it was found that his wallet, briefcase and two files had been taken from his room. A post-mortem examination showed sedatives in the stomach and the chambermaid from the room recalled that she had seen bloodstains on the sheets of the bed. There was an unfinished letter by his bedside dated 1 April indicating he probably intended to post it the next day. An hour before his body was found he had telephoned his parents telling them of the Bolivian mission and how much he was looking forward to it. The incontinence pad can be explained by the fact that over the previous days he had had diarrhoea.

On 30 March he had taken a flight to see Chilean airforce bases in Antarctica

---

* *The Times*, 30 May 1990.

but the trip had been aborted in Puntas Areas because of bad weather. One theory is that he learned something whilst speaking to people on the trip and was killed to prevent him publishing it.

It is difficult to accept the theory that he was murdered over the helicopter story. It had been known for some time that the helicopters had been manufactured. Nor had Mr Cardoen of Industrias Cardoen SA made any secret of dealing with Iraq. It appears that he and his press officer, Raul Montecinos, had met with Moyle at the hotel bar the evening before his body was found.

Another reason given for his killing was that, apart from the helicopter deal, he had discovered that a company was manufacturing seabed mines which also might have been purchased by the Iraqis. The theory goes that he was then killed on the orders of Saddam Hussein. The room service waiter who took Moyle his morning coffee was found dead two days later.

The question arises whether Moyle was acting for British intelligence, something the Foreign Office minister, Mark Lennox-Boyd, denied in December 1992. It seems, that whilst at Aberystwyth University, Moyle had written a thesis for his MA which was classified. His tutor confirms the work was completed but Defence officials deny its existence. In May 1993 Moyle's father Tony told *The Sunday Times* that he was giving up his search for his son's killers. Despite a reward of £5,000 and the hiring of private investigators he had, he said, bowed to Whitehall dirty tricks and obsessive secrecy.

Ellen, Michael and Norah Murphy

On Monday, 26 December 1898 Ellen, Michael and Norah Murphy drove to a dance at the Tarampa Divisional Board's Hall, nearly a hundred kilometres west of Brisbane, Australia. They arrived at 9 p.m. only to find that the dance had been cancelled because insufficient girls had attended. Michael turned the sulky around and a kilometre out of town they met their brother, Patrick, who was returning to college in Gatton. They told him of the cancellation and drove on towards their farm. When they had not returned by the next morning their father, Daniel, organised a search party. Their bodies were found by their brother-in-law, William McNeil, in a paddock outside Gatton.

Norah Murphy was lying on a blanket, her hands tied behind her back and her skirt undone at the back. A tightly buckled harness strap was around her neck. Ellen lay almost back to back with her brother. Her hands were tied and her underclothes torn. Both girls had been sexually assaulted. From marks on their bodies it appeared that the girls had put up a struggle against their attackers but, on the ground there were no signs of any fight. It looked as if the bodies had been laid out.

A post-mortem showed that each had been killed from a blow to the skull and in Norah's case she had also been shot, as had Michael and the horse. Michael was clutching an empty purse and his gold-handled riding crop had been taken.

The initial theory was that they had been lured to the paddock on the pretext that someone had been injured and needed help. Then attention turned to and against William McNeil. He was rigorously questioned over his movements: he had been in bed with his invalid wife that night, something Mrs Murphy, the children's mother, confirmed.

On 6 January 1899 the police arrested a swagman, Richard Burgess. He had a number of convictions, including one for indecent assault during which he had been shot in the buttocks. He had been released from the Moreton Bay prison and had made his way to the Brisbane area staying, on Christmas Eve, some sixty-four kilometres from Gatton. However, there does not seem to have been any evidence against him and he was released. Later he boasted that he was the Gatton killer but he was never taken seriously. He died in prison in Western Australia.

A far more likely suspect would seem to have been Thomas Day who had arrived in Gatton to work for Arthur Clarke, the Gatton butcher, less than two weeks before the murder. Little was known of him and the fact that he read such books as Lytton's *Rienzi* is unlikely to have endeared him to the community. He had been seen near some sliprails which led to the paddock on the night of the murder and a sweater of his was found to have blood on it. Clarke said it was from some meat. Although one young police officer voiced his suspicions over Clarke, no in-depth investigation seems to have been conducted into his story that he too was in his room on the night of the murders. He left Gatton on 10 January 1898 and his detractors say it points to his wishing to absent himself from the scene. Alternatively it may be that he was encountering a good deal of local hostility, as had McNeil. Day is thought to have joined the Queensland Artillery and may have died during the Boer War.

No more arrests were ever made. The most likely explanation is that the family was attacked by a sex maniac but, over the years, rumours persisted that there was a secret in the Murphy family and that the killings were in revenge for some slight.

Alan Sharpe, *Crimes That Shocked Australia*

Hilda Murrell

On Wednesday, 21 March 1984 seventy-eight-year-old Hilda Murrell was killed. She had last been seen near her home in Sutton Road, Shrewsbury. Her body was found in a wood near Haughmand Hill, a beauty spot near the town. The police said she had been sexually assaulted. She had suffered multiple stab and other wounds but the cause of death was hypothermia. She had crawled about 100 yards after she had been dumped but had died after about six hours. Her Renault 5 car was found three days later in a ditch 500 yards from the wood.

Murrell was a rose-grower of international repute and an ardent conservationist – she was due to read a paper on nuclear waste at the Sizewell B enquiry to be held that summer. Her death sparked a ten-year dispute into the role played by the secret services, something the authorities have steadfastly and hotly denied.

It appears that unfortunately the wrong car number was fed into the computer and it was not until the Saturday that the Renault was identified as hers and a search begun. The body was found by a gamekeeper's wife at 10.30 a.m. According to Miss Murrell's nephew, Rob Green, a former high-ranking naval intelligence officer, he was told that the police had found the body some three and a half hours earlier.

There appears to have been some discrepancy over the time Miss Murrell's cottage was searched. The police say they forced entry at 6 a.m. on the Saturday morning. A witness says that a group of men, one of whom was wearing what appeared to be a uniform, entered on the Friday night. In any event, the back door was unlocked and the light on in the kitchen. Her telephone was cut in such a way that whilst it did not ring in the house a caller would hear the ringing tone. In any event, Special Branch was called in to investigate.

Miss Murrell was probably attacked in her bedroom on Wednesday morning – she had failed to attend a luncheon appointment. She had drawn £50 from the bank and this money, together with her briefcase, was missing. It seems she was driven through Shrewsbury slumped in the passenger seat of her car. The sexual assault may have been no more than the fact that she was half dressed – perhaps she had been surprised whilst changing. At the inquest on 5 December 1984 Detective Chief Superintendent David Cole, head of West Mercia CID, said his officers could not find any link between her killing and her anti-nuclear views. 'I am left with the inescapable conclusion that this was an offence of burglary and the offender was, in the main, after cash.' Of course not too many burglars, after they have robbed their victims, drive them six miles in their own cars and dump them still alive.

Another possibility was raised by MP Tam Dalyell who suggested that Miss Murrell had died after a fight with British intelligence men searching her home for secret Belgrano documents which they thought had been left by her nephew, Rob Green. It was an allegation immediately denied by the Home Office minister, Giles Shaw. In a letter to Dalyell he wrote, 'I am able to state unreservedly that your allegations about the intelligence services being involved are totally without foundation.'

By January 1985 the police were no nearer a solution. They had taken the relatively unusual step of having certain witnesses hypnotised, without success. They had also put a professional burglar on an identification parade. He was identified by one witness as having been seen in the area but he was never charged.

In March 1994 the police completed an eight-month investigation in which, said David Thursfield, the Assistant Chief Constable of West Mercia, officers had been given access to security service, military and nuclear industry files. No links had been found with Miss Murrell. The findings of the police investigation were not accepted by author Gary Murray, who said, 'The police mean well but they have been manipulated and misled. I find it impossible to believe that Hilda Murrell was not on secret service files.'

Judith Cook, *Who Killed Hilda Murrell?*; Graham Smith, *Death of a Rosegrower*

Benjamin Nathan

At 6 a.m. on 28 July 1870, Washington Nathan went downstairs in his home at 12 West 23rd Street, New York, to obtain a glass of water. Passing by his father's bedroom he looked in. On the floor lay Benjamin Nathan, said by some

to be the richest man in the world. His status was almost certainly over-esti-
mated but at least when his death was announced the flag over the New York
Stock Exchange was flown at half-mast. Nathan Senior had been hit over the
head a number of times with a carpenter's tool. There were signs of a struggle
and a safe in the room had been opened. It appeared that the killer had washed
his hands in a basin in the room but had not bothered to remove a handprint
from the bedroom wall. The science of fingerprints was, however, unheard of
in America at the time.

Young Nathan was known to have been in financial trouble and to have
quarrelled with his father over money. He had, however, an alibi for most of the
relevant time of death, provided in part by what the newspapers coyly described as a 'lass of the pavements'.

Washington was not the only son of the family under suspicion. Frederick
Nathan was also in the house, as was William Kelly, the son of the housekeeper
and a man with at least a passing acquaintanceship with the Underworld. Neither of them appear to have heard anything of what must have been a violent
incident.

Over the months and years a number of people confessed to the murder. One
man, John T. Irving, was brought from California but was unable to persuade
the authorities of his guilt. A prisoner in Sing Sing later implicated a burglar,
William Forrester. He said that he had heard Forrester had intended merely to
rob the house but was surprised by Nathan and had killed him. Forrester denied, almost certainly falsely, that he was in New York that night but there was
no hard evidence against him and he was never charged.

One puzzle was the question of the street door. Everyone in the house said it
had been locked up for the night but when Washington Nathan went down to
get his glass of water he found it unlocked. In 1879 Washington was shot in the
neck by a former girlfriend, Fanny Barrett. The Chief of the New York police
then had the ingenious idea that whilst Nathan recovered from the anaesthetic
he would be questioned about his father's murder. Unfortunately the scheme
came to nothing when the bullet worked its way out of its own accord. He
remained under a cloud for the rest of his life, finally leaving America to live in
Europe where he died in 1892 at the age of forty-two. His hair was said to have
turned prematurely white.

Daniel Cohen, *The Encyclopedia of Unsolved Crimes*

Mary Anne 'Polly' Nicholls

There is no doubt that Mary Anne 'Polly' Nicholls was a victim of Jack the Ripper and most enthusiasts for the case agree that she was the first of the five who can definitely be attributed to the work of the same person. At 3.15 a.m. on 31 August 1888 her body was found by a carter lying in the entrance to the Old Stable Yard on what was called Bucks Row but is now Durward Street. Her throat had been cut and she had been disembowelled.

Just over a week later, at about 6 a.m. on 8 September, the body of Annie Chapman was found at 29 Hanbury Street. Again the head was almost severed and her body had been cut open. Her kidney and ovaries had been removed. In a corner of the yard was a torn envelope bearing the crest of the Sussex regiment and under a tap was a leather apron. A Jewish shoemaker named Pizer, known in the locality as Leather Apron, was arrested and released. There had been considerable local hostility towards him but he provided a detailed alibi. It is, however, possible that both these potential clues had been planted with a view to misleading the police.

Towards the end of the month the Central News Agency received a letter signed 'Jack the Ripper', saying the writer was 'down on whores and shant quit ripping them till I do get buckled'.*

The third and fourth victims came within a matters of hours of each other. First, on 30 September at 1 a.m., the body of a Swedish-born prostitute, Elizabeth Stride, was discovered in Berner Street. Her throat had been cut and it is possible that when the hawker Louis Deimschutz, who found the body, drove his horse and cart into the yard he disturbed the killer.

About this time the forty-three-year-old Catherine Eddowes was released from Bishopsgate police station. At 1.45 a.m. her body was discovered in Mitre Square, off Aldgate. Her face had been badly cut and her left kidney had been removed. Shortly after the murders the Central News Agency received a letter in red ink from the Ripper saying he was sorry he had been interrupted.

The final victim who can definitely be attributed to the Ripper was on 9 November when, at 10.45 a.m., a rent collector called at Miller's Court, a cul-de-sac off Dorset Street, knocked on the door of Mary Kelly, a rather younger and cleaner prostitute than the others, and discovered her body. Her head was almost severed and her heart had been put beside her on the pillow. Her entrails

---

* To be buckled was to be arrested. It was a slang expression which had come into use in the late 1870s.

were draped over a picture frame. Walter Dew was the first officer on the scene: 'It remains with me – and always will remain – as the most gruesome memory of the whole of my police career.'

The ensuing panic led to the resignation of the already unpopular Commissioner of Police, Charles Warren. He had, in an endeavour to find the killer, hired a pair of bloodhounds at the exorbitant cost of £100. Unfortunately they lost themselves on Clapham Common. There were suggestions by the Home Secretary that East End brothels should be closed. This idea was rejected as it would only have had the effect of driving the 1,200 women estimated to be working at the time into other districts. Certainly there were no further murders that winter which can be placed at the Ripper's door and possibly he did not kill again.

There were three other later deaths of prostitutes which some writers attribute to Jack the Ripper. In June 1889 Elizabeth Jackson, a prostitute from Chelsea, was found in the Thames. Her head had been cut off but she was identified from a scar on her wrist. On 17 July the body of Alice McKenzie, known as Clay Pipe Alice, was found on Castle Yard, Whitechapel. Her throat had been cut and there were stomach wounds. The last possible killing to be attributed to him was that of Frances Coles, known as Carrotty Nell, who was discovered on 13 February 1891 in Swallow Gardens, Whitechapel. Her throat had also been cut and she had stomach wounds. She was alive when she was found but died soon afterwards, thereby producing a nice symmetry with Emma Smith (*qv*).

Over the years there cannot have been a British case which has attracted more attention worldwide. Indeed a whole industry has grown up as one writer or another attempts to prove that their chosen person, or class of persons, was the killer. Probably the favourite is Montague Druitt, a failed barrister who was drowned in the Thames on 4 December 1888. If this is so then the last three women cannot have been killed by the Ripper. Other suggestions are that the killer was a medical student or doctor. In support of this, Annie Chapman's kidney had been removed with some skill. The name of George Chapman (otherwise Severin Antoniovich Klosowski and no relation to Annie) is mentioned in this connection: a hospital attendant in Poland, he would have had some rudimentary surgical knowledge. On 7 April 1903 he was hanged for the murder by poisoning of Maud Marsh. There is little doubt he killed a number of other women by poisoning and it seems unlikely he would have changed his *modus operandi*. It is also suggested that the Ripper was a slaughterman, again someone who might have a rudimentary knowledge of anatomy.

Another name which is bandied about is that of the prostitute poisoner,

Neville Cream. There are problems with this theory in that he was almost certainly in prison in America at the time of the killings. As he was executed he is said to have cried out, 'I am Jack ...' It may, however, have been that he was saying that he was ejaculating. Again, why should he change his *modus operandi*? Later suggestions have been that the killer was the Duke of Clarence, the eldest son of King Edward VII, and that the killings were part of a masonic plot. It has also been postulated that the killer was a woman carrying out abortions and disguising her handiwork when it went wrong. The latest theory, offered in 1993, was that the killer was James Maybrick for whose murder his wife, Florence Maybrick, was convicted and served a life sentence. The purported diary in which he wrote his confession was exposed as a hoax in 1994. Richard Whittington-Egan doubts that any of the theories is correct, believing that if the name of the killer was ever known it would mean nothing to any of the historians who have compiled papers on the case.

'Such speculation is little more than childish,' wrote Chief Inspector Dew in 1930, 'for there is no evidence to support one view any more than another.'

Donald Rumbelow, *The Complete Jack the Ripper*; Walter Dew, *I Caught Crippen*; Richard Whittington-Egan, *A Casebook on Jack the Ripper*

Ann Noblett

The body of the shy and retiring twelve-stone, seventeen-year-old daughter of a company director who lived at Wheathampstead, Hertfordshire, was found by two brothers walking their dog on 31 January 1958 in nearby Rose Wood Grove. Her glasses were still in place and twenty-five shillings from her purse was scattered on a bank of early snowdrops. On her cheek was a frozen tear. She had vanished on 30 December after being seen at a bus stop some seven miles from the wood at around 6 p.m., on her way home from a dancing class.

The police were convinced that she was strangled the day she vanished and that her body was kept in a deep-freeze refrigerator, possibly to foil attempts at pin-pointing the time of death. Tests showed that she had died within twelve hours of her midday lunch. Her clothing had been stripped from her and she had been re-dressed. She had been raped. They were also convinced that the body had been dumped in the wood only shortly before its discovery – the area had previously been comprehensively searched. It was thought that the dumping might have been done by more than one person because the frozen twelve-stone body would have been a substantial weight to carry. Over 150 deep-freezers owned by farmers in a radius of fifteen miles were examined. When there was no success, the search was expanded to include the whole of the south of England.

In July 1958 the family instructed two former Scotland Yard officers, ex-Detective Superintendent Reg Minter and ex-Detective Inspector Mick O'Sullivan who ran a detective agency, Q Men, to investigate the murder. In 1961 Interpol was asked to trace a man who had gone to Belgium with a twenty-four-year-old beauty queen, Ann Edwards. He had been born in 1919 in Dartford, Kent, the son of a Belgian and his British wife. There was now a warrant for his arrest on a fraud charge. In June that year the *Daily Express* interviewed the man, who, when questioned about the death of Ann Noblett, denied that he had ever been near Wheathampstead. He was, he said, willing to return to England to be questioned.

The next month the police spent a considerable time talking with the man's co-director. Together they ran a refrigeration company in Essex. No charges were ever brought.

Sir Harry Oakes

On the morning of 8 July 1943 the sixty-nine-year-old multi-millionaire baronet, Sir Harry Oakes, was found murdered in his bed at Westbourne, near Nassau in the Bahamas. His body had been soaked with petrol and set alight. His pillow had been slit open and the feathers had settled on his body. An electric fan was blowing, seemingly to accelerate the burning. A freak thunderstorm had doused the flames and minimised the damage to the house. Oakes had been hit on the head with a type of club which had left four triangular indentations in the form of a square. His skull had been fractured. In the next bedroom, separated from Sir Harry's room by a sitting-room, his friend Harold Christie had slept undisturbed throughout the killing. It was he who discovered the body the next morning.

Oakes was a self-made man who had prospected and found gold in Canada. He had come to the Bahamas in search of the knighthood which could be, and was, bestowed on him for his charitable work. He had substantially improved the quality of life for much of the island, providing a wing for the hospital, milk for the schoolchildren and establishing a cottage industry in conch shell designer jewellery. He had married in late middle age and had five children.

It was something of an unusual investigation by the police. At the time the Duke of Windsor was Governor-General of the islands and it was he who called in two police officers, with no particular practical homicide experience, from Miami. Captain James Barker, a personal friend of the Duke, had been a motorcycle patrolman, then a clerk in the Bureau of Criminal Identification. He had been dismissed for insubordination and then returned to the Bureau as Superintendent. Captain Edward Melchen was Chief of the Homicide Bureau in Miami but had principally been involved with guarding visiting diplomats. They were billed as fingerprint experts of the highest quality but, through some administrative oversight, failed to bring any equipment with them to Nassau. The local police were forbidden to interfere.

The missing equipment appears to have been little handicap to the Captains. Nor do mistakes in basic homicide investigation procedure, such as a failure to keep sightseers away from Oakes's bedroom. Three days after Oakes's death his son-in-law, the Mauritian-born playboy, Alfred de Marigny, now the husband of the nineteen-year-old daughter, Nancy, was charged with his murder.

One weakness in the case was the question of motive. Although Oakes and

A partial view of Sir Harry Oakes's house. Oakes was murdered in the bedroom marked B. Christie, in bedroom A, only ten yards away, claimed he heard nothing.

de Marigny did not get on, and there had been hard words between them on a number of occasions because the baronet suspected the playboy had married Nancy for her fortune, things were not seemingly so bad that de Marigny would kill his father-in-law. Nor, at the time, was de Marigny in financial trouble. Perhaps more importantly, the other weakness was a lack of evidence. The prosecution case was based on what was said to be de Marigny's fingerprint on a Chinese screen beside Oakes's bed.

De Marigny's loyal wife hired a New York private detective, Raymond Campbell Schindler, who, in one of the really great courtroom dramas, was able to discredit the procedure under which the fingerprint was examined. The police had taken no photograph of the print *in situ* on the screen and had, according to their evidence, dusted it with fingerprint powder and then removed the surface with transparent tape. This was not standard procedure. Schindler photographed the screen and found no evidence of the print having been there at all. The fingerprint appeared to have moisture marks surrounding it, something which could not be related to the screen and, alleged Schindler, had in fact been taken from a waterglass handed to de Marigny by one of the officers.

Whilst the jury returned a verdict of not guilty they also recommended that de Marigny and a friend of his be deported. The Duke of Windsor, whom de Marigny had described as 'not my favourite ex-King', endorsed the recommendation. An offer by Schindler to turn over his papers to the Bahamanian police was declined, as was an offer by Franklin D. Roosevelt to supply FBI officers.

Any number of theories have been put forward for the death of Oakes. They include an Obeah killing (the feathers were said to have religious significance) and, rather more likely, organised crime involvement. Oakes was known to be opposed to the establishment of a casino in the Bahamas. A version of the theory is that Harold Christie (who was later knighted) took Oakes to meet with representatives of the Mafia financier, Meyer Lansky. When Oakes proved obdurate he was killed on a boat, his body being brought home by car with Christie. Another is that it was a simple robbery-murder. Oakes was said to have a fortune in gold hidden on his property although none was ever discovered. Three other suggestions are that he was killed to prevent him moving his fortune from banks in the Bahamas to Mexico; that he had discovered an espionage operation on the Islands, and that he was killed by white supremacists who disapproved of the way he had improved the condition of the islanders. With cunning sleight of hand they had made it look like an Obeah killing.

James Leasor, *Who Killed Sir Harry Oakes?*; Kirk Wilson, *Investigating Murder*

Bridie O'Hara *see* **Hannah Tailforth**

Gertrude Dorothea O'Leary

About 3.30 p.m on the afternoon of 30 June 1949 the sixty-five-year-old off-licensee was beaten to death in her shop at 13 Thomas Street, Stokes Croft, Bristol. She loved flashy jewellery and almost certainly was killed because rumours spread in the neighbourhood of her supposed wealth. She was said to keep a tin box full of valuables. In the event the killer who strangled and then beat Miss O'Leary, hitting her at least twenty times, escaped with only her watch and a pendant valued at around £25. There had been a man who had been seen acting suspiciously in the neighbourhood the day before. He was described as 5'4" and 5'6" in height, with a tanned complexion and of slim build. He was thought to be forty-five to fifty years of age.

Initially the police were hopeful of an early arrest. A Vauxhall car with London registration plates was found on waste ground nearby, but this line of enquiry came to nothing when the owner, a commercial traveller, explained he had left his car and travelled by coach to save petrol. His clothing and property were searched and no bloodstains were found. He was eliminated from the enquiry.

The police then received an anonymous letter suggesting that the murderer might be the same as at that of Frances Buxton, the fifty-three-year-old murdered at the Cross Keys public house in Lawrence Street, Chelsea, on 18 January 1920. The man, a relative, suggested as the O'Leary murderer, had already been eliminated from the Buxton murder. He was six foot tall and so not a real candidate.

By the beginning of August some 114 suspects had been eliminated and statements taken from double that number of witnesses. Because of the ferocity of the attack on the lady, whom the police described as 'top heavy' and unstable on her feet, it was thought this might be the work of a madman. The police also had one fingerprint to go on but it was not thought to be helpful since it was either that of a woman or a boy.

In September another name came up. Witnesses made tentative identification of the man from photographs and he was arrested. He was able to provide an alibi and the police paid £3.3s costs to his solicitor for a Saturday afternoon spent in the police station.

There the matter really ended. Patrick Ridge, who was charged with the murder of Laura Buller in Whitehaven in 1950 in similar circumstances, was suggested as a name. So were two Poles, Roman Redel and Zgipniew Gower, who were charged with the murder of Robert Taylor after trying to rob a Bristol bank, but there was nothing really to connect any of the men.*

Alfred Oliver

On 22 June 1929 Alfred Oliver was found beaten in his tobacconist's shop at 15 Cross Street, Reading, England. At 6.15 p.m. his wife Annie returned from taking their Pekinese for a walk to find her husband lying against the wall behind the counter. He died from head injuries the next day without regaining consciousness. He had suffered a frenzied attack with multiple fractures of the skull and jaw. Money had been taken from the till. The only help the police had at that stage was a bloodied palm-print on one of the glass showcases in the shop. A pathologist thought that perhaps two weapons had been used – a coal-hammer, a jemmy or a tyre lever were suggested.

Two people were arrested and released. The first, a Scotsman who had been found stealing coats from a car, and the second an errand boy who admitted he had been in the shop, seen the body and run out in a panic. His prints did not match the palm-print on the showcase. Ascot races had been run that week and for a time it was thought that the killing might have been the work of a member of one of the racecourse gangs. Later, however, the police received information that a tall middle-aged man had been seen at the doorway of the shop.

Suspicion fell on the middle-aged American actor and silent film star, Philip Yale Drew, who was at the time touring in a melodrama *The Monster*. At one time Drew had appeared for four months at London's Lyceum as Indian Jim in a Western drama *The Savage and the Woman*. Throughout the 1920s his popularity had declined as his drinking had increased. On 25 July he was interviewed when the tour reached Nottingham and he denied that he even knew where Cross Street was. He was duped into giving his fingerprints but they did not match the palm-print in the shop. He was, however, identified by two witnesses who were invited to stand on a street corner and see if they could recognise the

---

* Redel and Gower, who shot Taylor in their effort to escape, were hanged at Winchester Prison on 7 July 1950.

man they had seen in Cross Street. The next day he was interviewed again and this time theatrically denied any involvement. His jacket was retrieved from a dry-cleaners and it was learned that he had already successfully tried to get a stain from it. Again he denied his involvement in a third interview on 7 August. The police were nevertheless convinced they had found the right man.

At that time a coroner's jury could return a verdict identifying the man whom they believed had committed the murder and the inquest took the role of committal proceedings. It was re-opened on 2 October 1929. Towards the end of the first afternoon a butcher, William Loxton, who worked two shops away from Oliver, told of a man with an accent who had come in and asked for some calves' liver. He had appeared confused. The man had then stood across the road from Oliver's shop. He was asked if he could see the man in the courtroom and identified Drew. He was only the first in a string of witnesses who now came forward to identify Drew as being in Cross Street and behaving oddly, probably drunkenly. Drew had been found intoxicated in his dressing room after the performance on the night of the murder.

By now Drew had obtained legal advice and was represented by the rising young barrister, Bill Fearnley-Whittingstall, who also appeared in the Birdhurst Rise inquest. Drew had public support on his side and was loudly cheered as he made his way to court on 7 October. Overall he made a good witness – he admitted his drinking habits and was just as vague about his movements as he had been when questioned by the police. On Wednesday 9 October, Albert Wells, a butcher's assistant, was called by Fearnley-Whittingstall to give evidence. He too had seen a man in a blue suit in Cross Street but he was convinced the man had a northern accent. When asked to look at Drew he said the actor was not the man he had seen. When the question was raised why he had not made a statement before he said he had – it transpired the police had overlooked it. It tallied in every way with his evidence.

This was the clincher for Drew. On 10 October, after a retirement of three hours, the jury returned a verdict of 'wilful murder by a person or persons unknown'. Drew made appearances on the balcony of his hotel in response to a cheering crowd. No further arrests were ever made.

The inquest was without doubt Drew's finest performance. From then on his career went further downhill. After his tour in *The Monster* was over he had only a further week's work in his life and at one time slept rough on the Embankment. In July 1937 he was awarded substantial damages for libel over a book, *Death to the Rescue*, by Milward Kennedy, published by Victor Gollancz. He died of cancer aged sixty in 1940.

Did Drew kill Oliver? Those who knew him said it was impossible and that
the man could not harm anyone. The police, suffering some chagrin, held an
opposite view believing the jury had been intimidated by the crowd outside.
Nevertheless they could still have charged Drew, and did not do so knowing an
acquittal would have been inevitable. Their view was that Drew had killed
Oliver in a fit of drunkenness and was immediately filled with remorse. The
palm-print turned out to be that of a local shopkeeper and had nothing at all to
do with the case.

Richard Whittington-Egan, *The Ordeal of Philip Yale Drew*

Patrick O'Nione
(aka Paddy Onions)

On 30 November 1982 Patrick O'Nione was killed near his son's wine bar,
Caley's, in Tower Bridge Road, London. He had been shot in the back of
the head. A police officer who saw the attack chased after but lost the killer.
O'Nione had been a major Underworld figure. In 1951 he had been acquitted of
acting as a decoy in a robbery and in 1963 he had been convicted in a conspiracy
to smuggle watches. There were a number of suggestions put forward as to why
he should have been executed. One was that he was a police informer, another
that it was over a drug deal which had gone wrong. A third is that he was killed
as a result of his financing of a protection network of South-east London clubs
and pubs. The most likely, however, is that he was murdered in revenge for the
death of Peter Hennessey, one of a number of influential South London brothers. Hennessey had been killed in a knife fight at a charity boxing evening at the
Royal Garden Hotel, Kensington.

It is unlikely the truth will ever be known. On 11 March 1983 Jimmy Davey,
a Coventry-based hardman, who had already served a six-year sentence for an
attack on a policeman, was in custody awaiting transfer to London for questioning over the O'Nione killing when he lunged at an officer. He was placed in a
chokehold and collapsed. After eleven days, with Davey still in a coma, the life
support machine was switched off. It was thought probable that Davey had
undertaken the O'Nione killing for a fee of £5,000.

Colin 'Duke' Osborne

On 3 December 1980, then aged fifty, Osborne was found dead on Hackney Marshes, East London. A minor public schoolboy and gambler who had once owed money to the Kray Twins and later became their armourer, he had served five years for possessing firearms. In prison he became something of a cigarette baron and in 1980 he put together a drugs importation scheme involving Lennie (also known as Teddy Bear or Silly Eddie) Watkins. Deals were set up in Pakistan and four successful runs were made, netting some £10 million at street prices. Watkins, however, had a predilection for lighting cigars in public with £20 notes, something which drew him to the attention of the authorities. The last operation, involving some £2.5 million of cannabis, was monitored by a joint police and customs exercise in the course of which Watkins shot and killed a customs officer, Peter Bennett, on 20 October 1980.

Both the Customs and Excise and other members of Watkins's team still at large wished to see Osborne. Certainly the former failed to do so but the latter may have managed it. An open verdict was recorded at the inquest. Suggestions of the cause of his death include suicide (a version favoured by Reggie Kray in his book *Villains We Have Known*), a drug overdose or that he died of a heart attack, possibly during questioning by his former colleagues. It was thought that his body had been kept in a freezer whilst a decision was made for its disposal. Watkins was sentenced to life imprisonment for the murder of Peter Bennett and committed suicide in prison.

Reggie Kray, *Villains We Have Known*; James Morton, *Gangland*

Johannes Otten *see* **Helen Smith**

Vera Page

On 14 December 1931 Charles Page of Notting Hill, London, reported his ten-year-old daughter Vera was missing. She had gone to her aunt's home to collect some swimming certificates, leaving there at about 4.45 p.m. Two days later a milkman found her body in a garden in Addison Road. There were marks on each side of her neck showing manual strangulation and across her throat there was a mark as if made by a cord. She had been raped. In the crook of her right elbow there was a finger-stall consisting of a piece of bandage and a piece of lint. The bandage had come from someone whose finger was suppurating and when tested smelled of ammonia. On her coat there were spots of grease. From an examination it seems the body had only been placed in the garden a couple of hours before it was found. Sir Bernard Spilsbury, the pathologist, was clear that Vera Page had been killed shortly after she had last been seen and that her body had been kept in a warm place for at least twenty-four hours. By the middle of January the police had made no progress in their investigation although they had a witness to say that she had seen a man with a wheelbarrow which contained a bundle done up in what appeared to be a red tablecloth.

Suspicion then fell on Percy Orlando Rush, who indeed used ammonia in his work at Whiteley's laundry near Olympia. He lived with his wife in Talbot Road, directly east of Blenheim Crescent where Vera had been seen looking in a shop window. There was evidence from a workmate that he was wearing a bandage on his little finger at the time of the child's death and candle grease from his home was compared with and found to be similar to that found on Vera Page's coat. He had a red tablecloth and in a pocket was found a pyjama cord. Not altogether surprisingly he possessed candles. Most people did.

At the inquest into Vera Page's death he admitted he had spoken once with the girl but Page denied that he had been wearing a bandage on the day of Vera's death and indeed that he had had anything to do with the killing. He said he had discarded his finger-stall two days before the murder; when the girl was last seen he was miles away, having started his long walk home from work. He told the coroner's jury that he had been at work and then at home all the next day. The scientific evidence was circumstantial – there must have been hundreds of people with finger-stalls in Notting Hill, the bandage and lint found did not exactly match that found on the body. Fortunately for Rush, the woman who had seen a man pushing the barrow in Holland Park Avenue failed to identify him. He was undoubtedly helped by the coroner who, summing up the matter to the jury, gave Rush the benefit of every possible doubt. 'There must be no missing link; no weak link. It must be a complete, strong, inevitable chain of evidence fixing the guilt upon the guilty.' Probably the jury could not believe that Rush would have killed the girl and then pushed her home in a wheelbarrow to where his wife was waiting for him. They retired for only five minutes before returning a verdict of murder by a person or persons unknown. They extended their 'sincere sympathy' to Mr and Mrs Page.

Percy Rush died aged seventy in Acton Hospital, London on 17 November 1961. He had cancer of the bladder. Articles in the newspapers suggested that although a number of alternative theories were advanced the police had not seriously considered any other person as a suspect for Vera Page's murder.

George Cornish, *Cornish of the Yard*; Douglas Browne and Tom Tullett, *Bernard Spilsbury*

Luther 'Jerry' Parks

The former associate of President Bill Clinton, Parks was shot dead on Markham Street in Little Rock, Arkansas, on 26 September 1993. Said to have criminal connections, ironically he owned American Contract Services Inc. which provided security during the Clinton-Gore presidential campaign.

He was driving home when a shot was fired at him from a White Chevrolet which followed his car. As it drew level a further four shots were fired. Once Parks's car had been stopped the gunman fired again. Some sources link the death with that of Vincent Foster, former Deputy White House Counsel (*qv*), as being all part of the Whitewater troubles which from time to time beset the Clinton administration.

Patricia Parsons

On Saturday 23 June 1990 the strikingly attractive forty-two-year-old Patricia Parsons, who liked to be known as Lee, was due to go to her Turkish boyfriend Oz's restaurant in Harlow, Essex, in the early evening. She never arrived and her body was found the next day in her Volkswagen Cabriolet in Epping Forest. She had been shot three times in the head and neck with what the police at first thought was a spear gun, but which turned out to be a crossbow.

Parsons had run a sauna in Camden Town for some twelve years and was a wealthy woman who owned at least three houses. After her death her parents received a demand from the Inland Revenue for £100,000. Her black book, which contained over two hundred names, was said to include at least one judge as well as barristers and television personalities.

The police believe her killer had forced her to drive from her home to Epping. It was thought to be a contract killing, possibly to prevent the disclosure of names in a story to be told to the Sunday papers. The name of James Moody (*qv*) has been conveniently suggested as the executioner.

'Lee loved her work and saw herself as a social worker to lonely men,' said a friend. 'She dressed to please them and relieved their fantasies.'

Mary Phagan

A fourteen-year-old girl, Mary Phagan was raped and murdered at the National Pencil Company's factory in Atlanta, Georgia, on Confederate Memorial Day, 26 April 1913. She had gone to the factory to collect her wages before she went to watch the parade. She was almost certainly killed by the janitor, James Conley, who accused the manager, Leo Frank (*qv*), who in his turn was convicted of her murder.

Sandra Phillips

On 19 June 1986 Wayne Darwell and his brother, Paul, were convicted of the murder of a Swansea sex shop manageress, Sandra Phillips. In June the previous year she had been sexually assaulted, savagely beaten and her shop was then set on fire in an effort to cover the traces of the murderer. Wayne Darvell, suggestible and with limited intelligence, was a compulsive confessor. He had earlier admitted the murder of a dentist he could not possibly have committed. Now he confessed to this murder and implicated his brother Paul.

When the case was referred back to the Court of Appeal in July 1992 the defence alleged that there had been a planted earring, false sightings and a doctored confession. The Crown Prosecution Service did not contest the appeal.

One crucial piece of evidence, that of a palm-print found on a pay-phone attached to the wall by the dead woman's body, was neither hers nor that of the brothers. This information was not passed to the defence. Instead they were told that the tests had been insufficient for positive identification.

Valerian Johannes Piecvnski *see* **Walter Wanderwell**

MaryAnn Plett

On 15 September 1971 the mother of two young children, MaryAnn Plett, who worked for a real estate office in Edmonton, Alberta, took a client who gave his name as James Cooper to see a tract of land near Looma, half an hour away. Cooper, who was described vaguely as a big man, had expressed interest in the land and had been shown it twice. On the morning of the 15th he had telephoned to say he would like to see the acreage one more time before making a bid. He said he had flown in from Winnipeg. On earlier occasions Plett had expressed her doubts about Cooper. He had, she said, made her uneasy and once had been seen arguing with himself outloud. Nevertheless she was extremely keen on closing the sale on behalf of her clients.

MaryAnn Plett left her office to meet Cooper at about 10 a.m. She was never seen alive again. At five in the evening her employer, Norman Schultz, telephoned Plett's husband, Jake, to say that he was worried because she had not returned to the office. Schultz and Jake Plett drove to Looma to make enquiries, with no success. They returned to the office of Graham Realty and it was arranged that the police would talk to Plett at his home. As he left the offices at Whyte Avenue, Plett saw his wife's two-tone green Pontiac being driven past the office by a man. Although he gave chase he was unable to stop him.

Two days later, two blocks away from the offices of Graham Realty, MaryAnn Plett's car was found. It had been thoroughly cleaned and no single fingerprint was discovered. There were, however, two spots of blood. One on the latch of the boot and the second on a rug kept in the boot.

On 30 October two men out hunting found her briefcase near Fort Assiniboine. The search for the body of MaryAnn Plett was intensified and some of her papers were unearthed. On 5 November five heavy snows suspended further searching for the duration of the winter. On 17 April the following year more pieces of clothing were uncovered near where her briefcase had been discovered. Later that day the top of her skull was found and an identification was made through her dental records.

No arrest was ever made. It is probable she was put in the boot of her car at some time but because the body had had a winter in the wilds it was not possible to say how she had died. All the police were able to say was that she had not died from a gunshot to the upper part of her head. According to one of the officers involved in the case, Al Gowler, the killer must have known the area well, counting on the body being destroyed by animals. He believed that Mary-Ann Plett had been chosen at random by a local man. Shortly after the disappearance of Plett another woman who worked in an estate agency reported she had been telephoned by a man from out of town. He said he wanted to view properties, preferably that evening. He told her he was staying at a city hotel but the police were unable to confirm this.

Jake Plett, a devout Christian as was his wife, arranged for donations to be made to the Gideons International. He was assisted in thanking the people who had supported him by a young woman, Marion Jeanne Craggs. Inside a year they married and had a daughter. Both Plett and his second wife were killed in an air crash in 1978.

Barbara Smith, *Deadly Encounters;* Jake Plett, *Valley of Shadows*

Florence Sawdey Polillo *see* **Kingsbury Run**

Edmund Pook *see* **Jane Clouson**

Helen Puttock *see* **Patricia Docker**

Stacey Queripel

On 24 January 1993 the body of seven-year-old Stacey Queripel was found in woods near her home in Bracknell, Berkshire. At the initial post-mortem examination it was thought that Stacey had accidentally strangled herself by catching her green plastic necklace on a branch of a tree. A subsequent examination showed that she had been strangled with a ligature. Her thirty-four-year-old mother Gilliane was arrested but later released. The evidence against her had been the linking of soil and pollen samples on her shoes to areas of South Hill Park where Stacey's body was found. Robert Wilson, the East Berkshire coroner, said at the inquest, held on 16 June 1994, that the number of samples taken could not make a '100 per cent tight case'. Nor, he added, were inconsistencies in timings given by Mrs Queripel able to point either to motive or to opportunity.

In a statement made by Mrs Queripel to her solicitor, she said that whilst running a bath in the evening she had gone to check on Stacey and her half-sister, Lynette, and found only Stacey's teddy bear in her bed. She called to her lodger to ask if she was with him and then went in search of her daughter. The door was kept on the latch and Stacey had been able to go out without being heard. A statement made to the inquest by Barry Queripel, Lynette's father, said his former wife could not cope with children. 'On one occasion, Gill told me that she got hold of Stacey by the neck and held her until she turned blue – until she realised what she was doing.' The lodger and friends who were in the house made statements to the effect that Mrs Queripel had said that as the children were all right in their beds she was going to have a bath. Half an hour later she told them Stacey was missing. Now she had changed her clothes and had muddy feet.

A verdict of unlawful killing was returned. Only new evidence would reveal the identity of the killer, said Robert Wilson.*

Peter Raisini

On Sunday, 24 March 1991 forty-seven-year-old antiques and cocaine dealer Peter Raisini was shot in the garden of his home in Palmers Green. Loyally his family said he had no enemies and suggestions for why he had been killed included the possibility that Raisini had accidentally stumbled across some major criminal activity and had been silenced, or that, in some way, he had offended a leading figure in the Underworld. A re-run of the events on the television programme *Crimewatch* failed to produce a charge. Once more the

---

* Given the infrequency of a repetition of names it is strange that Queripel should appear both as a victim and as a killer. On 29 April 1955 Elizabeth Currell was killed near the seventeenth tee at Potters Bar Golf Club, Middlesex. She had been beaten to death with an iron tee-marker which had a bloody hand-print on it. On 19 August it was matched to a seventeen-year-old local government clerk, Michael Queripel, who told the police that he had hit and tried to strangle Mrs Currell. He pleaded guilty to murder on 12 October 1955 and was ordered to be detained during Her Majesty's Pleasure.

name of James Moody (*qv*) has been bandied as the executioner of a contract killing over money owed for drugs.

Clive Raphael

On 6 March 1970 the British property millionaire, Clive Raphael, was killed in an aircrash in central France. The light plane, a twin-engined Beagle, plunged into a field and exploded, killing him, his parents and a woman friend. In his will he apparently left the bulk of his property to his barrister friend and man about the clubs, thirty-six-year-old Ronald Shulman. To his widow, the twenty-one-year-old model Penny Brahms, he granted only a shilling (5p) and four photographs of herself in the nude. The shilling was because of his nickname for her. It soon transpired that the will, made two days before Raphael's death, was a forgery and that Shulman had conspired with his one-time mistress and Eric Henry Alba-Teran, the fifty-one-year-old Duc d'Antin, to forge the will.

The woman's counsel said that Shulman had 'sold his soul to the devil'. A victim of Shulman's threats and violence, she had typed out the 'will' with one finger after the barrister had threatened to smash her head against the wall and kill her if she made a mistake.

At the trial Peter Bardon, of the Department of Trade and Industry, told the court that he had been called in to assist the French authorities' enquiry into whether the plane had been deliberately blown up. Shulman, when being questioned by him, had asked whether he had found any evidence of sabotage. When he told him there was not, he claimed, 'Shulman seemed surprised.' The mistress and Alba-Teran were convicted at the Old Bailey on 14 November 1972. She was given a suspended sentence and he three years' imprisonment, including an extra year for obtaining Raphael's white Rolls-Royce by deception. He was recommended for deportation at the end of his sentence. 'I accept you were under the domination of another man,' the Common Sergeant, Judge Mervyn Griffith-Jones, told the woman. 'If you take my advice you will see no more of this other man and forget this now. You are still young. Go back to your family and start again.'

Shulman failed to appear at the committal proceedings for the conspiracy charge and fled the country alleging that he had received death threats. He was thought to have gone to Brazil at a time when the extradition treaty with that country had lapsed. By the commencement of the trial Penny Brahms had married Michael 'Dandy Kim' Caborn-Waterfield, who in 1960 had been sentenced to four years imprisonment for an art-theft from film tycoon Jack Warner's home in the South of France.

Chelsea Ellen 'Nellie' Rault

On 9 May 1919 the twenty-one-year-old Nellie Rault, originally from Jersey but then a WAAC stationed at Bedford, England, was found stabbed to death at Haynes Park Wood near the town. She had been missing for three days and her body had been carefully hidden in a spinney. She had a knife wound in the heart, two in her breast and bruises on the face. It appears she had died whilst on her knees, probably begging for her life. Four days later thirty-year-old Sergeant Major Montague Cecil Hepburn, who was known to have been seeing her and was thought to be the last person to have seen her alive, was arrested and charged with her murder. After a number of remand hearings the Director of Public Prosecutions offered no evidence against Montague, although he entertained 'a strong personal opinion as to the identity of the person who committed the murder'.

The police received a number of 'confessions' including one from Canada in which a man, 'Frenchy', claimed that he had met Nellie Rault in the spring of 1919 and had killed her because he was jealous. Another letter, supposedly written by a W. F. Smith from Crowborough, Sussex, said that 'Frenchy' was a Leroy Morey, a deserter from the American Expeditionary Force, and that he had seen him in the Bedford area in May 1919. After extensive enquiries the police decided the letter was a hoax.

Elizabeth Ray

Elizabeth Ray, together with Dr J. O. LaChappelle and a wood cutter, John Timson, failed to complete a seventy-five-mile trip in LaChapelle's canoe from Stewart Island to Dawson City in Canada on the Yukon River on 5 October 1928. Miss Ray was reported to be carrying a quantity of jewellery. Their bodies were never discovered but the canoe in which they were travelling was holed

from the inside and the doctor's cocker spaniel, Rufus, was found alive. Blame
has been laid at the door of Arthur Nelson who was later shot to death at Eagle
River in the Yukon on 17 February 1932. Others who may have died at the hands
of Nelson include Charles Taylor (aka 'Yukon Fisher'), a trapper whose body
was found in 1927 near the headwaters of Flat River. His remains indicated he
had tried to defend himself and his cabin had been burned. Nelson may also
have been responsible for the deaths of Angus Hall, James Gilroy and Andrew
Hay who disappeared in the South Nahanni River area in May 1929. Phil Powers was also found dead in the burnt out cabin in the Fall River in 1932. His skull
had been crushed by timbers from the roof and again the blame is laid at Nelson's door.

Nelson, who was believed also to operate under the name of Albert Johnson,
was thought to be either a mass murderer or, at the very best, a grave robber. It
is believed he was part Swedish or certainly Scandinavian, a lone trapper who
eschewed company and worked without dogs in the Yukon from the middle of
the 1920s. On 26 December 1931 he shot and wounded a Royal Canadian
Mounted Policeman sent to question him over the springing of another man's
traps. An enormously powerful and resolute man, for forty-eight days he then
defied the teams of men and dogs (helped by supplies dropped from the air)
sent to capture him. White trappers, Indians and the RCMP were all engaged in
a running battle, followed with intense interest throughout the world, which
covered 150 miles along the Arctic Circle during the winter of 1931–32. At times
the temperature was some forty degrees below zero but Nelson, with neither
proper food nor heat, eluded his pursuers, surviving repeated fire and a gelig-
nite attack. During the chase he shot and killed RCMP officer 'Spike' Millen. He,
himself, was finally killed on the Eagle River, Yukon Territory, on 17 February
1932.

The wholly circumstantial evidence against Nelson as mass murderer was
some rudimentary identification and the fact that on him were found to be
pieces of gold dental work, which suggested he might have extracted these from
his victims. He was also known to favour out of the way places to camp, usually
just outside the town, which his critics use to mark him as a predator. He does
seem to have been in the vicinity of a number of murders at the right time and
he carried an unusual rifle of a similar type to that used by Johnson. He was also
taciturn in the extreme which did not act to his favour in the community. They
also point to the fact that on one occasion in 1928 he did not sell his trapped furs
at the trading post at Ross River and instead travelled some 200 miles to sell
them to another branch of the same company. The argument runs that he was

afraid to show his face in Ross River for fear he might be recognised as Johnson. Other stories about him include the suggestion that he was known as Coyote Bill and was wanted for the death of an irrigation company worker in 1930.

On the other hand he may have simply been a deeply misunderstood man.

Dick North, *The Mad Trapper of Rat River*

Karen Reed

On 30 April 1994 Karen Reed was shot dead on the doorstep of her home in Woking, Surrey. It is thought that, in a revenge killing, Mrs Reed was shot by mistake for her sister, Alison Ponting, a BBC World Service producer, who had been staying with her following the imprisonment of Alison's husband, Gagic Ter-Ogannisyan. A professional hitman is thought to have been used. A fortnight previously the sisters had been warned by the police that they might be the target of an attack when a car was abandoned after a chase and a gun was found together with a map marking the area of Woking where they lived.

The shooting related back to the murder in London in February 1993 of Rusland Outsiev, the self-styled Prime Minister of Chechenia, and his brother Nazerbeck for which two Armenians, Mkritch Martirossian and Gagic Ter-Ogannisyan were charged. Outsiev had been spending money like water during his time in London – £2,000 restaurant bills, £100 tips for waiters and a string of prostitutes visiting his flat in Marylebone. The Prime Minister, who was ostensibly in London to organise the printing of stamps and currency and was also in the market for missiles, was shot in the head, as was his younger brother. He had been invited by the Armenian KBG to desist in his negotiations for Stinger missiles but had declined.

Martirossian told the police, 'The murders were planned by the KGB. I had no choice but to obey the KGB. They would have harmed my family.' Apparently a hitman from Los Angeles had originally been recruited but, rather prosaically, he could not get a visa. When Martirossian was searched on his arrest he was found to have snake venom hidden in a bandage. He was to use this if he was caught. Instead, after a visit by an Armenian KGB agent to Belmarsh prison in South-east London, where Martirossian was on remand, he hanged himself. Ter-Ogannisyan was sentenced to life imprisonment for murder in October 1993.

Gwynneth Rees *see* **Hannah Tailforth**

Peggy Richards

A prostitute, Peggy Richards was found in the Thames near Waterloo Bridge on 23 June 1942. An attempt had been made to strangle her. A Canadian soldier, Joseph McKinstry, who had handed her handbag in to the police, was acquitted of her murder. His story was that, whilst he accepted he had had intercourse and then a quarrel with her, during which she had thrown her bag at him, he had left her alive. There was no evidence to disprove this story and it seemed unlikely the killer would draw attention to himself by handing in the woman's bag.

Sandra Rivett

On 7 November 1974 Sandra Rivett, the nanny of the children of the estranged Lord and Lady Lucan, was found beaten to death in the family's Georgian house at 46 Lower Belgrave Street, London SW1. Lady Veronica Lucan ran into the local public house The Plumbers' Arms shouting 'Help me, help me ... I've just escaped from a murderer ... my children, my children ... He's in the house ... He's murdered the Nanny.' She was bleeding from a cut to her head. The 'he', she claimed, was her estranged husband.

Lord Lucan, known to his friends as 'Lucky', was the son of the sixth Earl. He was educated at Eton, served in the Army, worked for six years in the City and then became a professional gambler. His wife, Veronica, was the daughter of an army major who died when she was two. Her mother then ran a small hotel in North Waltham, Hampshire. They married on 28 November 1963 and in 1964, Lucan inherited the title and the then reasonable fortune of £250,000. The marriage did not do well – for a start Lady Lucan was never really accepted by her husband's friends. After he separated from his wife in 1973 he snatched the children as they were in a park walking with their nanny, looking after them in his flat in Elizabeth Street until he lost the subsequent court action over their custody. It was an action which cost him £40,000.

From then on his financial position deteriorated. His gambling was at a level where he could win or lose £5,000 a day. He was paying £2,500 a year rent, a further £2,000 allowance to his wife and £1,250 for a nanny. He was in arrears with the rent of his flat and he was said to be paying private detectives £8,000 a year. At this time his income totalled only £7,000 from a family trust, the rest was supplemented by gambling. He then ran into a losing streak and not only fell behind with the hire purchase instalments on his Mercedes car but bounced a cheque at the Clermont, his gaming club, for £10,000. His credit facilities were for a time withdrawn. Then he tried to have his wife committed to a mental institution.

Shortly before the attack on Sandra Rivett, he confided to a friend that the only way out of his difficulties was to get rid of his wife. On the day of the murder Lucan played backgammon until four p.m., then went to a chemist to discuss medicine belonging to Lady Lucan. Following this he then met Michael Hicks Beach of Toby Eady's literary agency about an article on gambling, and finally dropped him off in Fulham. At about 8.30 p.m. he telephoned the Clermont and booked a table for five for 10.30 p.m. About 8.45 p.m. he went to the club in person and asked whether his friends had arrived. He drove off in his Mercedes.

When the police arrived at 46 Lower Belgrave Street they found what seemed to be bloodstains on the wallpaper leading to the basement. In an upstairs bedroom there was a bloodstained towel. Two of the three children were asleep; the eldest, Lady Frances Lucan, was awake and in another room. When the police returned to the basement they found Sandra Rivett's body inside a canvas mailbag. On the half-landing there was a nine-inch piece of lead piping. There were also extensive bloodstains on the ceiling, carpet and walls, at the head of the stairs to the basement and broken cups and saucers in the basement itself.

The police case against Lucan was that he knew Sandra Rivett usually took Thursday as her day off, and although plumper, she was the same height as his wife. She had a boyfriend, John Haskins, a barman in the Plumber's Arms. The reasoning was therefore that Lucan, thinking his wife was alone, attacked Rivett by mistake. When Lady Lucan heard the screams she went to the basement where, in turn, Lucan attacked her.

That night Lucan appears to have called on Madeleine Florman, whose children attended the same school as his, but she did not answer the street bell. Blood was found on her doorstep. The next day his friend, Bill Shand-Kydd, at whose wedding he had first met Lady Lucan, received two letters postmarked Uckfield. The first read:

Dear Bill,
　The most ghastly circumstances arose tonight, which I have briefly described to my mother, when I interrupted the fight at Lower Belgrave Street and the man left. V. accused me of having hired him. I took her upstairs and sent Frances to bed and tried to clean her up. She lay doggo a bit. I went into the bathroom and she left the house.
　The circumstantial evidence against me is strong in that V. will say it was all my doing and I will lie doggo for a while, but I am only concerned about the children. If you can manage it I would like them to live with you. [There is then a sentence about the financial arrangements.]
　V. has demonstrated her hatred for me in the past and would do anything to see me accused.
　For George and Frances to go through life knowing their father had been in the dock accused of attempted murder would be too much for them.
　When they are old enough to understand explain to them the dream of paranoia and look after them. Lucky.

The second letter explained that the family silver should be sold and the proceeds credited to banks at which Lucan was overdrawn.

It transpired that Lucan had driven to his friends in Uckfield, Ian and Susan Maxwell-Scott, arriving about 11 p.m. He told Mrs Maxwell-Scott that he had been passing the family home when he had seen a man attacking his wife in the basement. He had let himself in and as he went down the stairs had slipped in a pool of blood. He had not chased after the man but had comforted his wife. Whilst he went to find some towels to clean up the blood she had run out of the house. Mrs Maxwell-Scott had suggested he stay the night but he said he had to get back to clear things up. He drove away at 1.15 a.m. and has never been seen since. On Sunday, 10 November the car, which belonged to another friend, Michael Stoop, was found at Newhaven in East Sussex from where a cross-Channel boat leaves for Dieppe. It was parked there on the Friday morning. In it was a full bottle of vodka and a lead pipe wrapped in adhesive medical tape which Lady Lucan later identified as being similar to the weapon with which she had been attacked. There was some evidence that a man resembling Lucan had caught the 11 a.m. ferry.

Two days later Stoop received a letter.

My dear Michael, I have had a traumatic night of unbelievable coincidence. However, I won't bore you with anything to involve you except to say that when you come across my children please tell them that all I cared about was them. I gave Bill Shand-Kydd an account of what actually happened but judging by my last effort in court no one, let alone a 67-year-old judge, would believe me – and I no longer care, except that my children should be protected. Yours ever, John.

A warrant for the arrest of Lucan was issued at Bow Street Magistrates' Court on 12 November. It alleged the murder of Sandra Rivett and the attempted murder of Lady Lucan. An inquest into the death of Sandra Rivett was held in June 1975 when Lady Lucan gave evidence that she had been attacked that night by her husband. Efforts to probe into the marriage by Mr Michael Eastham QC, later a High Court judge, and instructed by the Dowager Lady Lucan, were severely restricted by Mr Gavin Thurston, the coroner. As they were permitted to do at the time, the jury returned a verdict of murder against Lord Lucan.

Subsequent to the inquest the officers involved in the murder investigation have given their views on the case. Superintendent Roy Ranson and Detective Inspector David Geering both believe he killed Sandra Rivett, mistaking her for Lady Lucan and, when he had discovered his mistake, committed a series of elementary errors such as leaving the murder weapon in the car. Geering believes that he lived on, aided by his legion of friends, possibly in South Africa.

In 1980 Lady Lucan told a Sunday newspaper that she was the target of a poison plot. In the October of that year she gave an interview which could be interpreted as admitting she might have been mistaken in her account of the incident. Lady Lucan had a breakdown in December 1983 and was, for a time, committed to Benstead Mental Hospital.

Efforts by the Dowager Lady Lucan to have the inquest verdict overturned came to nothing. Over the years there have been many sightings of Lord Lucan and at present (spring 1994) there is yet another rumour that he is back and living in London. However, one of the detectives in the case believes Lucan to be living in Botswana.

In her book *Lucan Not Guilty*, Sally Moore presents the case for the defence – one which is adhered to by a number of Lucan's friends. She argues that apart from Lady Lucan's allegations, the evidence was wholly circumstantial and that it was possible Sandra had been killed in the course of a robbery.

In January 1985 a second Lucan nanny, Christabel Martin, was killed by her husband, Nicholas Boyce. He strangled her, dismembered her body and boiled some of her flesh before dumping it around London in plastic bags. As for the head, he dropped this into the Thames whilst out walking with his young children. He received six years for her manslaughter.

Sally Moore, *Lucan: Not Guilty*; John Pensrose, *The One That Got Away*

Jane Roberts

On 7 January 1880 Jane Roberts, a nineteen-year-old housemaid, was killed by a blow to the back of the head at her employer's home in Harpurhey, Manchester. Her employer, Mrs Greenwood, discovered the girl lying in the kitchen. There were no footprints nor was a weapon found. Nothing was stolen and no attempt had been made to rape her. Mr Greenwood had received a letter asking him to meet the writer in the Three Tuns public house and it was thought the letter had been written to lure him from the house. His wife was also out at the time.

The writing on the letter to Greenwood was identified as being similar to that on letters inviting locals to subscribe to an assisted passage to Australia for a Robert Haild. He and his friend, Thomas Leycock, were arrested and it was popularly believed that Leycock had confessed to murdering the girl whilst Roberts kept watch. Nothing came of the story. Haild's family was able to produce a substantiated alibi.

Other suggestions for the murder included an attack by a jealous lover. An attempt was made to trace the killer through a photograph of the eyes of the dead girl. There was a common belief that the image of the murderer would be fixed on the retina.

Jerome Caminada, *Twenty-five Years of Detective Life*

Edwin Robert Rose

On 4 August 1889 the body of Edwin Rose, an English tourist, was found on Arran Goatfell, Ayrshire. He had been missing for a week after going climbing with John Watson Laurie, a petty criminal from a respectable Glasgow family, whom he had met by chance on holiday in Rothesay. His body had been placed under a boulder and covered with stones and heather. His head and face were smashed, his cap was neatly folded and found in the bed of a nearby stream. All his possessions had been taken and his boots were missing.

Suspicion fell on Laurie, who was seen sporting some of Rose's distinctive clothing and who disappeared from his lodgings shortly afterwards leaving the week's rent owing. He sent a number of letters to the *North British Daily Mail* denying his involvement in the murder and threatening suicide. He provided a somewhat vague alibi saying that he had left Rose with two other men on the top of Goatfell and had made the descent with two friends whom he declined to name.

> I could easily prove that what I say is true, but I decline to bring the names of my friends into this disgraceful affair, so will content myself by wishing them a last adieu.

Edwin Robert Rose.

He was captured on 3 September near the railway station at Tillietudlem on the Glasgow line. He had been spotted by the local stationmaster who had reported the sighting to an off-duty constable. After a short chase Laurie was found with his throat cut. He had, at the very least, made a gesture at suicide. His words to Constable Gordon on his arrest were, 'I robbed the man, but I didn't murder him.'

His trial was a short-lived affair. It began in Edinburgh on Friday 8 November when the presiding judge, Lord Kingsburgh, announced it would be finished on the Saturday. The evidence against Laurie was largely circumstantial. He now denied he had stolen the unfortunate Rose's possessions and there was no evidence that he had actually killed him. He persisted with his story of meeting the men at the top of the climb. The defence was, therefore, that Rose had fallen and there was medical evidence which, at the very least, allowed this to be a possibility.

As for the theft of the clothing, this was blamed on holiday-makers from the Glasgow Fair. There was a more interesting explanation for the missing boots: Gaelic superstition has it that if a man meets a sudden death his ghost will continue to walk until his boots are buried below high-water mark. One of the policemen who had been present at the discovery of the body had taken Rose's boots and rendered this service to him.

True to his word the Lord Justice-Clerk was to have a verdict in two days and began to sum up at 8.40 p.m. on the Saturday night. After three-quarters of an hour the jurors – who had complained about the conditions in which they were kept overnight in an Edinburgh hotel and were clearly fractious – returned a verdict of guilty by the bare majority of 8–7. Laurie was sentenced to death to be hanged in the prison at Greenock, on the Clyde.

Within three weeks over 138,000 signatures had been received in support of a reprieve. Laurie had help from a number of doctors who wrote explaining how easy it was to suffer from vertigo and that Rose's death might have resulted from a fall. An enquiry was set up into Laurie's medical condition and he now wrote to the Secretary of State for Scotland admitting stealing from the body and denying the killing. It is said that two days before his execution Laurie asked warders to whom he could make a confession. It was never made. The next day he was reprieved and his sentence commuted to penal servitude for life on the grounds that the Medical Commission had found him to be of unsound mind.

He was never released from prison, to which he was sent rather than a mental institution. He worked well in the prison workshops and led the singing in chapel. However he was involved in an abortive prison escape on 24 July 1893. He was next heard of in 1910 when he was transferred to the Perth Criminal Asylum. He died there on 5 October 1930. In the last few years of his life he had been permitted to take walks in the town. He appears not to have shown any remorse or sadness over Rose's death, remarking that the man had little in the way of money.

In his book *Murder Not Proven?*, Jack House argues that the correct verdict should have been just that and the jury, annoyed at the circumstances in which they were confined, returned a quick verdict without proper consideration of the conflicting medical evidence. On the other hand the pre-eminent chronicler of Edinburgh murder cases, William Roughhead, who attended the trial, had no sympathy for Laurie, referring to him as the callous murderer.

The case has notable similarities to the death on 1 April 1882 of Charles Wagner (see West Ham Vanishings).

William Roughhead (ed), *Notable British Trials*; Jack House, *Murder Not Proven*

Arnold Rothstein

One of America's great gamblers, bootleggers and fixers (including the World Series of 1919 in which he persuaded players of the Chicago White Sox to lose the games), the forty-six-year-old Rothstein was shot on 4 November 1928.

A millionaire several times over Rothstein had had a poor year from investments and loans. On Memorial Day 1928 he had lost over $130,000 at Belmont Park racetrack in Queens. In September he played in a two-day poker game with several West Coast gamblers, including 'Nigger' Nate Raymond and Titanic Thompson, and lost over $320,000. He declined to pay the IOUs he had signed, claiming that the game had been fixed.

It appeared his gambling luck had turned again on the day of his death. He had been betting on the presidential election favouring Herbert Hoover. About 10 p.m. he received a telephone call at Lindy's, the popular Broadway restaurant. One of the players in the game, George F. 'Hump' McManus, wished to see him he said. Rothstein was found by a lift attendant three-quarters of an hour later near the elevator at the Park Central Hotel. Asked by the police who had shot him, he replied, 'Never mind. Get me a taxi.'

According to the taxi driver who was called, the gun which had been used to shoot Rothstein was thrown from a window of the hotel and landed on the roof of his cab. Rothstein died two days later. McManus was indicted for the murder but never brought to trial. Both Thompson and Raymond had unshakeable alibis. It is possible Rothstein was killed over the gambling debts but it is more likely that the powerful syndicates thought his financial acumen was failing and he could soon be an expensive liability. His empire was divided between various interested parties, including Lucky Luciano who took over the bootlegging enterprise.

Damon Runyon, *New York American*, Nov-Dec 1929 (partly reprinted in Jonathan Goodman (ed), *Masterpieces of Murder*)

Walter Graham Rowland *see* **Olive Balchin**

Arnold Schuster

On 9 March 1952 the twenty-four-year-old Brooklyn clothing salesman was found dead on the street where he lived. He had been shot in each eye and twice in the groin. His mistakes which led to his death were, first, to see the legendary escaped bank robber, Willie Sutton, on a New York subway in February 1952, and secondly to give the police the information which led to Sutton's capture. Schuster achieved temporary fame with interviews on television but on 9 March he was killed. The execution was thought to have been ordered by Albert Anastasia after he had seen the pictures of Schuster on television on the grounds that he could not stand informants. The contract may have been carried out by Frederick J. Tenuto, a man on the FBI's list of the ten most wanted criminals. Tenuto was himself later killed, as was Anastasia.

Peter Maas, *The Valachi Papers*

Mary Seaward *see* **Eliza Carter**

Shark Arm murder *see* **James Smith**

Alison Shaughnessy

At about 6 p.m. on Monday, 3 June 1991 Alison Shaughnessy was stabbed to death in her flat in Battersea, South-west London. She had been struck fifty-four times. Police enquiries focused on twenty-two-year-old Michelle Taylor, a former girlfriend of John Shaughnessy, who had continued her relationship with him after his marriage. Their affair had ended in the autumn of 1990, some three months after Shaughnessy's wedding. Michelle Taylor remained good friends with both the Shaughnessys. The motive, the police believed, was jealousy and the elimination of a rival.

Michelle Taylor was able to produce an alibi. She had been working in her job as an accounts clerk at a private health clinic in Lambeth Road, South London with John, who worked as a gardener. On the evening of Alison's death she had been with him at about 6 p.m. arranging flowers in patients' rooms. She had then spoken to a porter and at 8 p.m. she had given John a lift to his flat to collect two large flowerpots. At half past eight that evening they discovered Alison's body. Michelle ran into the street screaming and called the police. When she was asked later that evening whether John had any girlfriends she said no. It was when, some weeks later, the police discovered the old relationship between Michelle and John that a theory was constructed that Michelle could have stabbed Alison to death in her flat and returned to the clinic before 6 p.m.

Alison's movements could be traced back to the time she left work in the Strand very shortly after 5 p.m.

There were problems with the theory. The first was a witness, a girl in the clinic called Jeanette Tapp, who said that Michelle and her younger sister, nineteen-year-old Lisa, had been at the clinic talking to her at 5.15 on the afternoon of Alison's death. The second problem was one of timing. How could Michelle and Lisa, who had also become a suspect, have killed Alison after 5.40 p.m. (the earliest time she could have arrived home), cleaned themselves of all the blood from what was a truly savage attack and Michelle been back at the clinic at 6 o'clock? Jeanette Tapp adhered to her story on three occasions but, on 7 August, the police came to her home at 5.40 a.m. and told her she was being arrested for conspiracy to murder. By the time she arrived at Tooting police station nearly three hours later she had changed her mind. She was now certain that she had not been with Lisa and Michelle at 5.15 p.m. In fact she had not seen them until 7 p.m. She was released without charge and the following day Michelle and Lisa were charged with murder.

There was no scientific evidence to link either of the sisters to the killing. Most surprisingly, no spot of blood could be found on the clothing of either of them. A doctor said he had seen two girls running from the flat at the time of the murder but he failed to pick out either of the sisters at an identification parade. There were five sets of unidentified fingerprints in the flat and there was some evidence that jewellery had been stolen. The defence was able to show that it was possible Alison had not arrived home until after 6 p.m. that day. What assisted to convict both sisters was the alarming coverage in the press of the affair John had had with Michelle. There were stories that she was a jealous mistress and when it came out that she had slept with John on the way to Ireland for his wedding a further volley of abuse was delivered at her. Much was made of an entry in her diary in October 1990 in which she had described Alison as an unwashed bitch and said, 'My dream solution would be for Alison to disappear as if she never existed.' She had also wrongly told the police that Lisa had never been to the Shaughnessy flat. The girls were convicted and sentenced to life imprisonment.

On 11 June 1993 the Court of Appeal released the girls, quashing their convictions which were ruled to be unsafe and unsatisfactory. The press coverage of the trial, described as 'unremitting, extensive, sensational, inaccurate and misleading', had, said Lord Justice McCowan, 'created a real risk of prejudice'. There was also an evidential problem: the Crown's eye-witness, Dr Michael

Unsworth, had made another statement, not disclosed to the defence, in which he had said that one of the girls he had seen fleeing from the flat was black.

A possible alternative theory for the killing comes from a social worker who, on 5 June 1991, had telephoned the police to say that a man, whom he named, had told him he had 'done a girl'. The man had been in a squat in Battersea, had also been sleeping rough in the Strand and had carried a knife. The social worker and a colleague telephoned the police on a number of other occasions but when detectives finally went to interview the named man he had disappeared.

Sally Shepherd

On Saturday, 1 December 1979 the body of twenty-four-year-old Sally Shepherd, restaurant manageress at the Old Vic theatre in London's West End, was found raped and battered in Staffordshire Street, Peckham, South-east London. The night before she had been to visit friends in Essex and had managed to catch the last bus at New Cross. The bus stopped in Clayton Road and Sally asked the conductress if she could stay on until the depot. She was told it was against the rules and so she began her walk of a few hundred yards to her home.

About 8.30 a.m. two workmen found first a pair of women's boots and then the naked body of Sally Shepherd. Her purse was gone and the remains of the Indian takeaway she had been carrying lay strewn around. She had suffered a number of broken ribs and damage to her spine. Ironically the killing had taken place on the other side of the police station yard. 'If only she had managed to scream or call out she might be alive today,' said Superintendent Graham Melvin. 'But the officers heard nothing unusual to alert them.'

The bus conductress was able to speak of seeing a white Cortina with a dark patch of primer on one wing parked in the High Street and a man running out of Staffordshire Street. Another witness saw a man weeping and banging his head against a wall where she died.

In September 1991 a fifty-five-year-old man was arrested and questioned over her killing. He was released on bail to return to Peckham police station. No charge was ever brought.

Marilyn Reese Sheppard

On 4 July 1954 the thirty-one-year-old Marilyn Sheppard, wife of Dr Samuel Holmes Sheppard (one of the most highly paid surgeons in Ohio), was killed by thirty-five blows to the head at their beachside family home at 28924 Lake Road, Bay Village, Ohio. The prosecution's case against Dr Sheppard, son of a prominent local osteopath, was that his wife had discovered his infidelity and he had killed her during a quarrel. The thirty-year-old surgeon's version was that both he and Marilyn had been attacked by an intruder. They had entertained friends, the Aherns, to dinner and he had fallen asleep on the couch before they left. It was Marilyn who had showed the Aherns out at around 12.30 a.m.

At about 5.45 a.m. Sheppard telephoned his friend, John Spencer Houk, the local mayor, to say, 'I think they've got [or killed] Marilyn.'

When Houk arrived it appeared the house had been ransacked and the contents of Sheppard's medical bag were strewn over the floor. There were no signs of a forced entry, nor were there any relevant fingerprints. Within half an hour Sheppard had been taken to the hospital owned by his family in Bay Village. In a statement made to the police on 10 July he said, 'I charged into our room and

saw a form with a light garment ... grappling with something or someone.' He went on to say he had been knocked out from behind and then, when he had come to, had taken Marilyn's pulse and discovered she was dead. He checked his son Chip's room to make sure he was all right and then ran downstairs because he had seen 'a form progressing rapidly somewhere'. He said he had chased the figure down on to the beach and lunged at him. The man, someone with bushy hair, caught his neck in a grip and knocked him unconscious. When Sheppard recovered for the second time he went back to the house to call Houk.

At the funeral of his wife, Sheppard arrived in a wheelchair, his neck in a brace. He had suffered a fractured cervical

Marilyn Sheppard.

vertebra. It is possible he would never have been charged but for the crusading attitude adopted by the *Cleveland Press* and the growing hostility towards him. 'Why no Inquest? Do it now, Dr Gerber?' ran the headline for 21 July 1954, and the coroner Dr Gerber duly announced it would begin the next day. He did not allow witnesses to be represented and Sheppard in his eight-hour examination denied he had committed adultery. On 30 July a crowd surrounded the home of Sheppard's brother, Richard, also a doctor, where Sam Sheppard was staying. There were cheers when the police arrived with a warrant for his arrest.

There were a number of questions to be answered at the trial, which began on 4 November 1954. The first was what had happened to the T-shirt Sheppard had been wearing. Another related to the disappearance of morphine from his medical bag. A third was whether a medical instrument had made the imprint on the blood on Mrs Sheppard's pillow. Sheppard was not helped by his inital denial of adultery when the prosecution called Susan Hayes, a twenty-four-year-old laboratory technician, who said not only had she had an affair with him but that he had spoken of leaving his wife.

There was not really a great deal of hard evidence against Sheppard. His friend, Nancy Ahern, called on his behalf, hesitated when asked about Sheppard's relationship with his wife. 'Mrs Sheppard always seemed very much in love with her husband, but I was never quite sure about Dr Sam.' Much was also made of the family dog, Koko, which does not seem to have barked when the 'intruder' came. It was argued that this meant there was no such person. John Mahon, prosecuting, also concentrated on Sheppard's admission of perjury at the inquest by denying his adultery, then a crime in Ohio. As for the other questions they were largely unresolved.

After a four-day retirement, the jury found him guilty of murder in the second degree on 21 December 1954 and he was sentenced to life imprisonment. Sheppard's family then engaged a forensic scientist, Dr Paul Kirk, to try to establish his innocence. Kirk's belief was that Marilyn was killed in a sexual attack. In support he found blood on the wardrobe door which did not match either of the Sheppards and, from the position of the blows, he formed the opinion that the killer was left-handed, which Sheppard was not. Sheppard's appeal was turned down on 20 July 1955 and five months later the US Supreme Court refused to review the case.

In July 1957 a Donald Wedler confessed to the killing, saying he had entered a house in the Lake Road area and struck a woman with an iron pipe before assaulting her husband. The confession contained many details which did tie in with the killing but it was dismissed by the police as a hoax. In May 1960 the US Supreme Court again refused to review the evidence.

In August 1961 Sheppard's trial lawyer William Corrigan died and the family engaged the then up and coming F. Lee Bailey to act for him. Five years later Bailey secured a re-trial. By now the moral climate in Ohio had changed and adultery was no longer seen as the disgraceful thing it had been. Bailey was able to establish that Marilyn had herself had lovers. Paul Holmes, a private investigator engaged by the family, believed that apart from the Sheppards there were two people in the house on the night of Marilyn's death. One theory advanced was that she had been killed by the wife of one of her lovers, and the lover who followed her to try to stop the attack. This, at least, would have explained why the dog did not bark at people he knew. In fact a woman's footprints were found on the beach leading away from the house but Corrigan had not brought this up at the first trial.

At the re-trial Bailey did not allow Sheppard (now out on bail), whom he thought was losing his grip in a world of drink and drugs, to testify. He effectively destroyed the police surgeon and described the evidence as 'ten pounds of hogwash in a five pound bag'. On 16 November 1966 Sheppard was found not guilty after a twelve-hour retirement by the jury. It emerged that there had been five ballots before a verdict was reached. On the first one, four of the older members had voted for a conviction.

Whilst on bail Sheppard had married German-born Ariane Tebbenjohns (or Tennenjohanns) – whose half-sister was the wife of Dr Paul Josef Goebbles – with whom he had corresponded in prison. After the acquittal he regained his licence to practice medicine but on 3 December 1968 he resigned after a malpractice claim which the hospital's insurance company refused to settle whilst he was on the staff. Later he was divorced on the grounds of extreme cruelty.

In August 1969, at the age of forty-five, he became a small-time professional wrestler and in the October married his manager's daughter, twenty-year-old Colleen Strickland. He claimed he had never been happier but, nevertheless, continued to drink heavily. He died of liver failure on 6 April 1970. At the time of his death he was almost penniless and facing a $300,000 medical malpractice claim. F. Lee Bailey was one of the pall-bearers at his funeral. His former wife Ariane attended, as did his brother Richard. His other brother, Stephen and son Chip did not – they were travelling in Europe.

Although he does not mention it in his book, Bailey later appeared in front of a Grand Jury regarding the allegation that there were two people involved in the murder. On 15 December 1966 the Grand Jury declined to issue a Bill of

Indictment saying that the suggestions made by Bailey were 'merely the opinion of an attorney representing a client and are wholly unsubstantiated'.

F. Lee Bailey, *The Defence Never Rests*; Paul Holmes, *The Sheppard Murder Case*; Sam Sheppard, *Endure and Conquer*; John Harrison Pollack, *Dr Sam – An American Tragedy*

Elizabeth Anne Short

The body of twenty-two-year-old Elizabeth Short was found on a vacant lot on South Norton Avenue, a block east of Crenshaw Boulevard, Los Angeles, on 15 January 1947. Her body, cut in half at the waist, was found five days later. The autopsy showed she had been tortured for two or three days, gagged and bound, possibly with wire, and that she had been hung head downwards and alive whilst she was stabbed and burned with cigarettes. Finally her throat had been cut from ear to ear. A rose tattooed on her thigh had been gouged out and the initials 'BD' had been carved on the other one. Every drop of blood had been drained from the body. Her hair had been shampooed and hennaed.

The first problem was identification. Fingerprints were taken and matched as Elizabeth Ann Short, not because of a criminal record but because during the war she had been a clerk in the United States Post Office Exchange. Born in Medford, Massachusetts, she had run away from home in Boston and travelled to California to become a would-be bit-part actress, and certainly a part-time prostitute. Short was known in the bars and hotels as the Black Dahlia because of her jet black hair and her predilection for wearing black clothing.

She had also been a waitress in Miami and a cocktail waitress in Chicago. When she was found in the El Paseo Restaurant in Santa Barbara drinking as a minor she was shipped back East. On the way she skipped from the train and returned to Santa Barbara where she became 'Cutie of the Week' at Camp Cooke. After several liaisons she had met, and probably become engaged to, a Matthew Gordon Jnr, an Air Force Major from Pueblo, Colorado. He was killed in an air crash just after the war. Certainly his mother sent her a telegram of condolence.

Shortly after that she had gone to San Diego and stayed with the French family in Bayview Terrace, having spun them the sob story of a dead husband and baby son. She left on 8 January 1947 in a tan coupé with a red-haired man

Elizabeth Short with Major Matthew Gordon Jnr.

– she had told Mrs French the man was an airline employee. From then on there were various sightings of her in a number of bars and clubs and a former boy-friend received a letter saying she was planning to move to Chicago with a man named Jack. She also seems to have returned to San Diego where she was seen in a drive-in restaurant with a red-headed man. On 10 January 1947 she was offered dinner by a salesman at the Los Angeles Biltmore, declined the invitation and at 10 p.m. went south on Olive towards Sixth. She was not seen alive again.

One man, Robert 'Red' Manley, was arrested and questioned. An ex-Air Force band saxophonist, he had been admitted to a psychiatric ward before being discharged from the service in 1945. He admitted he had been with Elizabeth Short, voluntarily submitted to a lie-detector test which proved inconclusive and his wife alibied him for the day of Elizabeth's death. He was released without charge. Seven years after he was committed to another psychiatric hospital where he was once again questioned over the death of the Black Dahlia and again released after taking truth serum. Later he committed suicide.

On 21 January, the city editor of the *Los Angeles Examiner* received a call giving details of the killing and saying that he could expect to receive some souvenirs. The caller said he would give himself up, 'But I want to watch the cops chase me some more.' Ten days after her body was found an unsealed envelope with her social security card, birth certificate and some personal papers were sent to the police. There was also a note clipped from the *Los Angeles Examiner* and other papers: 'HERE! is Dahlia's belongings ... Letter to follow.'

There were over fifty confessions which the police thought to be false, various people gave themselves up and were painstakingly eliminated from the enquiry and a number of copycat killings followed her death. The police came no nearer to a solution than to suggest the killer might either be a sadist who had picked her up, a repulsed lesbian or someone from whom Short had attempted to extort money who had made the killing look like a sex offence. A number of commentators, including Captain Donahoe, in charge of the investigation, have suggested that, because of the nature of the injuries and the spite with which they were inflicted, the killing was done by a woman. One line of enquiry tended to show that Elizabeth Short had had a lesbian relationship which she had broken off just prior to her death.

Richard and Molly Whittington-Egan, *The Bedside Book of Murder*

Benjamin 'Bugsy' Siegel

On the evening of 20 June 1947 forty-one-year-old Benjamin 'Bugsy' Siegel, racketeer extraordinaire, was shot dead in North Linden Drive, Beverly Hills, as he sat on the sofa at the home of his girlfriend, Virginia Hill, bag-lady for the Mob, who was conveniently away in Europe that night. Versions of the reason for her visit to Europe vary: the more romantic one is that she knew of the contract on him, warned him to leave and when he did not do so, fled herself; the more prosaic is that she was sent on a Mob mission to get her out of the way. He was hit with six shots fired through the window, the first of which blew his eye fifteen feet away on to the tile floor. The man sitting next to him, an old gambling friend, Allen Smiley, was unhurt. No one was ever charged with his murder.

On the face of it Siegel was one of the more engaging members of organised crime. In his later years he lived a dual life, exercising his undoubted charm in Hollywood where his friends included Jean Harlow, Clark Gable and Gary Cooper, whilst simultaneously functioning as a contract killer. He was known as a cowboy – a killer who is not content with the mere organisation but one who wishes to be at the scene.

He had grown up on the Lower East Side in New York and had been a childhood friend of Meyer Lansky with whom he had run gambling concessions before graduating into muscle for hire. He worked with Lucky Luciano and was instrumental in the removal of the old guard of racketeers. Siegel was sent to California to consolidate the West Coast operations and it was whilst he was there, organising the shipment of narcotics and the syndicate's bookmaking operations, that he dreamed up what would be his memorial, Las Vegas. Then a small town, he turned it into the gambling paradise it is today. The flagship Flamingo Hotel was named after his nickname for Ms Hill.

Siegel was ahead of his time. The Flamingo lost money and worse he was skimming money from the mob, which is claimed was the reason for his execution, voted by a council of which Meyer Lansky had the casting vote and approved by Luciano at a conference in Havana. Lansky denied any involvement. 'Ben Siegel was my friend until his final day,' he said ambiguously on one occasion. In 1975 he clarified things, 'If it was in my power to see Benny alive he would live as long as Matusula [sic].' Another theory, advanced by Martin Short, is that he was killed in the so-called 'race-wire' war. The head of the rival organisation to control the transmission of racing results across the States, James Ragen, had been killed the year before. It is possible that Siegel was murdered as a reprisal.

Virginia Hill did not attend Siegel's funeral nor did the Hollywood stars he had cultivated. She later thwarted an IRS investigation into her affairs by marrying a ski-instructor and going to Europe. She died in March 1966 of an overdose of pills. She had lain down in the snow. Suggestions that she had been murdered because she was about to publish a 'tell all' cannot be substantiated.

Robert Lacey *Little Man*; Jay Robert Nash, *World Encyclopedia of Organised Crime*; Martin Short, *Crime Inc*

Leonard Siever

On 11 December 1933 Russian-born dentist Leonard Siever was found shot dead in his parked car outside the Scottish Rite Cathedral in Pasadena, California. A great ladies' man Siever may have been killed because of his Gladstone-like hobby of rescuing girls whose virtue was a risk – in Siever's case from Hollywood clubs. It may have been because of his involvement with any number of married women. A Pasadena surgeon Dr Carl Wagner was repeatedly questioned before his death in a car accident. Both had courted the same divorcee Frances Cooke. A claim by Nellie Madison after her conviction for the murder of her husband, Eric, that he had killed Siever in a fight over a divorcee may have been made for tactical purposes. It was never substantiated. Nor were suggestions that his death was somehow linked to the Wanderwell killing (*qv*). In his book John Austin suggests that local informed gossip had it that both Siever and Wanderwell were chasing the same bit-part actress and were killed by her jealous boyfriend. Again it was a story which was never put to the test.

John Austin, *Hollywood's Unsolved Murders*

Stanley Silk *see* **David Brindle**

Karen Silkwood

A t about 7.30 p.m. on 13 November 1974, laboratory analyst and spokesperson for the Oil, Chemical and Atomic Workers Union (OCAW) at the Kerr-Mcgee plant in Crescent, Oklahoma, twenty-eight-year-old Karen Silkwood was found in her car which had crashed on Highway 74, the road leading from Crescent to Oklahoma City some thirty miles away. The police were called; she was cut from the car and taken to hospital but she was dead on arrival.

She had just left a union meeting at the Hub Café in Crescent and was due to meet a reporter from the *New York Times* to talk about her concerns for safety at the Kerr-McGee plutonium plant. She was known to be a good driver and had won a trophy in a women's competition. Her boyfriend, Drew Stephens, was a car enthusiast and had fitted her car with extra-traction tyres. The evening was cold and dry and the road virtually flat and straight. Her car was found, on its left side, by a lorry driver after it had crashed into a culvert about seven miles from the café. Some papers were on the ground outside the car and, in one version of events, were put back inside by the police. In her purse, outside the car, was found a sleeping pill and part of another tablet which could not be analysed.

Karen Silkwood's death has become a classic accident-versus-conspiracy theory, with the union spokesperson seen as a martyr by some, such as the

National Organisation of Women who declared 13 November Karen Silkwood Memorial Day, and derided by others as a drug-smoking unbalanced woman who abandoned her three young children and deliberately contaminated herself for her cause.

Silkwood worked as a laboratory analyst in a department which was considered a trouble spot by the management of the company, with suggestions that some of the employees had deliberately contaminated themselves either for dares or political purposes. If a contamination occurred the usual practice was for the laboratory to be closed. On 31 July 1974 it was suggested that she may have deliberately contaminated filters which had been found to be clean before she began her

Karen Silkwood.

shift. A week later she was elected to the union bargaining committee, much of whose role was to present the workers' concerns over health and safety at the plant. A report alleging thirty-nine cases, where it was said the company had failed to keep plutonium levels safe as well as failing to monitor exposure and train workers in safety, was compiled. Karen Silkwood also employed herself in putting together a report in which she sought to prove that quality-controllers at the plant were touching up photographs of fuel rods to cover flaws. Her argument was that faults, which showed up on negatives, were being eliminated from the prints. If this was correct and national medial coverage could be obtained, the union would have an extremely strong card to play in negotiations with management at Kerr-McGee.

There is little doubt that shortly before the meeting with the reporter from the *New York Times* Karen Silkwood was in a highly emotional state. She had been losing weight and telling her family she would soon be quitting her job. She claimed that forty pounds of plutonium was missing from the plant. In fact much of it was in the pipes at the plant. On 31 October she had a minor road accident, after which she said she had swerved off the road to avoid hitting a car. On 4 November she was found to have a level of plutonium contamination over forty times the AEC safety limit. On 5 November the level was even higher and there was contamination at her home. Again it was suggested that she had deliberately caused this.

When her car was pulled from the culvert it was clear it had banged against the concrete side. This tended to negate the belief, held by Silkwood supporters, that she had been deliberately forced off the road. There were no skid marks and her death was recorded as an accident. The investigating officer filed a report that he believed Silkwood, under the influence of a combination of drugs and alcohol, had fallen asleep at the wheel.

The union was not satisfied with the report and hired its own investigator, whose findings included that the dents in the back bumber were made by something moving from the rear as opposed to occuring when the car was hauled from the culvert. Because of the camber in the road, he also found it strange that, if she had indeed gone to sleep at the wheel, the car had veered to the right – left was much more normal. His third significant finding related to the steering wheel – it had been bent forward at the sides, indicating that the driver had been awake at the time of the accident and was trying to keep control of the car. Later a television programme would show that the car would have been likely to have stopped before it reached the culvert.

A Supporters of Silkwood (SOS) organisation was formed and demanded and received another enquiry into her death. No satisfaction was obtained from it and a civil action was filed against Kerr-McGee on behalf of her estate. At the ten-week trial beginning in March 1979 her children were awarded $10.5 million, a decision which was upheld in February 1984. The allegations of conspiracy against Kerr-McGee had been dismissed at an earlier stage. The family continues its fight to prove her death was no accident.

Harry Khom, *Who Killed Karen Silkwood?*; Richard Rashke, *The Killing of Karen Silkwood*; Irene Matthews in *Unsolved*

Debby Silverman

On 11 August 1978 the attractive twenty-one-year-old Debby Silverman went out dancing with friends in Toronto's Islington district. About 4 a.m. she left the house of one of the boys and drove home. There is little doubt she completed the journey, but about two hours later one of the tenants of the apartment block where she lived found two broken necklaces, together with a handbag, on the floor in the corridor. He also found a pair of torn pants. When her daughter had not arrived home by lunchtime, Debby Silverman's mother called the police. Further strands from the necklace were found in the car park. On 21 August, a man with a real or assumed stutter called the Toronto police to say that no one would see Debby Silverman again. Three days later a reward of $5,000 was offered for information leading to her discovery – there were no takers, nor was any kidnap demand made.

On 12 November her body was found in a shallow grave in Brock Township, forty miles east of North York. Her hands had been tied behind her back but, apart from her missing pants, her clothing had not been disturbed. Because the body had been attacked by animals it was not possible for an autopsy to decide exactly how she had died. No arrest was ever made.

Derrick Murdoch, *Disappearances*

Lloyd Simpson

On 7 November 1983 twenty-six-year-old Lloyd Simpson was shot in the head and stomach at his home in Shaftesbury Court, Shoreditch, London, as he watched television with his valuable pit bull terrier, which was left un-harmed. His body was discovered the next day by his father when he failed to turn up for work at the family's wastepaper business. Simpson's red Jaguar was found two days later in the East End. Simpson's spare-time hobby was buying and selling second-hand cars and the police believed his death may have re-volved around that. The killing, they said, 'has all the hallmarks of an execution'. His father could not accept this. 'Unless it's proved to me, I won't believe he was involved in gangland.'

Oscar Slater *see* **Marion Gilchrist**

Ambrose Small's will, leaving everything to his wife Theresa.

Ambrose J. Small

On 2 December 1919 the fifty-six-year-old Ambrose J. Small, a Toronto theatre owner, sold the shares in his companies for $1 million. His wife,

Theresa, banked the money and went home to await her husband for dinner. Small told his lawyer that he would be keeping his bookkeeper, John Doughty, and went to pay off his staff. He was never seen again.

Doughty disappeared shortly afterwards, together with some $100,000 of bearer bonds from Small's bank deposit boxes. Whilst there were a number of false sightings of Small, Doughty was traced to Oregon where in November 1920 he was found working in a lumber camp. In the meantime it had become apparent that Small was not the homeloving man he had been thought to be – he had kept a love-nest at the Grand Opera House furnished with oriental decor. It was also apparent that Doughty and Small did not get on and they had fought on at least one occasion.

When he was extradited to Canada, Doughty was convicted of stealing the bonds and received five years' imprisonment. Curiously, suspicion now fell on Theresa Smalls. There were suggestions that she had murdered her husband to provide money for the Catholic church and obscene pictures were printed of her. The family home was searched but nothing incriminating was found, let alone Small's body.

He was officially declared dead in 1924 and his wife died thirteen years later. When the Opera House was pulled down in May 1944 the police were on hand to see if any body had been hidden. Nothing was found.

Edward H. Smith, *Mysteries of the Missing*

Geoffrey Small

At about 5.30 a.m. on 6 September 1976 forty-four-year-old newsagent Geoffrey Small was shot seven times with a 7.65 9mm semi-automatic pistol as he stepped into his shop in Westmead Road, Sutton, Surrey. Small had been married for twenty years, during the latter part of which he had had a mistress. By all accounts that affair had dwindled and was effectively ended by the summer of 1976. He and his wife had then bought a house away from the shop and had spent the late summer doing it up.

The gunman had entered the premises through a ground-floor window and had sat and waited for Small. After the murder he then walked past an early customer who had come to collect a paper bidding him good morning. He was described as forty-five years old, 5'6", slim with brown hair and wearing a check

sports jacket and brown trousers. According to former Detective Superintendent Beavan Moss, who was in charge of the case, there was no doubt it was a
contract killing.

> Anybody but an absolute professional would find it very difficult in hitting the
> target. This bloke adopted what we call the double tap method of firing in as much
> as he fired two shots, bang bang, and then changed position, bang bang again'.*

The gun was never found and only two of the seven cartridges were retrieved
by the police.

The killer took with him Small's wallet containing £150 but no one believed
the motive was robbery. It was suggested that perhaps he was killed in mistake
for Bertie Smalls, the first of the British supergrasses who had once lived in the
area and on whom it was known there was a contract. The problem with that
theory was that Small and Smalls looked nothing like each other and Smalls had
given his evidence some four years earlier. In November 1976 a former mercenary in Angola was arrested and questioned before being released without
charge.

The *Sutton Herald* offered a £1,000 reward for information leading to the arrest
of the killer but it has gone unclaimed.

Isabella Smethurst *see* Isabella Bankes

Thayne Smika *see* Sidney Wells

Alan Smith

On the evening of Sunday 1 December 1985 loan shark and enforcer forty-
six-year-old Alan Smith, known as 'Mad Scouse' and/or 'The Gent', was
shot dead in the Duchess of Bedford public house in Islington, North London.
It is said he had gone there to discuss £40,000 he had loaned to a client. At one
time Smith, who physically resembled the actor Wilfred Brambell and once

---

* Fenton Bresler in the *Sunday Express*, 8 December 1985.

owned a green Rolls-Royce, was paranoid that he would be fitted up by the police over his links with organised crime – he was involved with the protection of clubs, pubs and market stalls and, it was said, male prostitution and drugs. He was shot as he stood at the bar of the pub. He staggered into the street and, said an eye-witness, 'One of the gunmen pivoted on his heel and calmly aimed a pistol with both hands like an American policeman. He was completely in control of that gun... he fired from point-blank range into the man's head'. No charges were ever made.

Emma Elizabeth Smith

On 3 April 1888, the forty-five-year-old prostitute Emma Smith returned to her lodging house at 18 George Street, Spitalfields, London at about 4.30 a.m. She told the deputy warden that she had been attacked and robbed by four men. She was in a dreadful condition with a cut ear and a weapon, possibly an iron bar, inserted into her vagina tearing the partition between her front and back passage. She was taken to the London Hospital where she died of peritonitis the next day. Her attackers were never found and some writers (including Chief Inspector Walter Dew) claim that she was the first victim of Jack the Ripper. Set against this there were, at the time, gangs of bullies, such as the Blind Beggar and High Rip gangs, who extorted money from prostitutes and beat them if they refused to pay.

Walter Dew, *I Caught Crippen*; Donald Rumbelow, *The Complete Jack the Ripper*

Helen Smith

On 20 May 1979 Helen Smith, a twenty-three-year-old English nurse, died from head injuries after attending an illegal drinks party thrown by an ex-patriate English surgeon, Richard Arnot, and his wife in Jeddah, Saudi Arabia. She was found outside the apartments and the initial statement by the Foreign Office was that she had fallen some seventy feet from a balcony. Also found dead was a young Dutch sea captain, Johannes Otten. His body was impaled on railings. The version of the matter given at the inquest was that

Helen Smith and Otten had, whilst drunk, attempted to have sexual intercourse on the balcony and had fallen over. The guard railing around the balcony was, however, an extremely high one. The post-mortem evidence did not appear to confirm a fall from a considerable height. There was a deep indentation in Otten's forehead but the severe damage to be expected in such a fall was missing. Arnot, his wife and seven guests were later imprisoned for alcohol offences.

Helen Smith's father, Ron, did not accept the Home Office statement and spent many years and thousands of pounds in an attempt to prove his daughter had been murdered. There was some medical evidence to show she had been sexually assaulted and considerable evidence to negate the suggestion she had fallen from a height of seventy feet. One pathologist, Professor Dalgaard, gave his opinion that the maximum Helen Smith could have fallen, if she fell at all, was ten feet. There was also a lesion which tended to show Helen Smith had been dead before her fall from the balcony. Ron Smith was eventually successful in obtaining an inquest for his daughter heard in Leeds on 18 November 1992. The Arnots' marriage had by this time been dissolved and Mrs Arnot was living in America and he in Australia. He attended the inquest whilst she declined to do so. The jury, though accepting she had fallen from the balcony, returned an open verdict.

Apart from the problems with the medical evidence, there are many questions which are unanswered about the death of Helen Smith. The first is why she and Mrs Arnot were the only women at the party. The second is the disappearance of Otten's trousers, although his passport and other belongings were found in the road. His spectacles and shoes were in the flat. Although Helen Smith had taken her camera to the party no film was found in it, and another guest who had taken photographs found that when the film was taken to be developed it had suffered from double exposure.

Gordon Wilson and Dave Harrison, *Inquest: Helen Smith, The Whole Truth*; Paul Foot in *Unsolved*

James Smith

On 25 April 1935 a captured tiger shark swimming in an aquarium at Coogee Beach, Sydney, Australia, suddenly regurgitated an arm on which was tattooed a pair of boxers. The limb was eventually identified as belonging to an ex-boxer, forty-year-old James Smith, who had been missing for a fortnight. He had been on vacation from his work with a Sydney boatbuilder, Reginald Holmes, and had rented a cottage with a well-known criminal, Patrick Brady.

Brady denied killing Smith, implicating the employer, Holmes, in forgery dealings. Holmes, when questioned, denied knowing Brady but, three days later after a high-speed chase in a speed boat, he was found with a gunshot wound to the head. Now he said that Brady had indeed killed Smith and disposed of the body. An inquest was held in which thirty-nine witnesses were called before an application was made to the Supreme Court to stay the proceedings on the grounds that there was no body, something to which the Court agreed.

Brady was charged with Smith's murder, for which Holmes would have been a prime witness had he not been shot dead in his car on 12 June. Two men charged with Holmes's killing were acquitted, as was Brady of the murder of Smith. His counsel argued that since there was no body it was impossible to be sure that Smith was dead.* There is no doubt they were involved together in drug dealing. Brady died in 1965 maintaining his innocence and suggesting the arm had bullet wounds, although how he could know this was never made clear by him.

The English pathologist, Sir Sydney Smith, who was holidaying in Australia at the time and who was invited to look at the arm, concluded that James Smith had been killed and his body placed in a tin trunk. He believed that the arm would not fit and so was roped to the outside. The trunk was dumped at sea but

---

* At one time it was thought that in law there could be no conviction for murder without a body. However, over the last century there have been a number of cases where no body has been found but which have, nevertheless, resulted in a conviction. They include that of Stanislaw Sykut, a Pole who disappeared in 1943, the Irish case of Edward Ball, convicted of the murder of his mother in 1936 and the Hosein brothers convicted in 1970 of the murder of Mrs Muriel Mackay. In the Ginger Marks and Frank Mitchell cases (*qv*) the defendants were acquitted. The most recent case was in May 1994 when Colin James received life imprisonment for the murder of his long-time business partner David Martin. The killing was proved after a schoolboy noticed a trail of blood leading from Martin's workshop. The blood was matched to Martin and bloody footprints in the garage to a pair of cricket shoes owned by James.

In fact the dangers of convicting where there is no body are apparent, never more so than in the case of the seventy-year-old William Harrison, who disappeared in the Cotswolds in August 1660 after setting out to collect rents for the Dowager Lady Campden. When he had not returned by the evening a servant, John Perry, was dispatched after him. The next morning a hat, comb and bloody neck-band were found by the roadside. Perry was accused and said that Harrison had indeed been murdered, not by him but by his (Perry's) mother and brother Richard. All were hanged. Two years later Harrison reappeared saying he had been robbed, kidnapped and sold into slavery from which he had eventually escaped – a palpably false story. He had probably been stealing the rent money and thought it prudent to disappear for a while.

the arm worked loose and was swallowed by the shark.

The beast died in captivity and on dissection was found to have no other pieces of body in its stomach, something which undoubtedly supported the pathologist's theory.

On 30 October 1952 Reginald Holmes's widow died in a fire at her home. Its cause was never discovered.

Sir Sydney Smith, *Mostly Murder*; Alan Sharpe, *Crimes That Shocked Australia*

Orma Smith *see* **Susan Becker**

Urban Napoleon Stanger

On 12 November 1881 a thirty-eight-year-old master baker, Urban Napoleon Stanger, disappeared from his home at 136 Lever Street, off the City Road, London. German born, he had come to England in about 1870 with his wife, Elizabeth, some seven years younger than he. He had set up a bakery and employed another German baker, Franz Felix Stumm, who still kept up his own shop. At the time of his death Stanger was described as unimaginative and mild-mannered with a compulsion for and a talent at making money. His better educated wife was stout and often decked out in cheap jewellery. It is said that she would sip brandy throughout the day and then throw her husband's loaves at him. Stumm was described as aged thirty-four, black bearded, fat and mercenary.

On 12 November Stanger took Stumm and another employee, Christian Zentler, out for a drink. He was seen to enter his home just before midnight by both Stumm and Zentler and, in case it is thought those two were lying, by two passers-by called Kramer and Lang. Stanger was never seen again.

When Zentler appeared for work the next day he was told by Elizabeth Stanger that her husband had been called away and that he should fetch Stumm who was to run the business. Within a fortnight Stumm had abandoned his own shop and now stayed with Mrs Stanger. The pair were seen walking out together and Stumm substituted his own name for that of the vanished Stanger on the shop fascia.

Now there was talk of a scream from the Stanger household on the night Urban disappeared and that Stumm had been seen staggering under the weight of a sack. In October 1882 the pair were arrested on charges not of murder but of conspiracy to defraud and forging and uttering a cheque. The case against Mrs Stanger, who was found to be pregnant, was withdrawn and in December 1882 Stumm, much to his fury, was sentenced to ten years' imprisonment by Mr Justice Hawkins. He disappeared from view after serving his sentence.

Benji Stanley

On Saturday, 2 January 1993 fourteen-year-old (but 6′1″ tall) Benji Stanley was shot dead in Alvino's Patty and Dumplin Shop takeaway, in Moss Side, the home of drug and gang warfare in Manchester. He had gone there with his friend, Neville 'Tito' Gunning.

Witnesses said that a stocky black man with a balaclava mask and combat coveralls shot him with a pump action shotgun. The first bullet caught him in the leg, the second in the thigh and, as Stanley lay on the ground, the gunman fired a third time into his chest.

Benji Stanley was wearing a red bandana, the colours of Manchester United football club, which unfortunately also happened to be that of the Gooch gang, one of the rival Moss Side factions.

At the conclusion of the inquest held nearly a year later the coroner appealed for witnesses. 'There are people who know and it is just horrific that they can stay quiet and allow this to happen to an innocent young man.' Benji's friend, Tito Gunning, had, it appears, changed his mind over the identification of the gunman. Despite the coroner's words it has never been quite established whether Stanley was involved in drug dealing or if his shooting was genuinely a case of mistaken identity. The killing of Benji Stanley produced a truce as there was a local, if not national, outrage at this seemingly random killing. This was, however, short-lived: in the early months of 1993 there was a string of shootings in the area culminating in a machine-gun attack on a public house.

James Morton, *Gangland 2*; Jon Silverman, *Crack of Doom*

William Starchfield

On the evening of 9 January 1914 the body of seven-year-old Willie Starchfield was found in a train at Shoreditch, North-east London, which had left Chalk Farm at 4.33 p.m. A boy who had apparently got on at Mildmay Park had noticed the body under the seat and called the guard.

Willie Starchfield, described as a mother's boy with long curly brown hair, hazel eyes and a missing tooth (in a photograph, he looked rather like Little Lord Fauntleroy) and whose parents were separated, had been strangled. There were marks of a cord or thin rope around his neck. His mother said she had sent Willie on an errand for their landlady, to change an advertisement for lodgings in a shop some 200 yards down the road. It was, it seemed, a complete mystery how he had ended up on the train. Two theories emerged: that he had been murdered on the train, or, alternatively that he had been murdered in the station lavatories and that his body had been carried on to the train. His teeth had been loosened and the medical evidence from Sir Bernard Spilsbury was that he had been killed between 2 and 3 p.m.

Initially his father, John Starchfield, a newspaper vendor with a pitch at Tottenham Court Road, satisfied the police that he had an alibi. Thomas Stickley, a hotel porter, who shared lodgings with Starchfield said he had seen him in bed at 12.50 and 2.50 that day.

The waters were then considerably muddied by Horatio Bottomley, the proprietor of the magazine *John Bull*. He put up £500 reward money leading to the conviction of the killer and out of the woodwork, amongst others, came John Moore to say he had seen Starchfield with his son. Others were also sure they had seen him at 3.30 p.m. in Endell Street, Covent Garden.

On 29 January Starchfield senior was arrested and charged with his son's murder. On 3 February a signalman gave evidence that, for a period of some ten seconds and from a distance of twenty-five yards, he had seen a man kneeling over a boy as a train passed by his box. The descriptions he gave tallied with those of the father and son. The inquest jury returned a finding of murder against John Starchfield who was committed for trial at the Old Bailey by the Old Street magistrate, Charles Biron.

Meanwhile John Moore was found on his bed in his room in Tolmers Square behind Euston Station with a gas tube attached to the stove in his mouth. As soon as he was well enough he was charged with attempted suicide. He said he was being hounded for giving evidence.

At the Old Bailey a jury was empannelled after a challenge to one who said he did not believe in capital punishment. He need not have worried. On the second day of the hearing the trial collapsed when Mr Justice Atkin stopped the case, saying to Sir Archibald Bodkin, prosecuting, that he did not consider 'the evidence of identity is sufficient in a case of life and death'. And, a nod being as good as a wink, Sir Archibald, who later became the Director of Public Prosecutions, agreed. Later commentators seem to have taken the view that Starchfield Senior was fortunate in his judge but the likelihood is that the child met his death at the hands of an unidentified maniac.

Before the murder of his son, John Starchfield had been something of a hero. In 1913 an Armenian had shot and killed the manageress of the Horseshoe Hotel in Tottenham Court Road near the junction with New Oxford Street. Starchfield had cut off his escape and, for his pains, had been shot in the stomach. He had been given a £50 award and a £1-a-week pension from the Carnegie Trust. He died from the effects of the injury two years after Willie's death.

H. L. Adam, *Murder by Persons Unknown*; Douglas G. Browne and Tom Tullett, *Bernard Spilsbury*; E. Spenser Shew, *A Companion to Murder*

Virgil Starks *see* **Richard Griffin**

Belle Starr

On 3 February 1889 the celebrated woman outlaw was shot to death near Eufaaula, Indian territory, Oklahoma. Born in Carthage, Montana in 1848, she had been the associate or mistress of some of the most notable of the post-Civil War villains in the West. Her brother, Ed Shirley, rode with the James-Younger gang and her daughter, Pearl, was the result of a short liaison with Cole Younger. After the death of her husband, Jim Reed, with whom she rustled horses, she took up first with Blue Duck, and later Sam Starr, a Cherokee. She received a six-month sentence for rustling from Judge Parker and then was offered a part as an outlaw in a Wild West show. The judge who had sentenced her played the part of a stage-coach passenger. After the death of Sam Starr her fortunes declined. She became involved with a Creek Indian, Jim July, and when he was accused of theft went with him to surrender at Fort Smith. He was acquitted by Parker and on the way back both were bushwhacked. A neighbour, Edgar Watson, with whom she had quarrelled, was arrested but the charges were dropped. It is likely she was killed by her son, the eighteen-year-old Ed Reed, with whom she was reputed to have had an incestuous relationship and whom she certainly physically abused, hitting him with a bullwhip. Ed Reed later became a deputy marshall at Fort Smith. In turn he was shot in a bar-room brawl at the age of twenty-four.

Gary Stoner

On 14 March 1982 the thirty-two-year-old small-time marijuana and psilocybin mushroom dealer was found stabbed sixty-three times in the back, chest and head at his home at 2251 Goss Street in Goss Grove near downtown Boulder, Colorado. It was never clear whether his death had been the result of a drug rip-off or was a homosexual murder. Two weapons were used but neither was found. In the flat was a woman's wallet. The owner denied any connection with Stoner and it was thought it had been stolen and that the man had been stabbed before its loss was discovered.

Mamie Stuart

The twenty-six-year-old chorus girl disappeared in 1920. In July 1917 she had met Everard George Shotton, a marine engineer from Newcastle, and they had lived together for a year in Wales before moving to London 'for a while'. He was a dapper little man who deliberately cultivated a Chaplinesque appearance and according to one neighbour 'charmed the girls of the village for five years with his dandy appearance and stories of high living'. On 25 May 1919 Mamie Stuart had gone through a ceremony of marriage with him in South Shields and they then lived first in rooms in Swansea and afterwards in a house, Ty-Llanwydd on the cliff-top near the village of Newton, five and a half miles out of Swansea. A week after moving into the house it was found deserted. No letters to Mamie from her parents were answered. She had written one letter to her mother:

He hit me across the head and my arms are all bruised. I am as sick as I can be. He said if he knocked the life out of me it was not your place to interfere. If you do not hear from me, inquire from Mrs Hulme and see if she knows anything about me. I'm afraid I won't live very much longer with him. My life is not worth living.

Her last letter to her mother read:

He has put me in a great big house away from everyone else and he just comes and goes when he likes. I came back to try and make him happy, but he starts again after two days. I will write more later – Mamie.

But she never did.

The following year some of her clothes were found along with her shoes, all of which had been destroyed, in a bag in the Old Grosvenor Hotel in Swansea. Towards the end of March that year a cleaner found her handbag, containing an old wartime ration card and £2, behind a washstand in the house.

Shotton was found and, when questioned, claimed his wife had left him after a quarrel. In accordance with standard police practice the garden of the house was dug over but there was no trace of either Mamie or her belongings. Local gossip was that she was dead and that her body had been disposed of in a limepool. Mamie Stuart's disappearance came at a time when there was a strongly held belief that in English law a murder charge could not be brought without a body. It was, however, discovered that Shotton was already married – they had an adopted son – and he received eighteen months on a charge of bigamy. At his trial he denied the charge saying someone had impersonated him at the ceremony with Mamie. After his release in 1922 Shotton was believed to have gone to America. In fact he went to live with his parents in Tintern for a short period and then disappeared from view.

On 6 November 1961 pot-holers found what turned out to be the body of Mamie Stuart, cut into three pieces, at the bottom of a disused lead-mine. The thigh bones of the skeleton were cut clean through just above the knee as though they had been sawn. A three-stone engagement ring and a thick gold wedding ring similar to the jewellery Mamie used to wear were found near the body. Then a postman came forward to tell the curious story of how back in 1920 he had seen Shotton carrying a sack from Ty-Llanwydd. 'Oh, My God,' Shotton had said. 'I thought you were a policeman.'

Efforts were made to trace Shotton in Swansea, the North and Balham where his mother once lived. He had lost contact with the family during the war and it was thought that for a time he had worked as a mechanic in a garage in Lydney in Gloucestershire. Old people's homes were visited but to no avail.

Finally it was discovered that Shotton had died in 1958 and had been buried in Arno's Vale Cemetery, Bristol.

Beatrice Vilna Sutton *see* **Norah Upchurch**

Joy Sweatman

On Derby Day, 1 June 1977, Joy Sweatman was battered to death in St Andrew's Road, Coulsdon, Surrey. The attacker then clubbed her five-year-old daughter Sarah with a hammer, so badly that the child was unconscious for four days. Joy Sweatman's body was found by her lodger when he returned about 1.30 p.m. A pillow and plastic bag were over her head. Sarah appeared to be dead on the sofa.

A pathologist, Dr Rufus Crompton, gave evidence at the inquest that he believed Joy had been standing when she had first been attacked. When she fell to the ground her murderer had then stamped on her body.

A witness recalled seeing a man in a fawn coat and with a flat cap leaving the house wiping a hammer. He appeared to have red paint on his face. He had driven off in an R registration white Austin Maxi saloon. Each of the 3,500 owners of these cars in mainland Great Britain was checked with no success.

Martha Tabram
(aka Martha Turner)

On 7 August 1888 the body of prostitute Martha Tabram was found at about 3 a.m. on the first-floor landing of George Yards Buildings in the East End of London. She had been stabbed thirty-nine times. Earlier in the evening she was known to have been in company with another prostitute who went under the name of Pearly Poll. They had picked up two soldiers and were seen drinking with them in the Angel and Crown public house. Tabram's soldier was traced and provided an alibi. The killer was thought to have been ambidextrous and that two weapons, one of which was possibly a bayonet, had been used. All soldiers stationed in the Tower of London were paraded for Pearly Poll to try to make an identification but she failed to do so. She was then ordered to attend the inquest and went into hiding. She was found in Covent Garden and taken to Chelsea barracks to see if she could do better. Out of pique she picked out the first two men she saw. Fortunately they were able to establish alibis. Martha Tabram is sometimes thought to have been the second victim of Jack the Ripper.

Walter Dew, *I Caught Crippen*

Hannah Tailford

On 2 February 1964 the body of thirty-year-old Hannah Tailford, a prostitute who also called herself Anne Taylor and Teresa Bell, was found in the Thames near Hammersmith Bridge. Her clothes were missing but her stockings were still around her ankles. She had facial bruising and her pants were stuffed in her mouth.

She had last been seen leaving her home in West Norwood, South London a week earlier and it was thought that she might have been killed by a former client to stop her attempts at blackmail. She was a known party-goer and in the flat she kept in Victoria she had studio lighting equipment and a camera. Her diary was missing. She was the first victim of a serial killer who became known as Jack the Stripper.

The jury at the subsequent inquest returned an open verdict – it was just possible she might have committed suicide and the facial bruising might have been caused by a fall.

A second body was found in the Thames, this time at Duke's Meadow on 8 April. Irene Lockwood had been strangled and again the police thought she might have been blackmailing her former clients. Irene Lockwood had provided the alibi for a man accused, a year earlier, of murdering another prostitute, Vicki Pender. Both women were involved in blue movies.

The body of the third victim, Helen Barthelemy, was found on 24 April, a little way from the river in a driveway near Swincombe Avenue, Brentford. Four of her teeth were missing and a dark ring around her waist indicated that her pants had been removed after she died. She had traces of paint spray on her which made the police think her body might have been kept in a paint-strip shop before being dumped. Traces of sperm in her mouth suggested she had either been orally raped or that she had performed fellatio before she died. Now it appeared that if one man was responsible for the murders the blackmail theory was wrong.

The next day the police must have thought their Sundays had indeed all come at once. Kenneth Archibald, a caretaker, walked into Notting Hill police station and confessed to killing Irene Lockwood. He was able to give a detailed statement of his movements with the woman, saying, 'I must have lost my temper and put my hands around her throat. She could not scream. I then proceeded to take her clothes off and rolled her into the river. I took her clothes home and burned them.' It was apparent, however, that he was not involved with the murders of either Tailford or Barthelemy.

Archibald was charged and indicted for Lockwood's murder. His trial began at the Old Bailey on 19 June and four days later the jury retired for only forty minutes before returning a verdict of not guilty. Afterwards, Archibald told reporters that he had confessed only because he was fed up. He was upset because he was being questioned about a break-in at the club where he worked and had drunk six pints of beer before he walked into the police station.

Superintendent John du Rose, who headed the investigation, later wrote, 'We had no reason to believe that Archibald had anything to do with the murder but he had to be charged and a jury had to decide the case because he had repeated his false confession twice before retracting it.'

Coincidentally, whilst Archibald was in custody the murders stopped. The police later believed that this was due to the extensive coverage the case had had and that prostitutes were being more careful in their choice of clients. The next murder came on 14 July when Mary Fleming, a mother of two, was found in a sitting position near a garage in Berrymead Road, Chiswick, West London. She too was naked and her dentures were missing. Again there was sperm in her mouth and traces of spray on her body. She also fell into the height pattern of the dead women: none was more than 5'3" tall.

On 25 November the body of yet another diminutive prostitute, Margaret McGowan, was discovered on a pile of rubble in a car park in Hornton Street near Kensington High Street. Again spots of paint covered her body and she had a tooth missing. She had disappeared on 23 October. The last of the killings was discovered on 16 February 1965, when the body of Bridie O'Hara was discovered behind a store shed off Westfield Road, Acton.

There was little doubt that the killings were the work of one man. Apart from their lack of height, all the prostitutes worked the Bayswater-Kensington beat, all were suffocated whilst clothed and all were kept in a store before their bodies were left to be found. All were discovered in or near the Thames.

The paint on the bodies was traced to a covered transformer near to a paint-spray shop on the Heron Factory Estate in Acton. Matters did not end there, however – there were over 7,000 people working on the estate. Then in June 1965 a married man living in South London killed himself leaving a note to the effect that he was unable to stand the strain any longer. The killings ceased and the police believed that this man was in fact Jack the Stripper. His name has never been made public but journalist Brian McConnell claimed that he was an ex-policeman who was a heavy drinker. Despite his grotesque sexual tastes and a lifetime obsession with prostitutes he had married and had only returned to drink when refused a transfer to the plainclothes division. He had then left the force.

The unsolved murders of two other women were at one time thought to be the work of Jack the Stripper. Elizabeth Figg was found dead in June 1959 and Gwyneth Rees, who had strong East London connections, was discovered in November 1963. In the case of Gwyneth Rees it is almost certain she died following an abortion. As for Elizabeth Figg her death was rather outside the timespan of the Stripper's operations.

Brian McConnell, *Found Naked and Dead*; John du Rose, *Murder was my Business*

Shirley Dean Taylor

The body of twenty-three-year-old prostitute Shirley Dean Taylor was found off Interstate 70 in Medina County, Ohio, on 20 June 1986. Her pants had been wrapped around her arm. She had last been seen two days earlier in the rear lot of the Union 76 truck stop in Austintown wearing a black camisole and pink hot-pants. Taylor was one of up to possibly 150 women who were victims of a serial killer who worked the I-70 in the mid-West from 1985.

Again, as is so often the case with serial killings, the first attacks were thought to be random ones. Investigation showed that the women, many of whom were unidentified, all worked truckstops. When they had finished with one client they used his CB radio to advertise their availability, speciality and price over the airwaves. The killer, who may have driven a dark blue or black Peterbilt truck, took the calls and arranged to meet the prostitutes. He does not appear to have disposed of the bodies immediately. One girl, who was six months' pregnant when she died, was thought to have been killed within two days of her disappearance but there was medical evidence that her body had been kept in a refrigerator for a month before it was discovered. The general *modus operandi*, however, was that he threw the victims out of the truck as he drove along. On one occasion he left pieces of clothing at mile intervals along the road.

The killings, which spread over Ohio, Illinois, Pennsylvania and upstate New York, ceased in 1980 and were once tentatively linked to the Green River killings, which themselves ceased shortly before the I-70 killings began. After the I-70 killings stopped a further series began in the Seattle area prompting suggesting that the killer might have moved to the West Coast.

Paulette Cooper and Paul Noble, *Reward*

William Desmond Taylor

The silent film director was found shot dead on 2 February 1922 at his home, Bungalow B, 404 Alvarado Street, Los Angeles. At first it appeared he had had a stomach haemorrhage and it was only when the body was moved that it was seen he had been shot in the back. Coming almost immediately after the Fatty Arbuckle trial for the murder of actress Virginia Rappe at a party, the Hollywood industry was sensitive to further difficulties.* Things were not

---

* On 9 September 1921 the twenty-five-year-old aspiring actress and international model, Virginia Rappe, died of peritonitis in a San Francisco hospital. She had been taken there after being injured four days earlier after an incident at a party thrown by the silent film comedian, Roscoe 'Fatty' Arbuckle. She had internal injuries. Few of those present at the party would admit seeing Rappe there. Eventually the girlfriend with whom she had gone to the party came forward and said that the 300-pound Arbuckle had dragged the model into a bedroom saying, 'This is the chance I've been waiting for.' A nurse at the hospital confirmed that Rappe had said, 'Fatty Arbuckle did this to me. Please see he doesn't get away with it.' The peritonitis had been caused by the bursting of Virginia Rappe's bladder and the coroner made public his opinion that it had happened during a forcible rape. Arbuckle's story was that the girl had been taken ill after drinking gin. A Grand Jury voted to indict him with manslaughter, but the district attorney pressed ahead with a murder charge. However, by the time the trial opened in November 1921, witnesses had disappeared and changed their minds and Ms Rappe's character was blackened by the defence. After a forty-three-hour retirement, the jury was hung ten to two in favour of an acquittal. The second jury also disagreed, this time favouring a conviction by the same majority. The prosecution offered no further evidence but Arbuckle's career was ruined and he was effectively blacklisted. On 28

helped by the fact that apparently the last person to see Taylor was Arbuckle's best known co-star, Mabel Normand. She was certainly there when the police arrived, going through drawers looking for some letters.

Taylor, born in England in 1867 as William Deane Tanner, had come to Hollywood in 1912, as an actor and had then turned to directing. In Taylor's bungalow a considerable amount of women's underwear, marked with the name of the donor and date of receipt, was said to have been discovered. Studio employees were also said to have been busy destroying letters from actresses and pornographic photographs. In any event none were discovered and the only piece of clothing identified was a nightdress with the initials MMM, said to belong to Mary Miles Minter who was being groomed by her studio to replace Mary Pickford.

There were also stories that Taylor was bisexual and that he was being blackmailed. A chauffeur, Strange, had robbed him and then forged cheques. No charges were brought but it is possible that this is because the man may have been Taylor's brother. On the day of his death Taylor had made a substantial withdrawal from his bank account. Other suggested motives included a revenge by Canadian soldiers from Taylor's time in the Canadian Army. More probable was a drug connection. Mabel Normand was a user and the alternatives on offer were that Taylor was a dealer or, more attractively, that whilst trying to wean Ms Normand off this destructive habit he had fallen foul of dealers who did not wish to lose such a good client.

In such a hotbed of gossip as Hollywood it is not surprising there were countless rumours and counter-rumours. Prime suspects were Mary Minter and her mother, Charlotte Shelby, who, in the 1930s, demanded the police put up or shut up. Nothing came of their request.

In the 1940s the Hollywood director, King Vidor, investigated the case, partly with a view to making a film. His theory was that Mabel Normand had not been at the Taylor bungalow on the night of the murder; that all the stories of women's clothing and love letters had been plants by studio publicity to divert attention

William Desmond Taylor.

June 1933 he completed the first in a series of comeback pictures and threw a modest party to celebrate – he died that night in his sleep.

from the fact that Taylor was homosexual; that there was no drug dealing involved; there was no chauffeur brother. The truth, he believed, was that, to the fury of her mother, Mary Minter had been obsessed with Taylor. The fiercely possessive Shelby had done what she could to stop the relationship, even from time to time locking her up. Vidor's theory was that Minter evaded her mother, who went searching for her, found Taylor and shot him. She certainly owned a .38 revolver. Minter then provided her mother with an alibi. Vidor also argued that Shelby bribed three Los Angeles district attorneys to suppress evidence. In support of this, Shelby and her daughter were by no means questioned thoroughly by the police. Against this explanation is the 'put up or shut up' action of the pair in the 1930s. In 1973 the last surviving of the district attorneys, Byron Fitts, shot himself, co-incidentally with a .38 revolver.

Sidney Kirkpatrick, *A Cast of Killers*; John Austin, *Hollywood's Unsolved Mysteries*

Arthur Allen Thomas *see* **Harvey and Jeanette Crewe**

Elizabeth Thomas

At about 6 p.m. on 10 January 1953 Ronald Jones, a laboratory technician, who lived in the fishing village of Laugharne near Carmarthen, was walking to collect his car from the village garage. As he passed the cottage of the seventy-eight-year-old Elizabeth Thomas, a retired schoolmistress, he heard screams and the old lady calling out to someone not to hurt her. He heard a name being shouted but was not sure who it was and went at once for the village police officer, Sergeant Morgan. On their return they found Miss Thomas lying in the doorway. Her head had been split with a heavy object, her right arm was fractured and she had been stabbed four times in the chest. She died of her injuries the next morning without regaining consciousness. Her neighbour, a Mrs Phillips, said, 'She had worked hard all her life. She was very independent and I don't suppose she owed a penny to anybody.'

Morgan, who had pulled down a window to get into the Thomas cottage, had previously looked through the keyhole. 'In the pale light reflected from the oil lamp I saw a person wearing a light-coloured man's cap in a bent position. I can't say whether this person was a man, woman or child.' When he had rattled the door of the cottage the lamp had been lowered.

No knife was found but by her body was a heavy stick with hairs matted to it. The police used mine detectors amongst Miss Thomas's apple trees in an effort to find the knife. A flagstone was taken away for forensic examination but unfortunately, as with so many cases, the police had not managed to keep the area sterile. The police believed that valuable evidence was destroyed when villagers ran to the scene of the crime. The motive was possibly robbery and, if so, it may be that the robber was disturbed because under the mattress in the murdered woman's bedroom was found £200, enough then to buy a small cottage. A fingerprint expert said that it had not been tampered with.

The police fastened on to their suspect with some alacrity. He was a forty-six-year-old odd-job man, George Roberts, who lived in the Ferry House in the village. He was illiterate and worse, from the point of view of the police, he was a deaf mute. Nor had he learned to communicate in anything more than the most rudimentary sign language.

The Carmarthenshire police called in Scotland Yard and Detective Superintendent Reginald Spooner was sent to assist the local force. He was able to trace Miss Thomas's movements quite easily. On the Saturday morning she had been to watch a wedding at the local church along with her next door neighbour, a retired headmistress, Miss Elizabeth Davies. In the late afternoon, about 5 p.m., she had gone to the sweet shop across the road to buy peppermints and had told the grocer's wife she was going home to have an egg for her tea.

So far as Roberts was concerned, he had been seen by another of Elizabeth Thomas's neighbours, a Miss Lewis. At about 4.30 p.m. Roberts had called round to show her a pair of gloves he had bought. About 5.30 he had been seen by Phillips, the grocer, standing on the pavement near his shop. Other people put Roberts near Miss Thomas's cottage up to a quarter to six. They said he was wearing a macintosh and cap.

A Roy Edmunds, who lived opposite Miss Thomas, saw Roberts outside his front door at about 6.15. All he could say was that the man was wearing wellington boots. From that time on Roberts was seen by a number of people up to about 6.40 p.m.

So far as clues were concerned, there had been far too many people in and out of the cottage for them to survive. There was a print of a wellington boot but this had been blurred and a footprint in the back garden was not capable of being cast. There was, however, a trace of green distemper on Roberts's macintosh similar to that in Miss Thomas's cottage.

With the help of his uncle, Roberts made a statement that he had come home about 4.45 p.m. and then later that he had come home at 5.30 p.m. The next day with a deaf and dumb interpreter he made a statement that at about 4.15 he had seen Miss Thomas on her doorstep and had waved to her. He said he had not been out after 5 p.m. The police version of events was that he was then told he could go home but he did not leave the police station. In fact it is agreed he stayed there for the next four days before he finally left. With the gift of hindsight it seems peculiar that the police should allow a man to camp out in their station.

On Sunday 18 January Roberts was brought back to the police where he made a statement to Detective Inspector Spooner without the benefit of an interpreter. Spooner had already carried out some simple tests on Roberts which had led him to believe that he was able to give intelligent answers to questions put to him. Now Roberts was shown two photographs of Miss Roberts's cottage. He then made a sign he wanted paper and a pencil and drew a sketch of the row of cottages. He drew a sketch of himself and, pointing to the middle of the five cottages, made thrusting motions.

> I showed him a knife and he nodded. He made a movement from that particular house in the middle, over its top, along the top of the two houses to the right and down by the side to the end of the house to where he had pictured himself. He then indicated walking along the road.

Roberts was then taken along a path to the cliff edge and where he stopped he made a cutting motion with his hand, drew his arm back and brought it over his head and made a throwing motion. The police officer with him, Detective Sergeant Millen, interpreted that as Roberts telling him he had thrown the knife into the sea. Roberts was then re-interviewed with two interpreters and, so Spooner believed, confessed to the murder of Miss Thomas.

Proceedings in the magistrates' court did not go well. The court interpreter failed to make Roberts understand the evidence of the first witness and Roberts' solicitor, Myer Cohen, told the court, 'From my observations and from the advice of people who have been with him it is believed it is impossible for any interpreter to interpret for this man anything but the most elementary phrases.' The magistrates committed Roberts for trial at the next Carmarthen Assizes.

He appeared there on 6 March 1953 in front of Mr Justice Devlin, who adjourned the question of whether he was fit to plead. If he had been found unfit he would have been committed to a lunatic asylum. 'To insist on the issue being tried first might result in a grave injustice,' said Mr Justice Devlin, 'to detain as a criminal lunatic a man who might be quite innocent. I can find no authority which would prevent the defence, which wishes to test the prosecution's case on the general issue, from having the right to do so.' Evidence was given that Roberts had not spoken in twenty-nine years and a jury found him mute by visitation of God.* The case was adjourned to the next assize town, Cardiff, where the trial re-opened on Monday, 23 March.

After the prosecution opened its case the judge asked whether, if the statements were ruled inadmissible, there was any evidence on which a jury could convict? Counsel for the prosecution replied there was not. The next day Mr Justice Devlin ruled the confession inadmissible and told the jury:

> The man was taken to Carmarthen Police Station on the night of January 10–11 after the crime and he was kept there until January 14. No charge of any sort had been made and during that time he was questioned and questioned in a manner that was not designed merely to elicit facts but was in the nature of a cross-examination.
>
> I am fully conscious of the fact that the police have a very difficult task to discharge. It is easy to criticise the way they discharge their duties. This case must no doubt have created at every stage difficult problems for them. But I should like to make it abundantly clear, a man cannot be detained unless he is arrested.

Devlin went on to say,

> The evidence comes down to the fact that Roberts was seen before and afterwards and the fact that he previously had a knife in his possession. Those things are coupled with certain statements said to have been obtained from a man with whom conversation is almost impossible. You could never have been asked to convict on evidence of that sort.

After his discharge Roberts drew two pictures for reporters: one was a man with a spade and the other a man fishing from a rowing boat. The interpreter said these meant he was going back to work after first taking a holiday.

Can Roberts possibly have been guilty? It seems extremely unlikely. According to his biographer, Spooner thought a man named Harry might have been involved until Roberts 'confessed'. First, when Jones heard a name being called out, he was sure it was not Booda, the name by which Roberts was known in the village. Jones thought it was more likely Harry. Secondly, could Roberts have gone home and wiped from his clothes all the blood there must have been, without leaving any trace? His fingerprints were not found on the piece of wood by the body. And why had the lamp been lowered? Roberts could not possibly have heard the policeman rattling the front door.

---

* The other verdict open to them was 'mute of malice'.

That leaves his apparent lies about the time he was in his own cottage and the 'confession'. It can never be known exactly what grasp Roberts had on the concept of time or indeed whether he was answering the questions put to him. As for the 'confession', he may just have easily been recounting in his own way what he saw the actual killer do.

Iain Adamson, *The Great Detective*

Claire Tiltman

On 18 January 1993 sixteen-year-old Claire Tiltman was found stabbed to death in an alley near her home in Greenhithe, Kent. She had been attacked as she walked to a friend's home and died in an ambulance on the way to hospital. On 3 May 1994 an inquest was told how on 1 February 1994, forty-four-year-old Peter Rivers had stabbed and strangled his mother. He then slashed his wrists, doused himself with petrol and ignited himself on a piece of waste ground. He had left a note saying, 'Mum was starting to suspect me of killing Claire.' After the inquest Detective Superintendent Owen Taylor said, 'We have to conclude that perhaps the Claire was Claire Tiltman. If he was capable of killing his mother he may well have been capable of killing Claire. There are a number of enquiries we want to carry out but there is still no direct evidence to link Peter with the murder of Claire. There are a lot of questions that remain unanswered.'

Alma Tirtschke

On Friday, 30 December 1921 the body of pretty twelve-year-old Alma Tirtschke was found in the dead-end Gun Alley in Melbourne, Australia, part of a complex known as the Eastern Market, a rag-bag of cheap shops, bars and curtained doorways which led to brothels. The girl had been raped and her body had been washed, which the police believed had been done to remove clues as to the killer's identity.

Along with his brother, Stanley, Colin Campbell Ross was the owner of a wine bar just over a hundred yards from where the naked body of the child was found. The floor of his wine bar had recently been scrubbed but, although he was one of the first to be questioned about the killing, Ross seems to have been unconcerned. He gave the detectives details of an alibi saying he had seen a friend, Gladys Wain, and that after he had shut his bar he had seen her to her house before catching the train at Spencer Street station to his own home.

This was one of those cases in which the police relied heavily on the evidence of known criminals and people with a grudge against Ross. They were later to share in the A£1,250 reward put up by the Victorian Government and the *Melbourne Herald*. Ivy Matthews, who had been questioned previously, decided on 9 January 1922 that Ross had confessed to her and that she had seen a girl, whom she believed to be the victim, peeping out of a cubicle in the wine bar. She, Matthews, had been given notice by Ross three weeks earlier. Another witness was a prostitute, Olive Maddox, who also said she had seen Alma in the wine bar and that Ivy Matthews had told her to tell the police.

Whilst on remand, Ross was said by Sidney Harding, a cellmate, to have confessed to the crime, a confession overheard by another prisoner who also gave evidence. He said he had seen the girl loitering in the street.

The witnesses were bitterly attacked by the defence who accused them of giving evidence in the hope that a conviction of Ross would bring reward money. In the case of Harding it does seem difficult to understand why Ross should confess to him – Harding was a known 'shelf' or police informer. In his alleged confession to Harding, Ross had said he had given the girl three glasses of wine. No alcohol was found in her stomach. Ivy Matthews said he had told her he'd been 'fooling about with her and had strangled her in his passion,' adding, 'I could have taken a knife and slashed her up, and myself too, because she led me on to do it.' Harding's version was that Ross had said, 'At six o'clock the girl was still asleep in the cubicle, and I could not resist the temptation.' Afterward the girl called out and he went in to silence her and must have choked her.

There was no forensic evidence except for some hairs similar to those of the girl's attached to a blanket. The forensic expert, Dr Charles Taylor, demonstrated the individual qualities of hair, something no longer regarded as an exact science. There were no bloodstains on the blanket nor on the floor of the bar. There was evidence, too, that Ross suffered from venereal disease.*

Ross's trial, which began on 20 February, lasted five days. It was carried out in an atmosphere of almost total public hostility towards him but the jury took

---

* An old wives' tale is that gonorrhoea can be cured by intercourse with a virgin.

over twenty-four hours to find him guilty. 'My life has been sworn away by desperate people. If I am hanged, I will be hanged as an innocent man,' he told the court.

As is so often the case, after the trial some witnesses came forward to support his story. One man said that he had been in the bar and the child could not have been on the premises without being seen by him. Another, a taxi driver, said he had heard a child scream, had looked for the source but although he could not find it he was sure that the cry had not come from Ross's wine bar. The Court of Appeal refused to hear the witnesses.

To his death Ross continued to protest his innocence, saying he had been framed by the Melbourne police. On the gallows on 24 April 1922 he said:

> I am now face to face with my Maker, and I swear to you that I am innocent. I never saw the child. I never committed the crime and I do not know who did. I never confessed to anyone. I ask God to forgive those who swore my life away, and I pray God to have mercy on my darling mother and my family.

His detractors point out that he had originally told the police he had seen the girl when she was loitering in the doorway of Madame Ghurka, a fortune-teller. One story told against him is that, after his death, an acquaintance said that Ross had told him he 'preferred them without feathers' – a reference to the lack of pubic hair among very young girls.

After his death Ross was championed by his junior barrister, the former journalist T. C. Brennan, who explains this remark by saying that 'never seen' meant never spoken to. Brennan, who died in January 1944, wrote *The Gun Alley Tragedy* defending his former client. Until his death at the age of seventy-four he believed evidence would be forthcoming which would clear Ross. Brennan became Acting Attorney-General of the Commonwealth and a Senator.

The reward money was shared out between the witnesses with Ivy Matthews receiving £350 and Harding £200. Madame Ghurka, whose real name was Julia Gibson, received £25 although it is not clear how she helped the case.

In 1963 Ivy Matthews, then known as Irene Cholet, died of a heart attack four days before she was due in court to answer charges relating to abortions. It was thought she was the last of the surviving witnesses.

T. C. Brennan, *The Gun Alley Tragedy*; Alan Sharpe, *Crimes That Shocked Australia*; Vince Kelly, *The Charge is Murder*

Unknown *see* **Brighton Trunk Murders; Castleman Floater; Hagley Wood; Harley Street**

Norma Upchurch

A prostitute, Norma Upchurch (also known as Laverick) was found dead on 2 October 1931 in an empty shop in New Compton Street, London W1. Her clothes were awry and her handbag was missing. Her body was discovered when Douglas Bartrum, the manager of a firm of sign contractors, and one of his employees, Frederick Field, broke open a wooden door at the rear of the shop to gain access to remove some signs.

There were a number of suspects for the murder of this twenty-year-old girl, who had been placed in care at the age of sixteen and who from time to time had tried to break out of the life. The first was a man called Peter Webb who, so Field said, had worn plus fours, and who had obtained the keys from Field several days earlier, showing him what appeared to be an authority from the estate agents. The keys had never been returned. At Richmond police station he had made an identification of Webb, something hotly denied by the man. The second suspect was a former England cricketer who had been the last person to see Upchurch alive. He had spent the night of 28 September with her. The third person was a sailor from Chatham Barracks who considered himself engaged to her.

The fourth was Field himself. Field was a married man who lived in Sutton. He had spent six years in the RAF and had been discharged with a good character. The police were not happy with his story, particularly when he identified Webb who turned out to have an unshakeable alibi. The coroner at the inquest, Ingleby Oddie, summed up Field's story about the keys to the jury:

> Does it sound a truthful story? Look at his identification of the man in plus fours – Webb. Does that ring true? You have to ask yourself seriously whether the chain of circumstantial evidence is as complete against Webb as it is against Field … Although the matter is one for you, you will allow me to suggest that the chain of evidence is not sufficiently strong and complete and secure. You may disbelieve Field's story altogether, but that does not prove that he is a murderer.

The jury followed the coroner's implicit instructions and returned a verdict of wilful murder against some person unknown. There the matter rested for some two years until, in July 1933, Field walked into a newspaper office and confessed. The paper had guaranteed his defence costs in 1931 if the jury had named him in returning the verdict of wilful murder.* His story was now that

---

* This is by no means as odd as it sounds. There was no such thing as legal aid in those days. Indeed it was about the only way a defendant could obtain the services of first-class counsel

he had met Norma Upchurch near the Hippodrome on the corner of Leicester Square, had gone with her to the shop but that, although she had agreed to fellate him, she would not lie on the floor with him. In rage he had strangled her and had then caught the underground train home to Morden. He said he had thrown her handbag in a water-filled ditch near Sutton by-pass. Why had he suddenly confessed? First, he wanted money to send his wife back to her family in Cardiff. Secondly, he had, he believed, committed the perfect murder. He had outwitted the police and the coroner but now his mates at work would not believe him. The newspaper sent a reporter and photographer to the ditch but it was dry and there was no handbag.

On trial at the Old Bailey he now denied he had killed Upchurch, saying that he wanted to clear his name as he had been offered a job in Ceylon on a tea plantation and when it had been learned he was involved in the Upchurch murder enquiry the offer had been withdrawn. Mr Justice Swift was impressed and summed up with what amounted to a direction to the jury to acquit; something they duly did.

In 1936, now a deserter from the RAF, which he had rejoined, and on a charge of larceny, Field confessed to the murder of another prostitute, Beatrice Sutton, strangled at her home in Clapham. Again, at the trial he withdrew his confession, but the investigating officer had obtained detailed descriptions from Field about the contents of the flat and the injuries to the woman so negating his story that Field had been there only because he thought something was wrong. He was hanged on 30 June 1936.*

Julian Symons, *A Reasonable Doubt*

---

on a murder charge. The implicit agreement was that, in the event of a conviction, the defendant would leave a death-cell confession to be printed in the appropriate Sunday paper the week after he was hanged.

* There have been a number of cases where a man has been acquitted of a murder and then hanged on his conviction for a subsequent one. For example, Walter Rowlands was convicted of the murder of Olive Balchin (*qv*). Frederick Murphy was hanged in 1937 for the murder of a prostitute, Rose Field. He had been acquitted of a murder in 1929. Like Rowlands he blamed his conviction on a determination by the police to get him convicted following his acquittal a decade earlier.

A sad little case is that of Freda Burnell. The eight-year-old disappeared on 5 February 1921. She had last been seen when she was served by fifteen-year-old Harold Jones in a shop in Abertillery. The next day she was found strangled and an attempt had been made to rape her. Almost the only evidence against Jones, who was tried for her murder, was that her handkerchief was found in the back of the shop. To great local acclaim he was acquitted. The murder would have remained unsolved had not, sadly, two weeks later, the body of another young girl, eleven-year-old Florence Little, been found. Jones was convicted of murdering her. He now admitted to the murder of Freda Burnell and was detained during His Majesty's Pleasure.

Stephen Varley

At about 7.45 on Sunday, 19 December 1948 a nursery gardener bicycling through allotments near St Albans, Hertfordshire, found the body of fifty-two-year-old Stephen Varley, a shop steward at the local aircraft manufacturers, De Havillands. It was covered with a dark overcoat. He had blue socks on but no shoes or boots. The pathologist, Professor Keith Simpson, thought that he had been killed about midnight.

The shoes were found some way away and it was apparent that the body had been dumped in the allotment. He had been struck in the face and then strangled. From his injuries it was clear he had been attacked by more than one person.

Varley had been drinking heavily that evening and had been seen very drunk in St Albans at 10.30 in the evening in the company of two men. There were no suggestions that he had made enemies in his work as shop steward and, despite extensive enquiries, the police never came near to finding his attackers in what seems to have been a straight forward robbery of a drunk who stood his ground and tried to fight back.

Michael Vengali

A four-year-old boy, sitting in a baby buggy, Michael Vengali was caught in machine gun fire in July 1931 on East 107th Street, New York, and died after being shot in the stomach. Vincent 'Mad Dog' Coll, an Irish gangster from the Hell's Kitchen district, was accused of the murder. The prosecution's case was that he had fired on Anthony Trobino, a member of the rival Dutch Schultz organisation, missing him but hitting five small children, including Vengali.

Coll hired Samuel Leibowitz, the celebrated New York attorney who later defended the Scottsborough Boys, for his defence. The principal witness against Coll was a self-proclaimed ice cream salesman, George Brecht, who, according to his evidence, sold Eskimo Pies, a popular brand, and who happened to be walking along East 107th Street at the crucial moment.

Leibowitz displayed consummate skill with the witness. During the luncheon adjournment he purchased a number of ice creams and distributed them amongst jurors, prosecution and the judge. He then asked Brecht questions, the answers to which every salesman should have known. They included a description of the wrapper, and how they were kept cold in July. Brecht had not heard of dry ice and believed that, on the thermos flask principle, ice creams kept themselves cold. From there it was only a step for Leibowitz to make him admit his previous convictions and that from the age of nineteen he had been a professional 'surprise' witness saying, 'That's the man.' Coll was freed on a directed verdict of acquittal.

Although the prosecution's testimony was clearly perjured, Coll was almost certainly the killer for he received the soubriquet 'Mad Dog' as a result of the incident. To finance his defence he had kidnapped an aide to another rival, Owney Madden, ransoming the man for $30,000.

The next year Coll made a call to Madden from a telephone booth in a drugstore, during which he threatened to kill him unless money was paid. The call was traced and Coll was shot to death in the booth. In turn, his killers were not traced.

Robert Leibowitz, *The Defender: The Life and Career of Samuel S. Leibowitz 1893–1933*; Quentin Reynolds, *Courtroom: The Story of Samuel S. Leibowitz*

Gregory Villemin

On 16 October 1984 the body of the four-year-old Gregory Villemin was dragged from the river Vologne in the Vosges. He was the son of Jean-Marie (known as the Chief because of his general superiority to his brothers and sisters) and Christine Villemin and his death was the culmination of a series of poison pen letters which had been flying about the villages of Gaichamp and its slightly more up-market neighbour, Paremont. It was also the beginning of a murder case which entertained *le tout France* for a decade and divided the villages where the Villemin family and their relations lived.

Poison pen letters are a particularly French form of crime. *Le Corbeau* (The Crow), a celebrated 1943 film by Henri Clousot, who later directed *Les Salaires du Peur* (Wages of Fear), gave the name to the genre, and the Villemins and their relatives had been subjected to a barrage of these letters over the previous two years. On the day of the death of Gregory, 'The Crow' telephoned a Villemin relative to say, 'Tell them I've taken the Chief's son and put him in the Vologne! His mother is already looking for him.'

The Crow was absolutely correct and, shortly after 8 p.m., the body of Gregory was dragged from the river.

The thinking behind the crime is that The Crow and the murderer must have been the same person – otherwise how would The Crow know that Gregory was in the water? Much of the venom in the poison pen letters had been directed at the Villemin family. It is difficult to argue that anyone outside the family would have had the interest or, indeed, ability to re-cycle the detail – such as work being done in the living room or the colour of a new suite of furniture – which the letters provided. One immediate suspect was a cousin of the Villemins, Bernard Laroche, who was reputedly something of a womaniser and who had been rejected by Christine. He was also the father of a slightly backward child Sebastian. It was thought that the poison pen letters had been directed at the Villemins because they had adopted a superior stance and moved away from the family. Another suspect was Jacky Villemin, the boy's uncle, who on investigation by the police always seemed to know a little more than he was prepared to divulge. There was another theory that the child might have been murdered by a gang who detested Jean-Marie.

The case seems to be one where the champions of the inquisitorial, as opposed to accusatorial, system may find themselves on weak ground. The investigation by Jean-Michel Lambert, the examining magistrate who had at least nominal control of the police enquiries, was later heavily criticised. On 5 November Bernard Laroche was arrested. This appears to have been done on the basis that his alibi, which was provided by his young sister-in-law Muriel, had been broken.

One of the crucial parts of the investigation was the tapes of The Crow, who not only wrote his or her letters but also made abusive telephone calls. One of the difficulties was that it was never established whether it was a man or a woman speaking. Finally tests, bitterly challenged by the Villemins, tended to show that The Crow, and therefore the murderer, was Christine Villemin, Gregory's mother. Bernard Laroche was released on 4 February 1985 after Muriel had changed her evidence once again. On 29 March he was shot dead outside his house by Jean-Marie who then surrendered himself to the police.

On 5 July Christine was arrested, not for complicity in Bernard's murder but for the killing of her own son. She was released a week later. Gregory's murderer has never been found and much of the blame for this has been laid at the door of the young examining magistrate who conducted the enquiries. Not that subsequent investigating magistrates did any better. On 3 February 1993 Christine Villemin was officially cleared of the murder. From the first Gregory's father, Jean-Marie Villemin, had accused his cousin, Bernard Laroche, of the boy's abduction and murder. On 16 December 1993 Jean-Marie Villemin was convicted of killing Laroche and sentenced to five years' imprisonment. One year of the sentence was suspended and because of the length of time he had been on remand it meant he would only serve a few months. He had appealed for an acquittal on the basis that the killing of Bernard Laroche had been on the grounds that he was 'grief stricken and felt justice had betrayed him'.

Charles Penwarden, *Little Gregory*

Charles Wagner *see* **Eliza Carter**

Julia Wallace

At 8.45 p.m. on 19 January 1931 Prudential insurance agent, William Herbert Wallace, returned to his home at 29 Wolverton Street, Liverpool, to find his fifty-two-year-old wife, Julia, savagely beaten to death. Her body was lying face down on a rug in front of the fire and she had received blows to the head opening her skull. There were at least ten wounds. According to a witness, milkboy Alan Close, he had seen Julia alive at 6.45 p.m. Later he changed his evidence to a quarter of an hour earlier.

Wallace told a neighbour, Mrs Jackson, and the police, that money had been taken from the cashbox in which he kept the insurance premiums. The amount he said had gone varied slightly. In his bedroom a jar filled with £1 notes was smeared with blood but the money remained, as did Julia Wallace's jewellery.

The Wallaces were a quiet couple who kept themselves much to themselves. She, half French and the daughter of a veterinary surgeon, painted a little and played the piano a little. His passion in life was chess. Their home was a typical Liverpool terraced house.

Wallace had been out at the time his wife was murdered because, he said, whilst at the Central Chess Club the previous evening he had received a telephone call from a man calling himself R. M. Qualtrough, to the effect that he would like to see him the next day at 7.30 p.m. over insurance he wished to arrange. Wallace told the police he had set out for the address at 25 Menlove Gardens East, Mossley Hill at 6.45 p.m. He had previously asked members of the chess club where exactly Menlove Gardens East was. One member had said he had heard of a North, South and West but no East and that it was a rough area. Wallace assured him he would manage.

He caught a tram at 7.06 p.m. at the Lodge Lane stop a few hundred yards from his home and arrived at Menlove Avenue at 7.20 p.m, having changed trams. He could not find Menlove Gardens East and asked around. No one knew the street and so Wallace went to 25 Menlove Gardens West in case he had made a mistake. The elderly resident knew of no one by the name Qual-trough. He continued to ask people, including a police officer and a newsagent, before he gave up and went home. He was, said the police, setting up an elabo-rate alibi. It would later be suggested that he himself had made the Qualtrough telephone call and had taken care to ensure that the operator had recorded the time.

The police questioned Wallace the next day and the day after. So far as foren-sic evidence was concerned there was no blood on his clothes to connect him with the murder, nor was there any more in the house than a minute spot on the rim of the lavatory. It was clear that the murderer had not cleaned himself up in the house. Wallace stood on an identification parade and was picked out as the man in Menlove Gardens. Insurance was examined as a motive for Julia Wallace's murder but it amounted to £20 and her savings were less than £100. A good deal of time was spent by the police seeing how fast the journey to Menlove Gardens and back could be made. (Liverpool police are known as Jacks and this little activity earned them the name Springheeled Jacks after a popular melodrama of the time.) Other suggestions were that Wallace had committed the murder naked and that he had dressed in his wife's clothing so that when the milkboy saw Mrs Wallace he was in fact seeing him. Since there was a great discrepancy in the height of the Wallaces this seems unlikely.

On 2 February, after the police had taken the advice of the Director of Public Prosecutions, Wallace was arrested and charged with his wife's murder.

It was accepted by both sides that Qualtrough was the murderer. Either Wal-lace had been lured away or he *was* Qualtrough, pitting his chess-playing abili-ties against the police. The pathologist, Professor MacFall, was certain that the time of death had been between 6 and 7 p.m. and the milk-boy stuck with his new time. The high point of the case against him was that Wallace did not check out the exact location of Menlove Gardens East before he started on his journey. It would have been quite easy – his superintendent, Joseph Crewe, lived in that area. On the other hand the prosecution could advance no real motive against Wallace.

Police mugshots of Richard Gordon Parry.

He was convicted at 2.20 p.m. on 26 April 1931 saying only that he was not guilty. On 19 May the Court of Appeal quashed the conviction, declaring that the case 'was not proved with that certainty which is necessary in order to justify a verdict of guilty'. Wallace did not live long after his acquittal. There was a whispering campaign against him in Anfield and in June 1931 he was moved to a job on the Wirral. He died on 26 February 1933 from kidney failure.

In 1969 Jonathan Goodman wrote *The Killing of Julia Wallace* in which he suggested that the killer was one of Wallace's colleagues and in a later edition he named him as a Richard Gordon Parry. The motive, he suggested, was robbery because it was known that from time to time there could be £30 or more in Wallace's cashbox. Parry had a number of criminal convictions and was dismissed from the Prudential for retaining and not declaring premiums. On 30 March 1966 Goodman had interviewed Parry who, unsurprisingly, declined to comment on the affair. He had already been interviewed in the course of the investigation and had given an alibi that he was with his fiancée, Lily Lloyd, a music hall pianist.

It is difficult to know why, without any apparent motive, the police were so keen to pin the killing on Wallace and it is suggested that there may have been something of a cover-up. One of Parry's uncles was the City Librarian and his father was a treasury official whose secretary was the daughter of one of the investigating officers. The evidence against Parry is, however, just about as circumstantial as that against Wallace.

Jonathan Goodman, *The Killing of Julia Wallace*

Daisy Edith Wallis

Daisy Wallis, the thirty-six-year-old proprietress of the small Adelphi Secretarial Agency, on the top floor at 157 High Holborn on the junction with New Oxford Street, London, who liked to be called 'Dorothy', was stabbed to death there on the evening of 15 August 1949. She lived with her parents in London and had saved from her earnings to set up shop with two secondhand typewriters, chairs and a filing cabinet. Two sisters who lived in the building heard her screams but did nothing about it. 'We often hear screaming and shouting,' said one, 'and take no notice of it.' The other commented, 'It was more than one scream. It seemed so close to us.' When asked if she could distinguish any words she said, 'Murder, I think.' It was a fairly rough area and much of the noise could be attributed to the postmen in the Drury Lane sorting office nearby.

Her body was found by her assistant, Sheila Bennett. When the police arrived they found that Daisy Wallis had been stabbed repeatedly with a stiletto-like knife. She was wearing a pink dress which was covered in blood. She had bled so much that when a sample was required for the autopsy, Professor Francis Camps had difficulty taking one. The only clue the police had was that a man seen running away was dark haired and of an Italian appearance. One witness described him as clean shaven, fairly thick set with dark hair brushed straight back from his forehead. Two witnesses said they had seen her on other occasions with a similar looking man, once in a restaurant in Piccadilly and the other in a public house in New Cavendish Street.

From her diary it was clear she had made an appointment to go out the night before but had cancelled it. The police found that every day she locked her office for a ninety-minute lunch break but were unable to find any local restaurant in which she took it. She was also a member of a number of clubs but enquiries showed she rarely went to them. What she did, however, was to keep a detailed account of her daily life in one of eleven diaries, much of it concerning her sex life, which she wrote up in an old-fashioned and indecipherable shorthand. Fingerprints were taken in the office and all but one set of prints were eliminated from the enquiry. The owner of that remaining set did not have a criminal record.

One of Dorothy Wallis's clients volunteered the information that she had telephoned about 6 p.m. on the night of the attack and had spoken to a well-educated man who said Miss Wallis had gone home. Earlier in the day a man, described by Miss Bennett as a well-educated Pole, had called twice saying he was desperate for work and also, curiously, offering Miss Wallis office space in a rather better building. He was never traced.

A month before the murder the office had been burgled. Curiously, only the older and bulkier of the typewriters was taken, with the thief disregarding a £20 new radio and a cashbox. At one time the police believed this to have some significance but Commander Harold Hawkyard said it was eventually recovered and its theft was of no significance.

When the office block was demolished in May 1957 workmen found a sword hidden behind packing cases filled with rubbish on the second floor. The case was re-opened but no arrests were made.

Robert Jackson, *Francis Camps*

Charles Walton

A seventy-four-year-old farm labourer, who on 14 February 1945, which was both St Valentine's Day and Ash Wednesday that year, was found dead in the village of Lower Quinton, Warwickshire. He had been pinned to the ground with his own hay-fork. His face had been slashed and two cuts on his chest were in the shape of a cross. His slash-hook was embedded in the chest wounds. His arms had marks of defence wounds and a bloodstained walking stick was found nearby. The case became known as the witchcraft murder.

The village had less than five hundred inhabitants but there was a prisoner of war camp two miles away at Long Marston and the belief grew up that, since this was such a savage killing, the murderer must have been foreign. The local vicar narrowed it down to Italian. Indeed one Italian prisoner had actually been seen wiping fresh blood from his hands and scrubbing blood from his coat.

Forensic evidence showed it was that of a rabbit which the man had poached to supplement the prison camp diet.

The case took its name from two pieces of local history-cum-superstition. In 1875 a young man, John Haywood, had killed an old woman with a hay-fork because he believed she was a witch and had gone on to say he would kill all the remaining sixteen witches in Long Compton. Sticking spikes into them – or in the old Anglo-Saxon term, stacung – was apparently the way to kill witches, something not, in fact, dissimilar from driving a stake through the heart of a suicide or even a suspected vampire. The second was that a man had seen a black dog on Meon Hill outside the village. The dog had metamorphosed into a headless woman in a silk dress and the next day the man's sister had died. The man was Charles Walton.

The celebrated Scotland Yard detective, Robert Fabian, was called in to assist the enquiry but, despite a painstaking investigation, he was unable to make any progress. He encountered the true hostility of a closed local community when outsiders, particularly Londoners, try to infiltrate it. 'Cottage doors were shut in our faces and even the most innocent witnesses seemed unable to meet our eyes,' wrote Fabian. There was also an echo of the headless woman incident. A police car ran over a dog and the next day a heifer died unexpectedly. Now the village shut its collective face to the outsiders investigating the murder. The enquiry, in which over 4,000 statements were taken and twenty-nine samples of clothing and hair were sent to laboratories in Birmingham, came to nothing. In the locality, at least, it was the long-held opinion that Walton had magic powers and was killed because of his involvement with witchcraft. The day of his death, a combination of both sacred and secular, was thought to be particularly significant.

More prosaically now, it is thought that Walton was a moneylender and his killer was Albert Potter, his employer and a church sidesman, who had a great interest in racing and was known in the community to have a violent nature after he had been drinking. Walton had certainly lent Potter money and the dates for repayment were overdue. Fabian's theory was that here was a man who could not repay his debt and who had savagely attacked his creditor in a quarrel. In support of this is the fact that it was Potter who was able to locate the body in the dark and that his accounts of seeing Walton during the day were inconsistent. Potter died in 1974.

Donald McCormick, *Murder by Witchcraft*; Robert Fabian, *Fabian of the Yard*

Walter Wanderwell

On the night of 5 December 1932 Captain Walter Wanderwell was shot dead on his boat, *Carma*, moored at Long Beach Dock south of Los Angeles. He had been planning an expedition to film a travel documentary in the South Seas. His fairly disparate crew members, including Lord Edward Montague, then a none too successful film extra but later to become Lord Montague of Beaulieu, had put up $200 each for the privilege of sailing with the *soi-disant* captain.

Shortly after 9.30 on the night of Wanderwell's death a man, said to be wearing a grey coat, had put his head through the porthole galley and asked the crew where he could find the good captain. They told him to go to the salon and a few minutes later heard a shot. Wanderwell had been killed with a .38 bullet. After paraffin tests the crew were eliminated from police enquiries.

The diminutive Wanderwell (who earlier in his life had been known as Valerian Johannes Piecvnski under which name he had been interned as an enemy alien in 1917), had made a travelogue *River of Death* with his second wife, the six-foot blonde Aloha. After his experience of internment he had married his first wife, Nell, and had set about forming an International Police Force 'to police the world so no nation can go to war against another'. In fact the American police forces were enquiring into Wanderwell as the promoter of various minor frauds. It was also alleged that his investors in *River of Death* had not only been swindled but left stranded in Panama.

Aloha, who had separated from the captain the previous week and was now living with her sister, came under police scrutiny. In turn she put them on to James 'Curly' Guy. He had been one of those stranded in Panama and his wife was still working as a bar-girl in clubs in the city. He was traced and denied his involvement saying that he was asleep at the home of a friend in Glendale, with whom he was probably rum-running from Mexico. He was identified by two female members of the crew, a grey raincoat was found in his room and it was learned he had shot a cat with a .38 revolver. The identification evidence was not impressive against him and he was acquitted after a three-hour retirement by the jury. He was deported to Australia and was killed in the Second World War when the bomber he was flying crashed off Newfoundland. Aloha's subsequent film career was both brief and unsuccessful.

John Austin, *Hollywood's Unsolved Mysteries*

Edgar Watson *see* **Belle Starr**

Kelley Lyn Watson

In the early hours of 13 October 1983 the body of Kelley Watson, twenty-one-year-old graduate of the University of Colorado, was found next to her boyfriend Keith Patrick Brown, in his car at the National Centre for Atmospheric Research, Table Mesa, Boulder. She had been strangled. The car engine was running and a length of green garden hose was extending from the tailpipe through the rear hatch into the passenger compartment. When Brown was revived he told the police that he and Watson had been petting in the car in a local but fairly isolated park, Chapaqua, when they had been approached by two men who had forced him to drive to Table Mesa some five miles away. There they had attacked him, knocking him unconscious. He described one of his assailants as white, about 6'1" tall, possibly bearded and wearing a baseball cap.

Brown had slight swelling to his forehead near his right eye, bloody nostrils and three two-inch scratches on the right of his jaw. There was a footprint made by Watson's tennis shoe on his sweatshirt and other footmarks made by her on the inside of the windscreen. The police did not accept his version of the event and charged him with first degree murder. Shortly after his release on bail he made a gesture at suicide.

The pair had met three years earlier on 14 October. Watson's family had called Brown 'Lance Romance' because of the flowers he sent her during the relationship. They had discussed marriage and Brown had bought Kelley a diamond in 1982. However, according to the prosecution, she was trying to extricate herself from the relationship.

Opening the case for the State at the Boulder District Court in April 1984, Paul Miller said, '[Brown] had a fiancée that was perfect and perfectly fit into his life's plans before Miss Watson decided she was not ready for marriage and wanted to date other men. We can suggest to you that Keith was so despondent about losing Kelley that he killed her; he strangled her that night.'

In support of this he called sorority sisters from the Pi Beta Phi house, where Watson had roomed, to say that she had been about to break up the relationship completely. 'She was going to lay it on the line and tell him she was tired of him bothering her,' Kerry Mohan told the jury.

Anniversaries were, said the prosecution, important to Brown. But he had learned, through an anonymous letter, that on their third anniversary Kelley was going to a square dance with another man.

At the close of the prosecution case Paul McCormick, defending Brown, asked for the charge to be dropped to manslaughter, arguing that at worst it was a crime of passion. The motion was denied by the trial judge, who nevertheless acknowledged it was a 'close call'.

Unusually for an American trial, Brown gave evidence. He said that whilst he and Kelley were petting a car drove up behind and flashed its lights. There was a knock on the window and a man said, 'Look straight ahead – don't look at me.' One man, he claimed, got into the passenger seat saying, 'Whatever you do don't look our way or we will kill the girl.' He was ordered to drive the five miles to Table Mesa and there they got out of the car. He heard Kelley screaming and 'swung wild punches' at the men. 'I could feel the adrenalin going through my body and I tried to get where she was.' He remembered nothing more. As for the footprint, he explained this by saying he had taken off his sweatshirt during the petting session and the footprint must have been made when it was on the floor of the car.

His watch, ring and a button ripped from his shirt were found behind the car. His wallet was inside but it had been emptied of credit cards – a card was later found in a trash can. It had on it a fingerprint which could not be connected to anyone in the case.

Brown also told the jury of two anonymous letters he had received. One had stated that Kelley was going to a square dance and the second read, 'The end is near. Soon our goal will be accomplished and you will both be broken up.' When asked about the words 'Kelley out all night' and 'The end is near' found in his notebook, he explained that they referred to the anonymous letters. One of Kelley's roommates testified on Brown's behalf that the relationship with Watson had been one of 'Patty Perfect'.

On Friday the 13th the jury, which had been sequestered throughout the trial, began deliberating and the next day returned a verdict of not guilty. After the verdict Brown said he was thinking of visiting Watson's grave in Texas.

Florence Weatherall

O n 2 February 1951 twenty-two-year-old Florence Weatherall, known as the 'prettiest woman in the district', the mother of newly born twins, left her home at Linby, Nottinghamshire, to go shopping at Mansfield. Her mother arrived to take care of the babies but, for some reason or another, Florence did not leave her home until 4 p.m. in an era when there was no late-night shopping. Her body was found at 8.15 a.m. on 23 February in Moor Lane, Bestwood. She had been strangled and Professor J. M. Webster, the pathologist, took the view that her body had been dumped before *rigor mortis* set in. Her clothes, which had been removed, had been placed in the ditch beside her, and her long fingernails were undamaged.

Her mother had seen her in the street walking on the pavement on the opposite side of the road from which she would catch the bus to Mansfield. There was no evidence that she did, in fact, ever board one.

Detective Superintendent Reginald Spooner was the Scotland Yard officer assigned to assist the local police and his enquiries showed that at the age of fourteen she had been described as 'promiscuous' and sent to a remand home from which she ran away and was traced to London. At the age of nineteen she was bound over at the Old Bailey for a post office fraud. She had admitted two counts of obtaining money by forgery and had asked for fifty-nine offences to be taken into consideration. A condition of the bind over was that she returned home to her mother. 'You chose to break away from a respectable home, scorned your mother's love and care, and deliberately went off with this man,' said the Recorder, Sir Gerald Dodson. Later she went into the Land Army.

Then in 1950 she married Edward Weatherall, a vacuum cleaner salesman, whom she had met while he was serving in the RAF.

Spooner's enquiries eliminated all the known men in her previous life but the fact remains that she must have gone quite voluntarily with her killer. The probable answer to her death is that, physically debilitated after the birth of the twins, she was accidentally strangled during sexual intercourse in a hold which would not normally have troubled her. An open verdict was returned but, despite an appeal by Scotland Yard, unsurprisingly the man who collected her from outside her house never came forward.

Iain Adamson, *The Great Detective*

Florence Weatherall.

Lionel Webb

A t about 5.30 p.m. on Sunday, 11 December 1989 Lionel Webb, an estate agent and property dealer who bought houses in the names of his girl-friends without telling them, was found shot dead in his office in Stoke Newington, London. A passer-by who knew him saw him sitting in his office at about five o'clock and then stretched on the floor half an hour later. It was thought he might have been killed because he was undercutting some rivals in overseas property transactions but a quantity of drugs was found in his safe and a drug connection seems a more likely explanation for his death. He was acquainted with John Lane (*qv*).

Albert Welch

I n the afternoon of 19 November 1947 forty-five-year-old railwayman Albert Welch, a morose and restless man known to his workmates as 'Snakey', left his council house in Cranborne Crescent, Potters Bar, Middlesex, putting a message on the kitchen table: 'Phyllis, I have gone for a walk. Shan't be in for tea. – Albert.' He took with him his ration book and identity card. Welch's home life had not been a happy one and there had been talk of his leaving Potters Bar, even going abroad to find work. When he had not returned Mrs Welch initially believed he had simply walked out on her, but the next day she took the advice of a retired police officer who was a neighbour and reported her husband missing. She then went out and got a job. Appeals by the police to make contact with them produced no result.

In May 1958 a young boy looking for golf balls in the pond by the seventh hole at Potters Bar Golf Club found a hand with manicured nails in the weeds. It had been there for some six months and the fingerprints had been wasted away. The pond was drained and raked and, piece by piece, the body of a man the police identified as Albert Welch was recovered. The head had been partially burned before being thrown into the pond, along with the hacksaw used for the dismemberment.

The identification was done by a process of elimination. The pathologist, Donald Teare, established that the body was of a man 5'5" to 5'6" tall, well built and with a protruding lower jaw. Thirty-six missing men fitted that description and thirty-five were eliminated. Welch was the one who remained. A plaster cast of the feet found in the pond fitted Welch's boots and, despite the long immersion in water, Superintendent Cherrill of the Fingerprint Bureau managed to obtain one nearly perfect print.

Despite extensive enquiries involving statements from 350 people, taking chimney soot samples and digging up gardens, the police never established the identity of the killer. Mrs Welch would never accept that the remains were those of her husband. He had, she said, rough workman's hands. His workmates claimed, however, that he had worn gloves to work and had spent his breaks manicuring his hands. Mrs Welch refused to attend the funeral.

Peter Beveridge, *Inside the CID*

Sidney Wells

At about 11.30 a.m on 1 August 1983 tuba player, journalism student at the University of Colorado and small-to-medium time drug dealer, Sidney Wells, was found shot, execution style, in the back of the head by a single blast from a .20 shotgun. Wells, the boyfriend of Shauna Redford, Robert Redford's daughter, shared a flat in mainly student-owned Spanish Towers, a condominium, with his brother Sam and Thayne Smika. Shauna Redford had a flat in the same block. There were no signs of forcible entry and few of a struggle, in what the police thought to be a gangland execution. Traces of cocaine were discovered in Wells's blood and drug dealing paraphenalia was found in the room. There was also a note from Smika:

> Sid/Sam. I've gone home to visit my folks for a couple of days and I'll be back Tuesday or Wednesday.

Shortly afterwards Smika was arrested. The basis of the police case, set out in an arrest affidavit, was that Wells had told a friend he had purchased a large quantity of cocaine and had suspected Smika of stealing some of it. He had also considered evicting Smika for non-payment of his share of the rent. The note left by Smika had no bloodstains on it although it was left on a table covered in blood. Smika had indeed returned to his mother's home in Akron in North-east Colorado on the day of the killing and had done some laundry. The police also found a shotgun at his home. Smika said it had been given to him by his father several years previously and he had not seen it for at least three years. The gun had recently been cleaned and oiled.

His family posted a bond of $100,000 bail and he was released. Darlene, Smika's mother, announced in the press that her son suffered from blackouts where 'he could not control his actions but could remember what had taken place.' Smika himself said, 'Hell, man, I didn't kill Sid. No way could I have done that.' A month later no charges were preferred against him and the District Attorney declared he would present the case to a Grand Jury and be guided by them. There was no evidence linking Smika's gun to the killing and the cartridge from the bullet which had killed Wells was never found. There was a flurry of excitement when a sawn-off shotgun was found in a trash can in Colorado Springs, but this died down. Although the Grand Jury met for the next twelve months they brought no charges against anyone and were discharged at the end of their term of office. It was then announced Smika was no longer an official suspect. Over 8,000 man hours and $150,000 had been expended on the investigation.

Smika was successfully sued by the landlord for the back rent of the condominium. By 1985 he had disappeared from view but a year later was arrested in Denver and charged with fourteen counts of second degree forgery involving the theft of $63,000 from his former employers. He was given bail in the sum of $50,000 and failed to surrender. An 'at large' warrant remains in existence.

Wells's mother denied her son was a drug dealer. She believed he had uncovered some facts in researching a television programme, *Cocaine in the Rockies*, and had been killed as a result.

West Ham Vanishings *see* **Eliza Carter**

Janice Weston

At 9 a.m. on Sunday, 11 September 1983 a body of a female was discovered in a lay-by on the northbound carriageway on the A1 near St Neots in Huntingdonshire. She had been badly beaten about the head, probably with a car-jack. When thirty-six-year-old Janice Weston, a London solicitor, failed to keep her Monday morning appointments at Charles Russell & Co in Lincoln's

Inn, her colleagues telephoned her sister, who in turn contacted the police. Later that day they identified her body.

Before she had joined Charles Russell, Janice Weston had been with another London firm of solicitors, Herbert Oppenheimer Nathan and Vandyk where she had met two married men. In 1975 when his wife died, the first, Heinz Izner, a man substantially older than herself, had asked her to marry him. She had declined but they continued to be close friends and, on his death two years later, she received the bulk of his estate.

Janice married the other man, Tony Weston, after he was divorced in 1982. They bought a property in Northamptonshire for conversion into flats, and, on the weekend of Janice's death, Tony was in Paris negotiating the purchase of a chateau.

Her movements could be traced until 5 p.m. on the Saturday. In the morning she had collected a tyre which her husband had left for repair and then had gone to her office where a colleague saw her at that time. It seems that afterwards she returned to their flat in Holland Park which she left in a hurry. She had eaten a meal but, unusually, had not cleared away the debris. She took a purse with her but not her handbag.

The motive for her death does not appear to have been robbery or of a sexual nature. She had not been assaulted and her purse, which contained £37, was found under the driving seat of her Alfa Romeo. The car was not at the scene of the crime but was found within twenty-four hours back in London in Camden Square NW1. The interior had bloodstains but there were no identifiable fingerprints. Some two hours after the body was discovered a man had bought spare number plates from a car-spares shop in Royston, Hertfordshire, also on the A1. Neither the man nor the plates were ever traced. The spare tyre and the repaired one were missing from the car although six people said they saw a man changing a tyre in the lay-by.

In December 1983 Tony Weston went to the police station for a progress meeting and was held for over fifty hours until his solicitor made an application to the High Court that he either be released or charged. He was able to establish that he had been in Paris on the evening of his wife's death: a concierge recalled him collecting his room key and he was later completely eliminated from the enquiries.

The questions which remain to be answered are why Janice Weston left in such a hurry and what was she doing well up the A1 on a wet Saturday night. It is unlikely she was intending to stay at their country house, Clopton Manor, some fifteen miles away as the conversion was unfinished.

In November 1991 Robert Delgado, then serving a life sentence for the murder of a man during a robbery, claimed that Mrs Weston had been killed by a
South London criminal, Charles 'Chic' Fowler. She had, he said, discovered a
drugs ring and been kidnapped by Fowler who, in panic, beat her to death. In
turn he had killed Fowler for bungling the kidnapping and had dumped his
body in Grafham Water reservoir in Cambridgeshire. The police said they had
no report of a Charles Fowler, described as in his mid-twenties and of stocky
build and medium height, being missing. Delgado, whose throat had earlier
been slashed in a prison fight, withdrew his claim.

John Canning (ed), *Unsolved Murders and Mysteries*

Lynette White

On 14 February 1988 twenty-one-year-old prostitute Lynette White was
killed in a frenzied attack in Cardiff, Wales. She had been the girlfriend of,
and had worked for, a small-time pimp, Stephen Miller. The week or so before
her murder she had fallen out with him – most of her earnings, between £10 and
£25 a time, were disappearing up his nose and she believed he was having an
affair with another woman. She was also due to give evidence in two cases, one
involving a member of a powerful local family who was alleged to have stabbed
a prostitute in the lung.

Lynette's body was found in the squalid Bute Town flat where she took her
punters. She had been stabbed more than fifty times and, from the defence
wounds on her hands, it was clear she had tried to fight off her attacker. Her
head and one breast were almost completely severed but there had been no
rape or mutilation of her genitals.

For ten months the South Wales Regional Crime Squad had no evidence
except that it seemed a white man had been seen covered in blood 150 yards
from her flat shortly before her body was found. Then in December five black
men, Stephen Miller, Tony Parris, Yusef Abdullahi and two cousins, Ronald and
John Astie, were arrested. The reason for this was that two prostitutes, Angela
Psaila and Leanne Vilday, suddenly told the story that they had been present
when Lynette was killed by the men and they had been forced to participate in
the slashing of her body.

What, if any, corroborative evidence was there? So far as Miller was concerned it was his own admission. He was questioned at length and, after denying the offence, he confessed. A supergrass, Ian Massey, said that Parris had confessed to him in prison and Abdullahi's girlfriend, Jacqui Harris, put him in the frame. She said that Yusuf had told her he had been in the room when Lynette was killed. There was no corroborative evidence against the Asties and there was no forensic evidence against any of the men. This was from a room which must have teemed with forensic material. The motive, the police decided, was revenge by Stephen Miller for Lynette's bad behaviour.

There is no doubt that from the start Psaila and Vilday told lies. Psaila also seems to have had some racist feelings: in court she called the defendants 'black monkeys'. The police were so concerned about Vilday's evidence and the changing of her statement between committal proceedings and the trials that she was taken to a hypnotist, something which had been effectively discredited if not quite outlawed in both the English and American courts by the mid 1980s.* Vilday had named a Martin Tucker as one of the killers and then withdrawn the allegation and Psaila made and withdrew an allegation against another man.

The case was transferred to Swansea and the evidence had been heard by Mr Justice McNeil when, at the start of his summing up in February 1989, he died of a heart attack. The second trial began in front of Mr Justice Leonard in the May and ended in November. At 197 days it was Britain's longest murder trial. He warned the jury of the dangers of convicting on the uncorroborated evidence of the girls alone and they must have listened to him because they acquitted the Asties. The others received life imprisonment.

Now began the campaign for the release of the Cardiff Three. It became known that the supergrass, Ian Massey, had given evidence against Ged Corley, the Manchester policeman whose conviction was quashed by the Court of

---

* Hypnosis has been used for a variety of legal and quasi-legal purposes including the obtaining of quick information by Israeli troops. There are two basic techniques – the crystal ball and age regression. In the first the hypnotised person is invited to 'Look into this ball and tell me what you see'. In the age regression the person is taken back in stages to the moment he is trying to recall. There are considerable difficulties in gauging the accuracy of the evidence obtained. Witnesses can lie deliberately or unknowingly and tend to guess at answers anyway. Once a person has been hypnotised the recollection, right or wrong, becomes that much stronger. Dr Martin Orne, a leading opponent of hypnosis in American courts, said at a Home Office conference in 1981 that 'hypnosis decreases reliability whilst making the witness more compelling'. In a trial at Maidstone Crown Court on 19 June 1987 the police had used a self-taught hypnotist who had learned his craft from reading books in the public library. The evidence he had obtained was ruled inadmissible. Earlier in 1987 the Home Office had issued guidelines to the effect that there be an uninterrupted video of the session and that a witness, who may be called to give evidence on material matters, should not normally be considered for hypnosis. (See also Marie Wilks.)

Appeal. Massey, a man with a record for violence, serving a fourteen-year sentence for robbery, was released after his first parole hearing. He had only served a third of his sentence. Jacqui Harris retracted her evidence and made a statement saying that Yusef would often say weird things and that she had made her statement to hurt him. That left the confession of Miller, a man with an IQ of 75, a point above sub-normal. It transpired that he had denied the offence some 300 times before confessing. As Lord Justice Taylor said in the Court of Appeal:

> If you go on asking somebody questions, and tell him he is going to sit there until he says what you want, there will come a time when most people will crack. Oppression may be of the obvious, crude variety or it may be just by relentlessness.

Twenty-nine days after the conviction of the men the body of another girl was found in the Fairwater area of Cardiff about two miles from Lynette's flat. She too had been savagely slashed. No one has been arrested for her killing.

John Williams, *Bloody Valentine*

Nick Whiting

On 8 June 1990 millionaire Nicholas Whiting, former British saloon car champion driver, went missing after a raid on his showroom, All Car Equipe, in Wrotham, Kent. Along with him went five cars including a Ford Escort Turbo and an Audi Quattro in total worth over £100,000. The cars were all recovered within a matter of days but of Whiting there was no sign.

Two weeks later it was suggested that Whiting had staged his own kidnap and had gone on the run with John 'Little Lew' Lloyd, wanted in connection with the Brink's Mat gold robbery. He had been a long-standing friend of Kenneth Noye, who earlier had been acquitted of killing an undercover policeman in the grounds of his home and then convicted of dishonestly handling gold bullion and sentenced to the maximum of fourteen years' imprisonment.

This unkind suggestion was proved totally wrong when on 2 July, following a tip-off, the police dug his body from a shallow grave on Rainham Marshes in Essex. They believed he had been beaten, bound and gagged, placed in the boot of a car and later been frog-marched for some two miles before being shot in the head.

One theory was that his killing had been ordered by a major criminal then serving time on the Isle of Wight. Whiting was believed to have borrowed stolen money from the man to build houses on a plot of land he had bought. Two men were charged but on 16 August 1990 Kenneth Stone was released when the Crown Prosecution Service offered no evidence. After he left court Mr Stone said that he had never met Whiting and that he had been charged as a result of a malicious call made to the police. On 13 December 1990 magistrates found that the second man, Stanley Wise, had no case to answer and he was also discharged.

Marie Wilks

On 18 June 1988 twenty-two-year-old Marie Wilks, seven months' pregnant, broke down whilst driving on the M50. She left her ten-year-old sister and her one-year-old baby in the car and walked to the nearest emergency telephone. Whilst she talked to the police operator she was attacked, stabbed in the neck and abducted. The killer drove her for two miles before throwing her over the motorway embankment, where she bled to death.

Thirty-six-year-old Eddie Browning, a former Welsh guardsman and a nightclub bouncer from Cwn-Parc, Rhondda, who had served a seven-year sentence for his part in a series of raids on antique shops, was arrested. At best the evidence against him was slender. Witnesses to the abduction said the man had spiky blond hair which Browning had. They also said the car in which Mrs Wilks was driven away was a silver Renault. And Browning had a silver Renault. When questioned he denied his involvement and said that on the evening of the murder he had driven to Scotland. The quickest route, and the one advised by his father, was the M50 but Browning said he had taken the M4 across the Severn Bridge. There were no traces of blood in his car although Mrs Wilks must have been bleeding badly after the stabbing. No witnesses identified him. The prosecution based its case on the premise that he was a violent man who had lied about the route he had taken. On 8 November 1989 he was convicted at Shrewsbury Crown Court and sentenced to life imprisonment with an order that he serve at least twenty-five years.

His first appeal, on the grounds that the trial judge did not point out the inconsistencies in the prosecution's case, failed in May 1991 but it later emerged that one of the key witnesses, an off-duty police officer, had been hypnotised and under hypnosis had given a description of a different make of Renault and a different number plate from the one owned by Mr Browning.* This was not disclosed to the defence, nor were the contents of two telephone calls to the police which were at variance with the way the prosecution put its case. The Court of Appeal judges ruled that had this been available to the jury they were not sure the same decision would have been reached. Browning was released.

Charles Wilson

On 24 April 1990 the former Great Train Robber, Charlie Wilson, was shot dead beside his swimming pool at his home in Marbella, Spain. He had been hosing down the pool area in the early evening when his wife, Patricia, answered a knock at the door. There was a man with a South London accent asking for her husband. She fetched Charlie and he and the young man went off together.

At the inquest, held in London in November 1991, Patricia Wilson said:

> I heard the man say 'I am a friend of Eamonn.' I had a feeling there were two people there, although I couldn't say why. I heard two very loud bangs and at first I thought it was from the building site next door, but then I heard the dog scream-ing. Charlie was lying at the side of the pool face down. The man had gone and the gate was open. I saw blood coming from his mouth and Charlie did a sort of a press-up and gestured in the direction the man had gone.

Initially it was reported he had been killed with a single karate blow but the autopsy showed he had been shot in the side of the neck and the bullet had lodged there. As the shot passed through the larynx it would have caused heavy bleeding and as he inhaled the blood he would have been unable to cry out. The dog had a broken leg and had to be destroyed.

The inquest was told by Detective Superintendent Alec Edwards that, although there was no direct evidence to link him with drug dealing, there was

---

* In some states of America once a witness has been hypnotised his evidence is inadmissible and in England in 1987 the Home Office produced draft guidelines on the conduct to be observed by a police force when a witness is hypnotised. These draft guidelines were never made mandatory. After the Browning case Dr H. B. Gibson, President of the British Society of Experimental and Clinical Hypnosis, wrote to *The Times* (24 May 1994) calling on the Home Office to make it 'mandatory for police forces totally to eschew the use of hypnosis'.

much circumstantial evidence, such as his lifestyle and his visits to Morocco.

> As far as the Spanish police and the British police are concerned there is circumstantial evidence that this is a drug-related incident. We know of his meeting British criminals who are known drug dealers and who have since been convicted of drug dealing and with one who has also been executed in a gangland killing.

A verdict that he had been shot by persons unknown was recorded. Paul Spencer, a solicitor for the Wilson family, said after the inquest that the drug allegations were strongly denied.

After his release from prison in 1978 – he was the last of the Great Train Robbers to be freed – Wilson had led something of a charmed life so far as the courts were concerned. In 1982 he had been one of seven men charged in a £2 million VAT fraud involving the melting down of gold Krugerrands valued at £16 million. Charges against him were dropped when the jury disagreed twice and he paid a £400,000 penalty to Customs and Excise. In 1984 he spent four months in custody awaiting trial for the alleged armed robbery of a security van. He was freed amidst allegations of police corruption.

One rumour current amongst the London Underworld is that the Spanish authorities wish to interview a criminal presently serving a twelve-year sentence.

Florence Wilson

The body of fifty-five-year-old Florence Wilson was found on the golf-course at Le Touquet, France, early one morning in May 1928. She had been stabbed and strangled but no effort had been made to take any of the quantity of jewellery she was wearing.

She and her husband had rented a villa 'My Rose' near the course and after tea in the club-house Wilson and a Captain Soanes had gone off to play golf. Mrs Wilson said she would walk to the Casino after arranging to meet her husband at the Cafe Central in Paris-Plage. When Mrs Wilson did not get to the rendezvous her husband and Captain Soanes went looking for her. During the evening Wilson reported the matter to the police and it was a gendarme who found the body at about half past four in the morning. The post-mortem showed that there had been a violent struggle and that intercourse had taken place shortly before or after death.

In turn the police arrested and released a deaf-mute, then a Portuguese man and thirdly Jean Matras who was the musical director of the Le Touquet Casino Orchestra. Two years later a French woman claimed she had been assaulted by a young boy, Andre Leloutre, in Paris-Plage. He was arrested and, according to the police, confessed to the murder of Mrs Wilson. He is alleged to have told them:

> I followed her until she reached a lonely spot, when I jumped out on her. She cried out, and seizing me by the hair, pulled my head back. She hurt me and I found she was very strong. At any moment someone might have come up, and I was desperate with fright. I found my knife, and I stabbed her time and again until her grip relaxed and she fell. [He had heard someone coming and continued] Mrs Wilson's body was out of sight but I noticed a large bloodstain on the edge of the path so I sat down to conceal it. A man came along, and I said, 'Good evening, Monsieur' as he passed. I then went away.

The boy, who would have fourteen at the time of the killing, had enormous hands and thumbs. He pleaded guilty to attacking two French women and withdrew his confession to the murder of Mrs Wilson. The police staged a reconstruction with M. Matras as the man who had passed the boy. Leloutre was charged with the murder and acquitted.

In 1933 a letter was sent to the police to the effect that it had been a contract killing and that the actual murderer had drowned in Etaples a little way down the coast. Mrs Wilson had known her killer, said the writer, because he had helped her with a secret correspondence she was carrying on with a man at the Cafe Central. No further arrests were ever made.

Harry J. Greenwall, *They Were Murdered in France*

James Wilson *see* Marion McDowell

Joan Mary Woodhouse

Shortly before 5 p.m. on 10 August 1948 the body of Joan Woodhouse was found strangled and raped at Box Copse in the grounds of Arundel Park, Sussex, by twenty-four-year-old labourer, Thomas Stilwell. He first found her handbag, then her dress and finally her partially clothed body. She was about five feet tall, of slim build and with blue eyes. The celebrated pathologist, Professor Keith Simpson, estimated the date of her death as between eight and ten days previously, so putting it over the August Bank Holiday which in the 1940s was taken during the first weekend in the month.

But what was Joan Woodhouse doing in Arundel Park in the first place? She was twenty-seven and worked as a librarian in Central London, living in the YMCA in Bennetts Park, Blackheath. She had arranged to spend the Bank Holiday with her widowed father in Barnsley, Yorkshire, and she told her roommate that that was where she was going when she left at 8.30 a.m. on the Saturday morning. She had said she planned to catch the 10.10 a.m. train. Instead she went to Worthing and checked her case into the left luggage office at the station.

Joan Woodhouse's body lay on its back stretched out on the slope of a hill. She was wearing pink cami-knickers, a brassiere, elastic suspender belt and stockings. The cami-knickers had fastened at the crotch by two buttons but now one was missing. Her clothes lay in a neatly folded pile about twelve yards away. Keith Simpson took the view that she had either taken off her clothes to sunbathe and had been surprised or had agreed to some form of sexual foreplay short of intercourse. On the pile of clothes was a necklace and her handbag was nearby. Simpson found fingertip bruises in the muscles on both sides of the voice box and the hyoid bone had been fractured. He thought she had been pressed on her back whilst the strangulation had taken place. The body was too infested with maggots to tell whether she had been a virgin before the attack.

The detective in charge was DCI Fred Narborough. A weekend case was recovered from the left luggage office and in it was a diary which contained the names of over 100 men. A previous boyfriend was found in Folkestone and eliminated from the enquiries. Joan Woodhouse had been deeply distressed by the break-up of her relationship caused by a difference of religious belief: she was an extremely High Church Anglo-Catholic and the man not so. A priest had advised her of the spiritual troubles she faced if she continued with the relationship. She had then had something of a nervous breakdown and for a time had returned north. Immediately after Stilwell had found the body he had been taken to the police station where he had been questioned for a number of hours. During the questioning he made a statement about taking a short-cut through the park, which he later retracted.

Despite three months of sifting through Joan Woodhouse's life, and the variety of 'sightings' of her alone and with a man over the Bank Holiday weekend, Narborough was never in a position to make an arrest. The diary with the names of 100 men turned out to be a red-herring. Far from the promiscuity this suggested there was a simple explanation: she was the Honorary Secretary of the Old Student's Association which linked librarians throughout Britain. She had also drawn up a code for living which was very strict:

1. I will offer the day's work to God on waking, pray for at least five minutes in the morning and at least ten minutes at night.
2. Say prayers each midday.
3. Make an examination of the day's work each evening.
4. Be at Mass on Sundays and make my Communion at least once each week.
5. Make two and a half hours meditation each week.
6. Make an annual retreat.
7. Do an hour's spiritual reading each week.
8. Read a chapter of the Bible each day.
9. Make my Confession monthly.
10. Seek out opportunities of helping others.
11. Give at least one-fifth of my personal money as alms.
12. Fast on Friday and all other fasting days.
13. Keep an account of my expenditure.
14. Practice inner mortification.
15. Be in bed by 11 p.m.

The inquest, begun and adjourned immediately after her death, was reopened on 22 November 1948 and this time there were solicitors representing the family of Joan Woodhouse, the police and Thomas Stilwell. Stilwell gave evidence after being warned that he was not bound to answer questions which might incriminate him. The jury returned a verdict of murder by a person or persons unknown.

The matter did not rest there. The family then offered a reward of £500 for information which might lead to the conviction of the man who had killed Joan. Nothing came of it. Next they instructed Thomas Jacks, a former CID officer from Bridlington, who had set up as a private investigator. He interviewed over 200 witnesses, at the end of which he presented a report to Scotland Yard saying there was enough evidence on which to launch a prosecution against Stilwell.

In turn Scotland Yard now appointed Reginald Spooner – Narborough had retired – to conduct an enquiry. His report, lodged six weeks later, was to say that there was no evidence on which a prosecution of Stilwell could be launched. This did not satisfy the Woodhouse family and at the end of August 1948 her father applied for, and was granted, a warrant for the arrest of Stilwell on a charge of murder. It was the first time such a warrant had been granted for eighty-five years. As is the custom, the Crown took over the prosecution.

The case against Stilwell, heard at Arundel Magistrates' Court, was based on what were said to be conflicting statements about his movements on the day Woodhouse died, and that on the day he discovered the body he had walked almost straight to the spot. One of the witnesses called Nellie Petley, a young woman with three children who had lung trouble, gave evidence that on the Saturday she had seen a young couple, of whom Stilwell was one, and had spoken to them. Later, under cross-examination, she admitted she was wrong and had not spoken to them. 'It was only in my mind,' she said. She admitted writing a letter to Jacks saying it was on the Sunday that she had seen the couple. She had also written, 'I thought long ago each time I lay in hospital I could claim the reward and go away and get well.' The prosecution, whose heart was by no means in its case, called a witness to contradict Mrs Petley. The evidence of another witness, who said she had seen Joan Woodhouse and re-called it because she was wearing a dress she admired and subsequently bought, was discredited when it was shown that she had bought the dress four days before Joan had disappeared. The magistrates retired for two hours and on their return, to great cheers, announced there was insufficient evidence to com-mit Stilwell for trial.

The family complained and a letter was written to the then Attorney-General saying that the opening by Mr J. S. Bass for the prosecution had been an invita-tion to acquit. The matter was raised in the House of Commons by their MP and in reply Sir Hartley Shawcross replied, 'It is the duty of the prosecution to prosecute, not to persecute.' Three months later the relatives sought a bill of indictment from Mr Justice Humphreys at Lewes Assizes against a named per-son. He refused to grant it.

Spooner's theory was that Joan Woodhouse was not murdered. He believed that because of the decomposition of the body Simpson was wrong and that she had not been raped. He thought that she was a young woman who, because of the break-up of her relationship and hearing how the other girls in the hostel were off for the weekend with their boyfriends, decided to commit suicide. Given her religious beliefs it is difficult to accept this. Certainly it was not a theory that was shared by Narborough who wrote, 'Down the years I had waited for a man to make his mistake. To take a drink too many perhaps and talk too loudly ... All the time there is that murder on my mind.'

Fred Narborough, *Murder on my Mind*; Iain Adamson, *The Great Detective*; Keith Simpson, *Forty Years of Murder*

John Wortley

On the evening of 5 June 1975, a day when he was standing in for a sick workmate, the sixty-six-year-old car park attendant was found battered to death near his kiosk in the Arundel Gate multi-story car park, Sheffield. Wortley, a frail man weighing only seven stone, had been battered with a fire extinguisher. The till contents of £59 had been taken.

A wage slip was found nearby and some bloodstained clothing was noticed by a local dry cleaner. An anonymous caller telephoned the police claiming that there were two people involved in the attack. A tape of the call was played on the local radio station but the caller was never identified.

One line of thought was that John Wortley knew, or at least could recognise, his attacker and had been killed so that he could not name him. There were also lines of enquiry which could have been helpful but which petered out. The first was that just before his death he had been seen talking to a man at the kiosk. The man never came forward to be eliminated from the enquiries. A twenty-year-old green Hillman Minx was parked in the car park but the driver was never traced. About the time of the robbery a man took a taxi from nearby Fitzalan Square to Manchester. He did not book into the hotel at which he was set down and he too was never traced.

Over the years the police received calls offering evidence but no one was ever arrested and the £1,000 reward on offer from National Car Parks went unclaimed.

J. P. Bean, *Crime in Sheffield*

Margery Wren

At about 6 p.m. on 20 September 1930 eighty-five-year-old Margery Wren was found bleeding sitting in a chair in her shop in Church Road, Ramsgate, Kent when a young girl called to buy some blancmange mix. She said she had been attacked about a quarter of an hour earlier. She died on 25 September in hospital after making a number of conflicting statements about her attacker. Robbery was almost certainly the motive because, although in reality she had an income of £13 a year from her sister's estate and the money from the small shop, she boasted of a number of properties she claimed she owned.

Initially she said she had tripped and fallen but it was clear from her injuries that she had been repeatedly beaten, probably with a pair of tongs. Sir Bernard Spilsbury, the pathologist, said that an attempt had been made to strangle her. When questioned further she made contradictory statements saying that a man had attacked her, two people had attacked her and yet again that she had simply fallen. She went on to describe a red-faced man with a moustache. In all there were six suspects, said Superintendent Hambrook at the inquest. Three of them were found to have cast-iron alibis and the murderer had to come from the remaining three.

When Margery Wren was invited to make a dying declaration she refused to do so with some satisfaction. Finally she said, 'I do not wish him to suffer. He must bear his sins. I do not wish to make a statement.' Both the police and the coroner believed she was deliberately shielding someone, and preferred to rely more on a remark she had made whilst drifting into unconsciousness: 'You can't take it. Oh don't.' No arrests were ever made.

Bella Wright

The twenty-one-year-old factory worker, Bella Wright, was found shot on the morning of 5 July 1919 in what became known as the Green Bicycle case and which was another of Sir Edward Marshall Hall KC's great triumphs. Her body was found beside her bicycle in a lane in Leicestershire. There were no signs of a sexual assault. She had left her uncle's house with a man who had a green bicycle, not much more than a half hour before she was found dead. Eight months later a green bicycle was found in a local canal and through the number of the frame, even though it had been partially obliterated, it was traced to Ronald Vivian Light, a former Army officer in the Royal Engineers who had been invalided from France with severe shell-shock and was now a master at Dean Close School, Cheltenham. A revolver holster and some .45 ammunition were also dredged from the canal. Light denied that the bicycle was his.

At the trial the evidence, at least of Light's ownership of the bicycle, was overwhelming. There was no doubt he had been riding with the girl and he gave evidence that he had lied to save his invalid mother from distress. So far as the evidence of the ammunition was concerned, Marshall Hall was able to establish that a bullet from a .45 would have made a much larger exit hole. He aired the suggestion that the girl might have been shot accidentally by a stray

The green bicycle at the centre of enquiries into the murder of Bella Wright.

bullet from a farmer aiming at rooks and indeed a dead bird had been found near the body. Light said in evidence that he had indeed met Bella Wright, who had something wrong with the wheel of her cycle and who had asked for the loan of a spanner. He did not have one but had gone with her to her uncle's cottage and then ridden a short way with her. He now had a defective tyre and kept stopping to pump it up. She left him and pedalled off in a different direction.

Marshall Hall appears to have been at his most brilliant in the first part of his speech to the jury until he was interrupted by the judge, Mr Justice Horridge, who had seen a press photographer about to take a picture in court. Even though he then lost much of his fire, Hall had done sufficient to persuade the jury that Light was not guilty. One problem the defence had, that of a discrepancy in the evidence of when Light disposed of his bicycle – he said one time, his mother another – seems to have gone almost unchallenged by the prosecution. The Attorney General had begun the case but had left halfway through. There are a number of reasons suggested for this. One is that he was called to London on Parliamentary business, a second is that the case was not going well and he simply bailed out.

This is another case in which, overall, critics take the view that the defendant was fortunate to have obtained an acquittal.

C. Wendy East, *The Green Bicycle Murder*; H. Montgomery Hyde, *Norman Birkett*;

H. R. Wakefield, *The Green Bicycle Case*; N. Warner Hooke and G. Thomas, *Marshall Hall*

William York *see* **Kate Bender**

Thomas Young *see* **Pat McAdam**

Zodiac *see* **David Arthur Faraday**

Tony Zomparelli *see* **Nicholas Gerard**

BIBLIOGRAPHY

Adam, H. L., *Murder by Persons Unknown*, Collins (London, 1931).

Adamson, I., *The Great Detective*, Frederick Muller (London, 1966).

Allen, J., *Inside Broadmoor*, W. H. Allen (London, 1952).

Anderson, F., *The Carbon Murders Mystery*, Frontier Publishing (Calgary, 1973).

Austin, J., *Hollywood's Unsolved Mysteries*, Ace Publishing Corporation (New York, 1970)

Bailey, F. L., *The Defence Never Rests* (London, 1972).

Bavin, B., *The Strange Death of Freddie Mills*, Howard Baker (London, 1975).

Bayer, O. W. (ed) *Cleveland Murders*, Duell, Sloan & Pearce (New York, 1947).

Bean, J. P., *Crime in Sheffield*, Sheffield City Libraries (1987).

Bennett, B., *Some Don't Hang*, Howard Timmins (Cape Town, 1973).

Berry-Dee, C. and Odell R., *A Question of Evidence*, W. H. Allen (London, 1991).

Beveridge, P., *Inside the CID*, Evans Brothers (London, 1957).

Blom-Cooper, L., *The A6 Murder*, Penguin (London, 1963).

Bolitho, W., *Leviathan*, Chapman & Hall (London, 1923).

Boot, A., *Psychic Murder Hunters*, Headline (London, 1994).

Brennan, T. C., *The Gun Alley Tragedy* (Melbourne, 1922).

Bresler, F., *Lord Goddard*, Harrap (London, 1977)

Bridges, Y., *Poison and Adelaide Bartlett*, Hutchinson (London, 1962)

—— *How Charles Bravo Died*, Jarrolds (London, 1956).

Browne, D. G. and Tullett, T., *Bernard Spilsbury*, George G. Harrap & Co (London, 1951).

Bryson, J., *Evil Angels*, Penguin (London, 1986).

Caminada, J., *Twenty-five Years of Detective Life*, John Heywood (Manchester, 1895).

Canning, J. (ed) *Unsolved Murders and Mysteries*, Michael O'Mara (London, 1987).

Celebrated Trials:

—— Cecil, H. (ed), *The Trial of Walter Rowland*, David and Charles (London, 1975).

Chamberlain, L., *Through My Eyes*, Heinemann (Australia, 1990).

Chandler, R., *Raymond Chandler Speaking*, Hamish Hamilton (London, 1962).

Clark, Sir George (ed), *The Campden Wonder*, Oxford University Press (Oxford, 1959).

Clarke, Sir Edward, *The Story of My Life*, John Murray (London, 1918).

Clarke, K., *The Pimlico Murder*, Souvenir Press (London, 1990).

Clegg, E., *Return Your Verdict*, Angus and Robertson (Sydney, 1965).

Cohen, D., *The Encyclopaedia of Unsolved Crimes*, Dodd, Mead & Co (New York, 1988).

Conan Doyle, A., *The Case of Oscar Slater*, Hodder & Stoughton (London, 1912).

Cook, J., *Who Killed Hilda Murrell?*, New English Library (London, 1985).

Cooper, P. and Noble, P., *Reward*, Pocket Books (New York, 1994).

Cornish, G. W., *Cornish of the Yard*, The Bodley Head (London, 1935).

Crispin, K., *The Dingo Baby Case*, Albatross Books (Australia, 1987).

Cyriax, O., *Crime*, Andre Deutsch (London, 1993).

de Marigny, A., *More Devil than Saint*, Beechurst Press (New York, 1946).

Dew, W., *I Caught Crippen*, Blackie (London, 1938).

du Rose, J., *Murder Was My Business*, W. H. Allen (London, 1971).

Eddowes, J., *The Two Killers of Rillington Place*, Little Brown (London, 1994).
Fabian, R., *Fabian of the Yard*, Heirloom Press (London, 1955).
Fido, M., *The Chronicle of Crime*, Little Brown-Carlton (London, 1993).
Foot, P., *Who Killed Hanratty?*, Jonathan Cape (London, 1971).
Fox, J., *White Mischief*, Jonathan Cape (London, 1982).
Fraser, F., *Mad Frank*, Little Brown (London, 1994).
Gifford, Lord, *The Broadwater Farm Inquiry*, Karia Press (London, 1986).
Goodman, J., *The Burning of Evelyn Foster*, Headline (London, 1988).
—— *The Modern Murder Yearbook*, Robinson Publishing (London, 1994).
—— *The Passing of Starr Faithfull*, Piatkus (London, 1990).
—— *Acts of Murder*, Harrap (London, 1986).
—— *The Killing of Julia Wallace*, Headline (London, 1969).
—— (ed) *Masterpieces of Murder*, Hutchinson (London, 1964).
Graysmith, R., *Zodiac*, St Martin's Press (New York, 1986).
Greenwall, H. J., *They Were Murdered in France*, Jarrolds (London, 1957).
Gribble, L., *They Got Away with Murder*, John Long (London, 1971).
Guiliano, G., *Paint it Black: The Murder of Brian Jones*, Virgin Books (London, 1994).
Gurr, T. and Cox, H. H., *Famous Australasian Crimes*, Frederick Muller (London, 1957).
Gwynn, G., *Did Adelaide Bartlett?*, Christopher Johnson (London, 1950).
Hale, L., *Hanged in Error* (London, 1961).
Hecht, B., *The Mystery of the Fabulous Laundryman* (short story)
Holmes, P., *The Sheppard Murder Case*, David McKay (New York, 1961).
Hooke, N. W. and Thomas, G., *Marshall Hall*, Arthur Baker (London, 1966).
House, J., *Murder Not Proven*, Penguin (London, 1989).
Hunt, P., *Oscar Slater: The Great Suspect*, Carroll & Nicholson (London, 1951).
Hyde, H. Montgomery, *Norman Birkett*, Hamish Hamilton (London, 1964).
Jackson, R., *Coroner*, Harrap (London, 1963).
—— *Francis Camps*, Hart-Davis MacGibbon (London, 1975).
Jones, R. J., *Still Unsolved*, Xanadu (London, 1990).
Justice, J., *Murder vs*, Olympia Press (Paris, 1964).
Kelly, V., *The Charge is Murder*, Rigby (Adelaide, 1965).
Kennedy, L., *The Airman and the Carpenter*, Viking (New York, 1985)
Kent, D. and Flynn, R. A., *The Lizzie Borden Sourcebook*, Brandon Publishing (New York, 1992).
Kirkpatrick, S., *A Cast of Killers*, Hutchinson (London, 1986).
Kohm, H. *Who Killed Karen Silkwood?*, Summit, (New York, 1981).
Knox, B., *Court of Murder*, John Long (London, 1968).
Kray, R., *Villains We Have Known*, M. K. Publications (Leeds, 1993).
Kray, R. and Kray, R., *Our Story*, Sidgwick & Jackson (London, 1988).
Lacey, R., *Little Man*, Random Century (London, 1991).
Lane, B. and Gregg W., *The Encyclopedia of Serial Killers*, Headline (London, 1992).
Lane, M., *Rush to Judgment*, The Bodley Head (London, 1966).
Leasor, J., *Who Killed Sir Harry Oakes?*, Mandarin (London, 1983).
Leibowitz, R., *The Defender: The Life and Career of Samuel S. Leibowitz, 1893–1933*, Engelwood Cliffs NJ (1981).
Lincoln, V., *A Private Disgrace*, G. P. Putnam's Sons (New York, 1967).
Linklater, E., *The Corpse on Clapham Common*, Macmillan (London, 1971).

Lock, J., *Dreadful Deeds and Awful Murders*, Barn Owl Books (Taunton, 1990).
Lowther, W., *Arms and The Man: Dr Gerald Bull, Iraq and the Supergun*, Macmillan (London, 1991).
Maas, P., *The Valachi Papers*, Panther (London, 1970).
Marnham, P., *Trail of Havoc*, Viking (London, 1987).
Martin, J. B., *Butcher's Dozen*, Harper & Brothers (New York, 1950).
McConnell, B., *Found Naked and Dead*, New English Library (London, 1974).
McCormick, D., *Murder by Witchcraft*, John Long (London, 1968).
Moore, S., *Lucan: Not Guilty*, Sidgwick & Jackson (London, 1987).
Morshead, I., *The Life and Murder of Henry Morshead*, Oleander Press (London, 1982).
Morton, J., *Gangland*, Little Brown (London, 1992).
—— *Bent Coppers*, Little Brown (London, 1993).
—— *Gangland 2*, Little Brown (London, 1994).
Mosley, L., *Lindbergh*, Hodder & Stoughton (London, 1976).
Murder Casebook (1989–1993), Marshall Cavendish (London)
Murdoch, D., *Disappearances*, Doubleday (Toronto, 1983).
Narborough, F., *Murder on my Mind*, Allan Wingate (London, 1959).
Nash, J. R., *World Encyclopedia of 20th Century Murder*, Headline (London, 1992).
—— *World Encyclopedia of Organised Crime*, Headline (London, 1993).
North, D., *The Mad Trapper of Rat River*, Macmillan, (Toronto, 1972).
Notable British Trials:
—— Adam, H. L. (ed), *The Trial of George Chapman*, William Hodge & Co (London, 1930).
—— Henderson, W. (ed), *The Trial of William Gardiner*, William Hodge & Co (London, 1934).
—— Roughead, W. (ed), *The Trial of J. W. Lawrie*, William Hodge & Co (London, 1932).
—— Fletcher Moulton, H. (ed), *The Trial of Steinie Morrison*, William Hodge & Co (London 1922).
—— Roughead, W. (ed), *The Trial of Oscar Slater*, William Hodge & Co (London, 1929).
Park, W., *The Truth About Oscar Slater*, The Psychic Press (London, 1927).
Pearson, E., *Murder at Smutty Nose*, William Heinemann (London, 1927).
—— *The Trial of Lizzie Borden*, Heinemann (London, 1937).
Penwarden, C., *Little Gregory*, Fourth Estate (London, 1990).
Plett, J., *Valley of Shadows*, Horizon House (Beaverlodge, 1975).
Pollack, J. H., *Dr Sam – An American Tragedy* (Chicago, 1957).
Price, C. and Caplan, J., *The Confait Confessions*, Marion Boyers (London, 1977).
Radin, E., *Lizzie Borden, The Untold Story*, Victor Gollancz (London, 1961).
Rashke, Richard, *The Killing of Karen Silkwood*, Houghton Miflin (Boston, 1987).
Rawlings, T., *Who Killed Christopher Robin?*, Boxtree (London, 1994).
Read, L. and Morton, J., *Nipper*, Macdonald (London, 1991).
Renshaw, P., *The Wobblies*, Eyre and Spottiswode (London, 1967).
Reynolds, Q., *Courtroom: The Story of Samuel S. Leibowitz* (New York, 1950).
Roughhead, W. N. (ed), *Tales of the Criminous*, Cassell & Co (London, 1956).
Rowland, J., *Murder Mistaken*, John Long (London, 1963).
Rumbelow, D., *The Complete Jack the Ripper*, W. H. Allen (London, 1987).
Sabljak, M. and Greenberg, M, H., *A Bloody Legacy*, Gramercy Books (New York, 1992).
Scaduto, A., *Scapegoat*, Secker and Warburg (London, 1976).

Sharpe, A., *Crimes That Shocked Australia*, Atrand Pty (NSW, 1987).

Sheppard, S., *Endure and Conquer* (Cleveland, 1966).

Shew, E. S., *A Companion to Murder*, Alfred Knopf (New York, 1961).

Short, M., *Crime Inc*, Mandarin (London, 1991).

Sifakis, C., *The Encyclopaedia of American Crime*, Facts on File (New York, 1982).

Silverman, J., *Crack of Doom*, Headline (London, 1994).

Simpson, K., *Forty Years of Murder*, George G. Harrap & Co (London, 1978).

Slipper, J., *Slipper of the Yard*, Sidgwick & Jackson (London, 1981).

Smith, B., *Deadly Encounters*, Hounslow Press (Toronto, 1993).

Smith, C. and Guillen, T., *The Search for the Green River Killer*, Onyx (New York, 1991).

Smith, Edward H., *Mysteries of the Missing* (New York, 1927).

Smith, G., *Death of a Rosegrower*, Cecil Woolf (London, 1985).

Smith, S., *Mostly Murder*, Harrap (London, 1959).

Spoto, D, *Marilyn Monroe: The Biography*, Arrow (London, 1994).

Stoddard, C. N., *Bible John*, Paul Harris Publishing (Edinburgh, 1980).

Sullivan, R., *Goodbye Lizzie Borden*, Chatto & Windus (London, 1975).

Summers, A., *Official and Confidential*, Victor Gollancz (London, 1993).

Symons, J., *A Reasonable Doubt*, The Cresset Press (London, 1960).

Taylor, B. and Knight, S., *Perfect Murder*, Grafton (London, 1987).

Taylor, B. and Clarke, K., *Murder at the Priory*, Grafton (London, 1988).

Thompson, C. J. S., *Poison Mysteries Unsolved*, Hutchinson (London, 1937).

Thurber, J., *My World and Welcome To It*, Harcourt Brace Jovanovich (New York, 1942).

Toughill, T., *Oscar Slater*, Canongate Press (Liverpool, 1993).

Tullett, T., *Murder Squad*, Grafton (London, 1981).

Unsolved (no editor ascribed), Blitz Editions (Leicester, 1992).

van den Bergh, T., *Who Killed Freddie Mills?*, Constable (London, 1991).

Vincent, A., *Killers in Uniform*, Headline (London, 1994).

Wakefield, H. R., *The Green Bicycle Case* (London, 1930).

Walker-Smith, D., *The Life of Sir Edward Clarke*, Thornton Butterworth (London, 1939).

Waller, G., *Kidnap*, Hamish Hamilton (London, 1961).

Weld, O. (ed), *Cleveland Murders*, Bayer, Duell, Sloan & Pearce (New York, 1947)

Wensley, F. P., *Detective Days*, Cassell (London, 1931).

Whittington-Egan, R., *A Casebook on Jack the Ripper*, Wildy (London, 1975).

—— *The Riddle of Birdhurst Rise*, Penguin (London, 1988).

—— *The Ordeal of Philip Yale Drew*, Penguin (London, 1989).

Whittington-Egan, R. and M., *The Bedside Book of Murder*, David & Charles Publishers (Newton Abbot, 1988).

—— *The Murder Almanac*, Neil Wilson Publishing (Glasgow, 1992).

Williams, J., *Bloody Valentine*, Harper Collins (London, 1994).

Wilson, C., *The Mammoth Book of True Crime*, Robinson Publishing (London, 1988).

Wilson, C. and Pitman, P., *The Encyclopedia of Murder*, Arthur Barker (London, 1961).

Wilson, F. and Day, B., *Special Agent*, Holt, Rinehart and Winston (New York, 1965).

Wilson, G. and Harrison, D., *Inquest: Helen Smith, The Whole Truth*, Methuen (London, 1983).

Wilson, K, *Investigating Murder*, Robinson Publishing (London, 1990).

Yallop, D., *Beyond Reasonable Doubt*, Hodder & Stoughton (London, 1978).

Young, W., *The Montesi Scandal*, Faber & Faber (London, 1957).